T0213726

Lecture Notes
in Business Information Processing

271

Series Editors

Wil M.P. van der Aalst
Eindhoven Technical University, Eindhoven, The Netherlands
John Mylopoulos
University of Trento, Trento, Italy
Michael Rosemann
Queensland University of Technology, Brisbane, QLD, Australia
Michael J. Shaw
University of Illinois, Urbana-Champaign, IL, USA
Clemens Szyperski
Microsoft Research, Redmond, WA, USA

More information about this series at http://www.springer.com/series/7911

Sofia Ceppi · Esther David
Chen Hajaj · Valentin Robu
Ioannis A. Vetsikas (Eds.)

Agent-Mediated Electronic Commerce

Designing Trading Strategies and Mechanisms for Electronic Markets

AMEC/TADA 2015, Istanbul, Turkey, May 4, 2015
and AMEC/TADA 2016, New York, NY, USA, July 10, 2016
Revised Selected Papers

 Springer

Editors

Sofia Ceppi
School of Informatics
University of Edinburgh
Edinburgh
UK

Esther David
Department of Computer Science
Ashkelon Academic College
Ashkelon
Israel

Chen Hajaj
Department of EE and CS
Vanderbilt University
Nashville, TN
USA

Valentin Robu
Smart Systems Group
Heriot-Watt University
Edinburgh
UK

Ioannis A. Vetsikas
Information Technology
The American College of Greece
Agia Paraskevi, Athens
Greece

ISSN 1865-1348   ISSN 1865-1356 (electronic)
Lecture Notes in Business Information Processing
ISBN 978-3-319-54228-7   ISBN 978-3-319-54229-4 (eBook)
DOI 10.1007/978-3-319-54229-4

Library of Congress Control Number: 2017933558

Printed on acid-free paper

This Springer imprint is published by Springer Nature
The registered company is Springer International Publishing AG
The registered company address is: Gewerbestrasse 11, 6330 Cham, Switzerland

Preface

Electronic commerce and automatic trading have become a ubiquitous feature of modern marketplaces. Algorithms are used to buy and sell products online, trade in financial markets, participate in complex automated supply chains, regulate energy acquisition in decentralized electricity markets, and bid in online auctions.

The growing reliance on automated trading agents raises many research challenges, both at the level of the individual agent and at a higher system level. In order to design mechanisms and strategies to tackle such challenges, researchers from AI and multi-agent systems have used techniques from a variety of disciplines, ranging from game theory and microeconomics to machine learning and computational intelligence approaches.

The papers collected in this volume provide a collection of such mechanisms and techniques, and are revised and extended versions of work that appeared at two leading international workshops on electronic markets held in 2015 and 2016. The first of these is the Workshop on Agent-Mediated Electronic Commerce and Trading Agent Design and Analysis (AMEC/TADA 2015), co-located with the AAMAS 2015 conference held in Istanbul, Turkey, and the second is the Workshop on Agent-Mediated Electronic Commerce and Trading Agent Design and Analysis (AMEC/TADA 2016), co-located with the IJCAI 2016 conference held in New York, USA. Both workshops aim to present a cross-section of the state of the art in automated electronic markets and encourage theoretical and empirical work that deals with both the individual agent level as well as the system level.

Given the breadth of research topics in this field, the range of topics addressed in these papers is correspondingly broad. They range from papers that study theoretical issues, related to the design of interaction protocols and marketplaces, to the design and analysis of automated trading strategies used by individual agents – which are often, though not exclusively, developed as part of an entry to one of the tracks of the Trading Agents Competition (TAC).

Two of the papers study auction design. Specifically, Alkobi and Sarne discuss the benefit an information broker can get by disclosing information to the general public for free in the context of the Vickrey Auction, while Gujar and Faltings analyze several auction-based matching mechanisms that take into account the worker's preferences in the scenario of dynamic task assignments in expert crowdsourcing. Moreover, Niu and Parsons present a genetic algorithmic approach to automated auction mechanism design in the context of the TAC Market Design game.

Another five papers focus on the problems related with the development of autonomous agents for the current games of the Trading Agents Competition (TAC).

Four of them are concerned with the study of the Power TAC game, a competitive simulation of future retail electric power markets. Specifically, Hoogland and La Poutré describe their Power TAC 2014 agent, while Özdemir and Unland present the winning agent of the 2014 PowerTAC competition.

Natividad et al. and Chowdhury et al. study the use of machine learning techniques to improve the performance of their respective Power TAC agents. Specifically, Natividad et al. focus on using learning techniques to predict energy demands of consumers; while Chowdhury et al. investigate the feasibility of using decision trees and neural networks to predict the clearing price in the wholesale market, and reinforcement learning to learn good strategies for pricing the agent's tariffs in the tariff market.

Finally, motivated by the Ad Exchange Competition (AdX TAC), Viqueria et al. study a market setting in which bidders are multi-minded and there exist multiple copies of heterogeneous goods.

Problems related to energy and electric vehicles are also considered by a further two papers of this volume. Specifically, Hoogland et al. examine the strategies of a risk-averse buyer who wishes to purchase a fixed quantity of a continuous good, e.g., energy, over a two-timeslot period; while Babic et al. analyze the ecosystem of a parking lot with charging infrastructures that acts as both an energy retailer and a player on an electricity market.

We hope that the papers presented in this volume offer readers a comprehensive and informative snapshot of the current state of the art in a stimulating and timely area of research.

We would also like to express our gratitude to those who made this collection possible. This includes the paper authors, who presented their work at the original workshops and subsequently revised their manuscripts, the members of the Program Committees of both workshops, who reviewed the work to ensure a consistently high quality, as well as the workshop participants, who contributed to lively discussions and whose suggestions and comments were incorporated into the final papers presented here.

October 2016

Sofia Ceppi
Esther David
Chen Hajaj
Valentin Robu
Ioannis A. Vetsikas

Organization

AMEC/TADA Workshop Organizers

Sofia Ceppi	University of Edinburgh, Edinburgh, UK
Esther David	Ashkelon Academic College, Israel
Chen Hajaj	Vanderbilt University, Nashville, USA
Valentin Robu	Heriot-Watt University, Edinburgh, UK
Ioannis A. Vetsikas	The American College of Greece, Greece

Program Committee

Bo An	University of Massachusetts, Amherst, USA
Merlinda Andoni	Heriot-Watt University, UK
Mohammad Ansarin	Erasmus University, The Netherlands
Tim Baarslag	University of Southampton, UK
John Collins	University of Minnesota, USA
Shaheen Fatima	Loughborough University, UK
Enrico Gerding	University of Southampton, UK
Maria Gini	University of Minnesota, USA
Mingyu Guo	University of Adelaide, Australia
Noam Hazon	Ariel University, Israel
Wolfgang Ketter	Erasmus University, The Netherlands
Christopher Kiekintveld	University of Texas at El Paso, USA
Ramachandra Kota	University of Southampton, UK
Daniel Ladley	University of Leicester, UK
Jérôme Lang	Université Paris-Dauphine, France
Kate Larson	University of Waterloo, Canada
Tim Miller	University of Melbourne, Australia
David Pardoe	UT Austin, USA
Steve Phelps	University of Essex, UK
Juan Antonio Rodriguez Aguilar	IIIA, Spain
Alberto Sardinha	Instituto Superior Técnico, Portugal
David Sarne	Bar-Ilan University, Israel
Paolo Serafino	Teesside University, UK
Lampros C. Stavrogiannis	University of Southampton, UK
Sebastian Stein	University of Southampton, UK
Taiki Todo	Kyushu University, Japan
Meritxell Vinyals	CEA, France
Dongmo Zhang	University of Western Sydney, Australia
Dengji Zhao	University of Southampton, UK

Contents

Strategic Free Information Disclosure for a Vickrey Auction

Shani Alkoby[(✉)] and David Sarne

Bar-Ilan University, 52900 Ramat-Gan, Israel
shani.alkoby@gmail.com

Abstract. In many auction settings we find a self-interested information broker, that can potentially disambiguate the uncertainty associated with the common value of the auctioned item (e.g., the true condition of an auctioned car, the sales forecast for a company offered for sale). This paper extends prior work, that has considered mostly the information pricing question in this archetypal three-ply bidders-auctioneer-information broker model, by enabling the information broker a richer strategic behavior in the form of anonymously eliminating some of the uncertainty associated with the common value, for free. The analysis of the augmented model enables illustrating two somehow non-intuitive phenomena in such settings: (a) the information broker indeed may benefit from disclosing for free some of the information she wishes to sell, even though this seemingly reduces the uncertainty her service aims to disambiguate; and (b) the information broker may benefit from publishing the free information to the general public rather than just to the auctioneer, hence preventing the edge from the latter, even if she is the only prospective customer of the service. While the extraction of the information broker's optimal strategy is computationally hard, we propose two heuristics that rely on the variance between the different values, as means for generating potential solutions that are highly efficient. The importance of the results is primarily in providing information brokers with a new paradigm for improving their expected profit in auction settings. The new paradigm is also demonstrated to result, in some cases, in a greater social welfare, hence can be of much interest to market designers as well.

1 Introduction

Information disclosure is a key strategic choice in auctions and as such vastly researched both theoretically and empirically [8,11]. One of the main questions in this context is the choice of the auctioneer to disclose information related to the common value of the auctioned item [4,10,12,19,20,24]. For example, the board of a firm offered for sale can choose the extent to which the firm's client list or its sales forecast will be disclosed to prospective buyers. Various other examples are given in the literature cited throughout this paper. The disclosed information affects bidders' valuation of the auctioned item and consequently the winner determination and the auctioneer's profit.

© Springer International Publishing AG 2017
S. Ceppi et al. (Eds.): AMEC/TADA 2015/2016, LNBIP 271, pp. 1–18, 2017.
DOI: 10.1007/978-3-319-54229-4_1

In many cases, the information is initially not available to the auctioneer herself, but rather needs to be purchased by her from an external information broker. This is typically the case whenever generating the information requires some specific expertise or special equipment that the auctioneer does not possess. For example, in the firm selling case the information may pertain to the financial stability of key clients of the firm, hence typically offered for sale in the form of business analysts' reports. The auctioneer thus needs to decide both whether to purchase the information and whether to disclose it to bidders whenever purchased. The problem further complicates when the information broker herself is acting strategically, e.g., setting the price of the information offered in a way that maximizes her profit.

Prior work that dealt with uncertain auction settings with a self-interested information broker [33] allowed the information broker to control only the pricing of the information offered for sale. In this paper we extend the modeling of the information broker's strategy, enabling her also to disclose for free some of the information she holds. Specifically, we allow her to publicly eliminate some of the possible outcomes, narrowing the set of possible values that the common value may obtain. For example, prior to offering a firm the purchase of a market prediction report, the analyst can publicly publish its preliminary version that eliminates some of the possible outcomes. This behavior might seem intuitively non-beneficial, because now the information service disambiguates between less values, hence seemingly "worth" less. Nevertheless, our analysis of the augmented model enables demonstrating, numerically, that this choice can be sometimes beneficial. A second somehow surprising choice that we manage to illustrate is the one where the information broker finds it more beneficial to disclose the free information to both the auctioneer and the bidders rather than to the auctioneer only. The latter choice strengthens the auctioneer in the adversarial auctioneer-bidders interaction, allowing her to make a better use of the information offered for sale, if purchased, hence potentially enabling charging more for the service.

As explained in more details in the following paragraphs, the information brokers' problem of deciding what information to disclose for free is computationally extensive. Therefore another contribution of the paper is in presenting and demonstrating the effectiveness of two heuristics for ordering the exponential number of solutions that need to be evaluated, such that those associated with the highest profit will appear first in the ordering.

In the following section we provide a formal model presentation. Then, we present an equilibrium analysis for the case where the free information is disclosed to both the auctioneer and the bidders and illustrate the potential profit for the information broker from revealing some information for free, as well as the ordering heuristics and their evaluation. Next, we present the analysis of the case where the free information is disclosed only to the auctioneer. Finally we conclude with review of related work and discussion of the main findings.

2   The Model

Our basic auction model considers an auctioneer offering a single item for sale to n bidders using a second-price sealed-bid auction (with random winner selection in case of a tie). The auctioned item is assumed to be characterized by some value X (the "common value"), which is a priori unknown to both the auctioneer and the bidders [13,14]. The only information publicly available with regard to X is the set of possible values it can obtain, denoted $X^* = \{x_1, ..., x_k\}$, and the probability associated with each value, $Pr(X = x)$ ($\sum_{x \in X^*} Pr(X = x) = 1$). Bidders are assumed to be heterogeneous in the sense that each is associated with a type T that defines her valuation of the auctioned item (i.e., her "private value") for any possible value that X may obtain. We use the function $V_t(x)$ to denote the private value of a bidder of type $T = t$ in case the true value of the item is $X = x$. It is assumed that the probability function of types, denoted $Pr(T = t)$, is publicly known, however a bidder's specific type is known only to herself.

The model assumes the auctioneer can obtain the value of X from an outer source, denoted "information broker" (for the rest of the paper will be called "broker"), by paying a fee C set by the broker. Similar to prior models (e.g., [33]), and for the same justifications given there, it is assumed that this option of purchasing the information is available only to the auctioneer, though the bidders are aware of this possibility.

If purchasing the information, the auctioneer, based on the value obtained, can decide either to disclose this information to the bidders or keep it to herself (hence disclosing $\emptyset$). If disclosing the information, then it is assumed that the information received from the broker is disclosed as is (i.e., truthfully and symmetrically to all bidders), e.g., in case the auctioneer is regulated or has to consider her reputation. Finally, it is assumed that all players (auctioneer, bidders and the broker) are self-interested, risk-neutral and fully rational agents, and acquainted with the general setting parameters: the number of bidders in the auction, n, the cost of purchasing the information, C, the discrete random variables X and T, their possible values and their probability functions.

Up to this point our model resembles those found in prior literature. For example, it generalizes the one found in [10,24] in the sense that it requires the auctioneer to decide on purchasing the external information rather than assuming she initially possesses it. It is also equivalent to the one found in [33] where the broker is self-interested agent that controls C, the price of purchasing the information. Our model, however, extends prior work in the sense that it allows the broker also to anonymously publish some of the information for free before the auctioneer makes her decision of whether to purchase the information. The anonymity requirement in this case is important as discussed later on in the analysis section. Yet, there are numerous options nowadays for publishing such information anonymously, e.g., through an anonymous email, uploading the information to an electronic bulletin board or anonymous file server, sending the information to a journalist or an analyst. The typical case, which we use for our analysis, is the one where the broker, knowing the true value $x \in X^*$, eliminates a subset of values $D \subset X^*$ (where $x \notin D$), leaving only the values $X^* - D$ as applicable values the common value may obtain. Doing so, our model distinguishes between the case where the free information is disclosed to all and the one where it is disclosed to the auctioneer only (allowing the latter to decide what parts of it to disclose further to the bidders prior to starting the auction).

3   Disclosing Information for Free

Consider the case where the true common value is x. In this case, if the broker publicly eliminates (i.e., anonymously publishes that the common value is not part of) the subset $D \subset X^*$ then the auctioneer and bidders are now facing the problem where the common value may receive only the subset $X^* - D$ and the a priori probability of each value in the new setting is given by $Pr'(X = x) = \frac{Pr(X=x)}{\sum_{x_i \in X^* - D} Pr(X=x_i)}$. Since the auctioneer needs to decide both whether to purchase the true value $x \in X^* - D$ and if so whether to disclose it to the bidders, her (mixed) strategy can be characterized using $R^{auc} = (p^a, p_1^a, ..., p_k^a)$ where p^a is the probability she purchases the information from the broker and p_i^a ($1 \leq i \leq k$) is the probability she discloses to the bidders the value x_i if indeed $X = x_i$. The dominating bid of a bidder of type t, when the auctioneer discloses that the true value is x, denoted $B(t,x)$, is given by $B(t,x) = V_t(x)$ [36]. If no information is disclosed ($x = \emptyset$) then the dominating strategy for each bidder is to bid her expected private value, based on her belief of whether information was indeed purchased and if so, whether the value received is intentionally not disclosed by the auctioneer [10]. The bidders' strategy, denoted R^{bidder}, can thus be compactly represented as $R^{bidder} = (p^b, p_1^b, ..., p_k^b)$, where p^b is the probability they assign to information purchase by the auctioneer and p_i^b is the probability they assign to the event that the information is indeed disclosed if purchased by the auctioneer and turned to be x_i.[1]

The bid placed by a bidder of type t in case the auctioneer does not disclose any value, $B(t, \emptyset)$, is therefore:

$$B(t, \emptyset) = \sum_x V_t(x) \cdot Pr^*(X = x) \tag{1}$$

where $Pr^*(X = x)$ is the posterior probability of x_i being the true common value, based on the bidders' belief R^{bidder} and is being calculated as:

$$Pr^*(X = x_i) = \frac{Pr(X = x_i)(p^b(1 - p_i^b) + (1 - p^b))}{(1 - p^b) + p^b \sum(1 - p_i^b)Pr(X = x_i)} \tag{2}$$

The term in the numerator is the probability that x_i indeed will be the true value and will not be disclosed. If indeed x_i is the true value (i.e., with a probability of $Pr(X = x_i)$) then it will not be disclosed either if the information is not purchased (i.e., with a probability of $(1 - p^b)$) or if purchased but not disclosed (i.e., with a probability of $p^b(1 - p_i^b)$). The term in the denominator is the overall probability that the information will not be disclosed. This can happen either if the information will not be purchased (i.e., with a probability

---

[1] Being rational, all bidders hold the same belief in equilibrium.

of $(1 - p^b)$) or when the information will be purchased however the value will not be disclosed (i.e., with probability of $p^b \sum (1 - p_i^b) Pr(X = x_i)$).

Consequently, the auctioneer's expected profit when using R^{auc} while the bidders use R^{bidder}, denoted $EB(R^{auc}, R^{bidder})$, is given by:

$$
\begin{aligned}
EB(R^{auc}, R^{bidder}) &= p^a \sum Pr'(X = x_i) p_i^a \cdot ER_{auc}(x_i) \\
&+ ((1 - p^a) + p^a \sum (1 - p_i^a) Pr'(X = x_i)) \cdot ER_{auc}(\emptyset) - p^a \cdot C
\end{aligned}
\tag{3}
$$

where $ER_{auc}(x_i)$ is the expected second highest bid if disclosing the true value x_i ($x_i \in \{X^* - D, \emptyset\}$). The broker's expected profit is $p^a \cdot C$. The first row of the equation deals with the case where the auctioneer discloses the true value to the bidders (i.e., p^a is the probability that the information was purchased and $\sum Pr'(X = x_i) p_i^a \cdot ER_{auc}(x_i)$ is the probability that x_i is the true value multiplied by the auctioneer's expected profit for this case). The second row deals with the case where the information was not disclosed to the bidders (i.e., when the information is not purchased by the auctioneer (with probability $(1 - p^a)$) and when the information is purchased but not discloses (with probability $p^a \sum (1 - p_i^a) Pr'(X = x_i))$).

A stable solution in this case (for the exact same proof given in [33]) is necessarily of the form $R^{auc} = R^{bidder} = R = (p, p_1, ..., p_k)$ (as otherwise, if $R^{auc} = R' \neq R^{bidder}$, the bidders necessarily have an incentive to deviate to $R^{bidder} = R'$), such that [33]: (a) for any $0 < p_i < 1$ (or $0 < p < 1$): $ER_{auc}(\emptyset, R) = ER_{auc}(X_i)$ (or $ER_{auc}(\emptyset, R^{bidder}) = ER_{auc}((1, p_1, ..., p_k), R^{bidder})$); (b) for any $p_i = 0$ (or $p = 0$): $ER_{auc}(\emptyset, R^{bidder}) \geq ER_{auc}(X_i)$ (or $ER_{auc}(\emptyset, R^{bidder}) \geq ER_{auc}((1, p_1, ..., p_k), R^{bidder})$); and (c) for any $p_i = 1$ (or $p = 1$): $ER_{auc}(\emptyset, R^{bidder}) \leq ER_{auc}(X_i)$ (or $ER_{auc}(\emptyset, R^{bidder}) \leq ER_{auc}((1, p_1, ..., p_k), R^{bidder})$). Therefore one needs to evaluate all the possible solutions of the form $(p, p_1, ..., p_k)$ that may hold (where each probability is either assigned 1, 0 or a value in-between). Each mixed solution of these $2 \cdot 3^k$ combinations (as only one solution where $p = 0$ is applicable) should be first solved for the appropriate probabilities according to the above stability conditions. Since the auctioneer is the first mover in this model (deciding on information purchase), the equilibrium used is the stable solution for which the auctioneer's expected profit is maximized.

If the information is provided for free ($C = 0$) then information is necessarily obtained and the resulting equilibrium is equivalent to the one given in [10] for the pure equilibrium case and [24] for the mixed equilibrium case.

Being able to extract the equilibrium for each price C she sets, the broker can now find the price C which maximizes her expected profit. Repeating the process for all different sets $D \subset X^*$, enables extracting the broker's expected-profit maximizing strategy (D, C).

Figure 1 depicts the expected profit of the auctioneer (vertical axis) as a function of the information cost C (horizontal axis), for five of the possible D sets. The setting used is given in the table at the bottom of the figure. It is based on four possible values the common value may obtain: $X^* = \{x_1, x_2, x_3, x_4\}$, where x_3 is the true value. The subset D that is used for each curve is marked

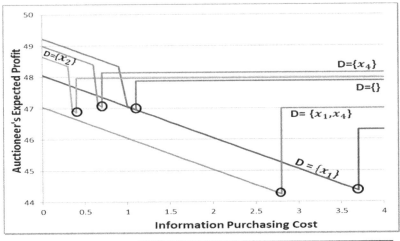

n=3		private values			
		x1	x2	x3	x4
Type	p(value) p(type)	0.626	0.159	0.143	0.072
1	0.252	54	25	84	10
2	0.33	79	56	0	53
3	0.386	21	59	46	69
4	0.032	25	94	69	93

Fig. 1. Auctioneer's expected profit as function of information purchasing cost, for different a priori eliminated subsets.

next to it. For each set D the information provider discloses, the auctioneer chooses whether to purchase the information and what values to disclose, if purchasing, according to the auctioneer's expected-profit-maximizing equilibrium. For example, the lowest curve depicts the auctioneer's expected profit when the broker initially eliminates the values $\{x_1, x_4\}$ and the auctioneer's strategy is to disclose to the bidders the value x_2 in case it is the true value of the auctioned item. Since equilibria in this example are all based on pure strategies, the expected-profit-maximizing price C, and hence the expected profit, equals the highest price at which information is still purchased (marked by circles in the graph, as in this specific example the last segment of each curve applies to an equilibrium by which the information is not being purchased at all). From the figure we see that indeed in this sample setting, anonymously eliminating some of the applicable values is highly beneficial - for example, the elimination of x_1 results in a profit of 3.7, compared to a profit of 1.2 in the case no information is being a priori eliminated (i.e., $D = \emptyset$).

As discussed in the introduction, benefiting from providing some of the information for free may seem non-intuitive at first—seemingly the broker is giving away some of her ability to disambiguate the auctioneer's and bidders' uncertainty. Yet, since the choice of whether the information is purchased or not at any specific

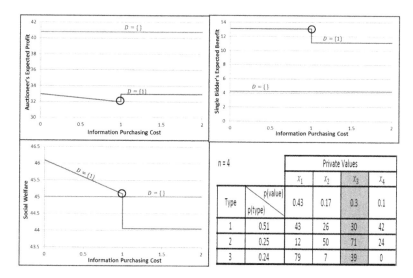

Fig. 2. An example of an improvement both in the broker's expected profit and the social welfare as a result of free information disclosure. The true common value of the auctioned item in this example is x_3.

price derives from equilibrium considerations, rather than merely the auctioneer's preference, it is possible that providing information for free becomes a preferable choice for the broker.

The benefit in free information disclosure does not necessarily come at the expense of social welfare. For exemplifying this we introduce Fig. 2. The setting used for this example is given in the bottom right side of the figure. Again, the auctioneer's strategy is to disclose the set which will benefit her the most. In this example the broker's expected profit increases from 0 to 1 by publicly eliminating the value x_1 (the information is not purchased otherwise), and at the same time the social welfare (sum of the bidders' and auctioneer's profit) increases from 45 to 45.2, due to the substantial increase in the bidder's profit (from 4.2 to 13.1). If including the broker's expected profit in the social welfare calculation, the increase is even greater.

Finally, we note the importance of disclosing the information anonymously or without leaving a trace of a strategic behavior from the broker's side. If the auctioneer and bidders suspect that the broker may disclose free information strategically, then the equilibrium analysis should be extended to accommodate the probabilistic update resulting from their reasoning of the broker's strategy. This latter analysis is left beyond the scope of the current paper—as discussed in the previous section there are various ways nowadays for anonymous disclosure of information, justifying this specific modeling choice.

4   Sequencing Heuristics

The extraction of the broker's expected-profit-maximizing subset D is computationally exhausting due to the exponential number of subsets for which equilibria
need to be calculated — the broker needs to iterate over all possible $2^{|X^*|-1} - 1$
D subsets (as there are $|X^*| - 1$ values that can be eliminated, and eliminating
all but the true value necessarily unfolds the latter as the true one). Therefore, in this section we present two efficient heuristics—Variance-based (Vb) and
Second-Price-Variance-based ($SPVb$)—that enable the broker to predict with
much success what subsets D are likely to result, if eliminated for free, with
close to optimal expected profit. The heuristics can be considered sequencing
heuristics, as they aim to determine the order according to which the different
subsets should be evaluated. The idea is to evaluate early in the process those
subsets that are likely to be associated with the greatest expected profit. This
way a highly favorable solution will be obtained regardless of how many subsets
can be evaluated in total.

Variance-based (Vb). The value of the information supplied by the broker derives
from the different players' (auctioneer and bidders) ability to distinguish the true
common value from others, i.e., to better identify the worth of the auctioned item
to different bidders. Therefore this heuristic relies on the variance between the
possible private values that the information purchased will disambiguate as the
primary indicator for its worth. Specifically, if the broker a priori eliminates the
subset D, we first update the probabilities of the remaining applicable values,
i.e., $Pr^*(x \in X^* - D) = \frac{Pr(X=x)}{\sum_{y \in X^* - D} Pr(X=y)}$. The revised probabilities are then
used for calculating the variance of the private values in the bidder's type level,
denoted $Var(T = t)$: $Var(T = t) = \sum_{x \in X^* - D} Pr^*(x)(V_t(x) - B(t, \emptyset))^2$, where
$V_t(x)$ is the private value of a bidder of type $T = t$ if knowing that the true
common value is x, as defined in the model section, and $B(t, \emptyset)$ is calculated
according to (1), based on a setting $X^* - D$. The overall weighted variance is
calculated as the weighted sum of the variance in the bidder's type level, using
the type probabilities as weights, i.e., $\sum_{t \in T} Pr(T = t) \cdot Var(T = t)$. The order
according to which the different subsets $D \subset X^*$ should be evaluated is thus
based on the overall weighted variance, descending.

Figure 3(a) illustrates the performance of Vb (middle curve) as a function
of the number of evaluated free disclosed subsets (horizontal axis). Since the
settings that were used for producing the graph highly varied, as detailed below,
we had to use a normalized measure of performance. Therefore we used the
ratio between the broker's expected profit if following the sequence generated
by the heuristic and the expected profit achieved with the profit-maximizing
subset (i.e., how close we manage to get to the result of brute force) as the
primary performance measure in our evaluation. The graph depicts also the
performance of random ordering as a baseline. The set of problems used for this
graph contains 2500 randomly generated settings where the common value may
obtain six possible values, each assigned with a random probability, normalized
such that all probabilities sum to 1. Similarly, the number of bidders and the

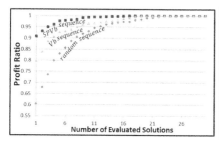 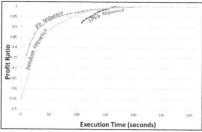

Fig. 3. Performance (ratio between achieved expected profit and maximal expected profit): (a) Vb and $SPVb$ versus random ordering; and (b) all three methods as a function of running time. All data points are the average over 2500 random settings with 6 possible values the common value obtains.

number of bidder types in each setting were randomly set within the ranges (2–10) and (2–6), respectively. Finally, the probability assigned to each bidder type was generated in the same manner as with the common value probabilities. For each setting we randomly picked one of the values the common value may obtain, according to the common-value probability function. Each data point in the figure thus represents the average performance over the 2500 randomly generated settings.

As can be seen from the graph, Vb dominates the random sequencing in the sense that it produces substantially better results for any number of subsets being evaluated. In particular, the improvement in performance with the heuristic is most notable for relatively small number of evaluated solutions, which is the primary desirable property for such a sequencing method, as the goal is to identify highly favorable solutions within a limited number of evaluations. As expected, the performance of both Vb and random ordering monotonically increase, converging to 1 (and necessarily reaching 1 once all possible solutions have been evaluated). This is because as the number of evaluated subsets increases the process becomes closer to brute force.

Second-Price-Variance-based (SPVb). This heuristic is similar to Vb in the sense that it orders the different subsets according to their weighted variance, descending. It differ from Vb in the sense that instead of depending on the variance in bidders' private values it uses the variance in the worth of information to the auctioneer, i.e., in the expected second price bids. The variance of the expected second price bids if disclosing D for free, denoted $Var(D)$, is calculated as: $Var(D) = \sum_{x \in X^* - D} Pr^*(x)(ER_{auc}(x) - ER_{auc}(\emptyset|D))^2$, where $Pr^*(x)$ is calculated as in Vb, $ER_{auc}(x)$ is the expected second highest bid if disclosing to the bidders that the true value is x, as given in the former section. $ER_{auc}(\emptyset|D)$ is the expected second highest bid if the auctioneer discloses no information to the bidders however the bidders are aware of the elimination of the subset D by the broker, i.e., bid according to $B(t, \emptyset) = \sum_{x \in X^* - D} V_t(x)Pr(X = x) / \sum_{x \in X^* - D} Pr(X = x)$.

Figure 3(a) also illustrates the performance of $SPVb$ (upper curve) as a function of the number of evaluated subsets D using a similar evaluation methodology and the same 2500 settings that were used for evaluating Vb, as described above. As can be seen from the graph, $SPVb$ dominates random sequencing and produces a substantial improvement, especially when the number of evaluated subsets is small. In fact, comparing the two upper curves in Fig. 3(a) we observe that $SPVb$ dominates Vb in terms of performance as a function of the number of evaluated sets. One impressive finding related to $SPVb$ is that even if choosing the first subset in the sequence it produces a relatively high performance can be obtained—91% of the maximum possible expected profit, on average. This means that even without evaluating any of the subsets (e.g., in case the broker is incapable of carrying the equilibrium analysis) but merely by extracting the sets ordering, the broker can come up with a relatively effective subset of values to disclose for free.

This dominance of $SPVb$ is explained by the fact that it relies on the variance between the winning bids rather than the bidders' private values. Meaning it relates to the true worth of the information to the auctioneer and consequently to the broker's profit. While this is $SPVb$'s main advantage, compared to Vb, it is also its main weakness: from the computational aspect, the time required for calculating the expected second-price variance of all applicable subsets D is substantially greater than the time required for Vb to calculate the variance between the possible private values. The expected profit of the auctioneer when disclosing the information $X = x$, denoted $ER_{auc}(X = x)$, equals the expected second-best bid when the bidders are given x, formally calculated as:

$$ER_{auc}(X = x) = \sum_{w \in \{B(t,x)|t \in T\}} w(\sum_{k=1}^{n-1} n\binom{n-1}{k}$$

$$\sum_{B(t,x)>w} Pr(T = t)(\sum_{B(t,x)=w} Pr(T = t))^k(\sum_{B(t,x)<w} Pr(T = t))^{n-k-1} \quad (4)$$

$$+ \sum_{k=2}^{n} \binom{n}{k}(\sum_{B(t,x)=w} Pr(T = t))^k(\sum_{B(t,x)<w} Pr(T = t))^{n-k})$$

The calculation iterates over all of the possible second-best bid values, assigning for each its probability of being the second-best bid. As we consider discrete probability functions, it is possible to have two bidders placing the same highest bid (in which case it is also the second-best bid). For any given bid value, w, we therefore consider the probability of having either: (i) one bidder bidding more than w, $k \in 1, ..., (n-1)$ bidders bidding exactly w and all of the other bidders bidding less than w; or (ii) $k \in 2, ..., n$ bidders bidding exactly w and all of the others bidding less than w. Notice that (4) also holds for the case where $x = \emptyset$ (in which case bidders use $B(t, \emptyset)$ according to (1)).

The mentioned calculation results in a combinatorial (in the number of values the common value may obtain) run time. The $SPVb$ method thus requires more time to run for producing the sequence according to which sets need to be

Table 1. Average time in seconds for extracting the broker's equilibrium profit in a single setting as a function of $|X^*|$.

# of possible values	3	4	5	6	7	8
Execution time (seconds)	0.16	0.58	3.57	20.07	103.19	708.46

evaluated, however the ordering it produces is substantially better than the one produced by Vb. Similarly, random sequencing does not require any "setup" time and the different subsets can be evaluated right away.

In order to weigh in this effect in the heuristics' evaluation we present Fig. 3(b). Here, the performance is depicted as a function of the actual run-time (in seconds, over the horizontal axis) rather than the number of subsets evaluated once the ordering is completed.[2] Here, we can see the tradeoff between the initial calculation required for the ordering itself and the improvement achieved within the first few evaluated subsets. The shift of each curve over the horizontal axis, till its first data point, is the time it took to generate the sequence of subsets. From the graph we see that if the amount of time allowed for running is relatively small then one should choose to use a random sequence for evaluation. If the broker is less time-constrained, the best choice is to use Vb and then evaluate subsets according to the generated sequence. We notice that the same typical behavior was observed for the case of five and seven possible values that the common value may obtain. Evaluating for settings with more than six values is impractical, as it requires solving for thousands of such settings each, as seen from the Table 1, takes substantial time to solve.

Table 1 depicts the average time it took to extract the equilibrium solution for a setting according to the number of values in X^*. Each data point is the average for the 2500 problems described above. This justifies our use of six values settings in the numerical evaluation, and generally motivates the need for the sequencing heuristics we provide by showing that evaluating all possible sets is in many cases impractical — indeed in many cases the total number of values in X^* is moderate,[3] however, even with 8 values it takes more than 10 min to extract the broker's equilibrium profit for a single instance.

5   The Influence of Bidders' Awareness

Next we consider the case where instead of revealing the information for free to all, only the auctioneer receives it (e.g., using anonymous email). In this case the auctioneer needs to decide whether to reveal this information (or part of it)

---

[2] Our evaluation framework was built in Matlab R2011b and run on top of Windows7 on a PC with Intel(R) Xeon(R) CPU E5620 (2 processors) with 24.0 GB RAM.

[3] For example, in oil drilling surveys, geologists usually specify 3–4 possible ranges for the amount of oil or gas that is likely to be found in a given area. Similarly, when requesting an estimate of the amount of traffic next to an advertising space, the answer would usually be in the form of ranges rather than exact numbers.

to the bidders. This complicates a bit the structure of the game: (a) First, the broker needs to decide on the set D of values to be eliminated for free and the price C of her service of disambiguating the remaining uncertainty; (b) then, she needs to transfer D anonymously to the auctioneer; (c) next, the auctioneer needs to decide what part $D' \subseteq D$ to further disclose to the bidders; (d) then, the auctioneer needs to decide whether to purchase the true value from the broker, and if purchasing, upon receiving the value, whether to disclose it to the bidders or leave them uncertain concerning the true value; (e) finally, the bidders need to bid for the auctioned item.

The analysis of this case relies heavily on the analysis given in the former sections. The resulting adversarial setting if using D and D' is one where bidders bid $V_t(x)$ whenever the information is purchased and disclosed by the auctioneer, and otherwise $B(t, \emptyset)$ according to (1), except that this time the probabilities $Pr^*(X = x_i)$ used by bidders result from the equilibrium of a setting where the original values are $X^* - D'$. Therefore, upon receiving the information D from the anonymous source, the auctioneer needs to calculate her expected profit from disclosing any subset $D' \subseteq D$ and choose the one that maximizes it. The auctioneer's expected profit calculation in this case is, however, a bit different, due to the asymmetry in information. When initially disclosing D' to bidders, the auctioneer needs to calculate the expected second best bid from disclosing any value $x \in X^* - D$, based on the bidders' type distribution and their bidding strategy as given above. The auctioneer should choose to disclose any value x for which the expected second best bid if disclosed is greater than the expected second best bid when no information is disclosed (i.e., when bidders bid $B(t, \emptyset)$ according to the equilibrium for the $X^* - D'$ instance of the original problem, as explained above). This allows the broker deciding what subset D to disclose, such that her expected profit is maximized.

Figure 4 is an example of a case where the information broker discloses the free information only to the auctioneer and it is to the auctioneer's choice which parts of the information (if at all) to disclose to the bidders prior to the start of the auction. It relies on a setting of three bidders, two possible types and four different values the common value may obtain $(x_1, ..., x_4)$, out of which x_4 is the true common value. The full setting details are given in the table in the right hand side of the figure. The leaf nodes provide the expected profit of the auctioneer (inside the rectangle) and the broker (below the rectangle) for each combination of selections made by these two players (the subset D disclosed for free and the subset $D' \subseteq D$ disclosed to the bidders), according to the resulting equilibrium as analyzed above. The yellow colored leafs are therefore those corresponding to the auctioneer's best response given the subset D picked by the broker, hence the expected-profit maximizing strategy for the broker is to anonymously disclose to the auctioneer the subset $\{x_2, x_3\}$ as in this case the auctioneer will choose not to disclose any of these two values to the bidders, resulting in expected profit of 0.9 (compared to 0.8,0.6,0.6,0.8,0.4 and 0.4 if eliminating $\{\emptyset\}, \{x_1\}, \{x_2\}, \{x_3\}, \{x_1, x_2\}$ and $\{x_1, x_3\}$, respectively).

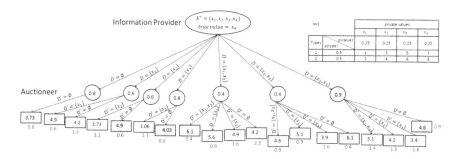

Fig. 4. Disclosing the free information to the auctioneer only: the broker needs to decide on the subset D to eliminate and then the auctioneer needs to decide on the subset $D' \subset D$ to disclose to bidders. (Color figure online)

Interestingly, if the broker chooses to anonymously disclose to both the auctioneer and the bidders that x_2 and x_3 can be eliminated, her expected profit, calculated based on the analysis given in former sections, is 1.4. This is substantially greater than in the case where the bidders are unaware of the information that was disclosed for free. Furthermore, eliminating x_2 and x_3 for free is not necessarily the broker's expected-profit-maximizing strategy for the scenario where the free information reaches both the auctioneer and bidders. It is possible that there is another subset which elimination results in an even greater improvement in profit when compared to disclosing the elimination of x_2 and x_3 to the auctioneer only. This outcome, as discussed in the introduction is quite nonintuitive because by eliminating the asymmetry in the information disclosed to the different players the broker seemingly reduces the auctioneer's power against the bidders in this adversarial setting. Indeed, when the choice is given to the auctioneer she would rather not disclose this information to the bidders and increase her profit. Since the auctioneer is the potential purchaser of the broker's service information offered by the broker, it might seem that by disclosing the free information only to her, she will have a greater flexibility in making use of the remaining information (that is offered for sale) hence will see a greater value in purchasing it. Yet, the improvement in the auctioneer's competence by disclosing the free information to her only does not translate to an improvement in the broker's profit—eventually the broker's profit depends on the range of prices and the corresponding probabilities at which her information is indeed purchased. These latter factors result from the equilibria considerations, leading to behaviors such as in the example above.

Even for this case, the sequencing heuristics Vb and $SPVb$ are of much importance. Figure 5 presents the performance evaluation for these two heuristics, for settings with six values, demonstrating that highly efficient solutions can be extracted even with a small number of evaluations.

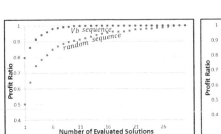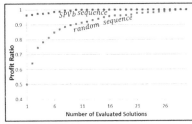

Fig. 5. Performance (ratio between achieved expected profit and maximal expected profit) when the information is disclosed for free only to the auctioneer and she chooses which information to disclose to the bidders: (a) Vb versus random ordering as a function of number of evaluated subsets; (b) $SPVb$ versus random ordering as a function of number of evaluated subsets. All data points are the average of 2500 random settings with 6 possible values the common value obtains.

6   Related Work

Over the years auctions have focused much interest in research, mostly due to their advantage in effectively extracting bidders' valuations and the guarantee of many auction protocols to result in efficient allocation [5, 7, 18, 21, 34, 35]. The case where there is some uncertainty associated with the value of the auctioned item is quite common in auctions literature. Most commonly it is assumed that the value of the auctioned item is unknown to the bidders at the time of the auction and bidders may only have an estimate or some privately known signal, such as an expert's estimate, that is correlated with the true value [14, 22]. Many of the works using uncertain common value models assumed asymmetry in the knowledge available to the bidders and the auctioneer regarding the auctioned item, typically having sellers more informative than bidders [1, 10]. As such, much recent emphasis was placed on the role of information revelation [8, 11, 12, 19]. In particular, several works have considered the computational aspects of such models where the auctioneer needs to decide on the subsets of non-distinguishable values to be disclosed to the bidders [9, 10, 24]. Still, all these works assume the auctioneer necessarily obtains the information and that the division into non-distinguishable groups, whenever applicable, is always given to the bidders a priori. Our problem, on the other hand, does not require that the auctioneer possesses (or purchases) the information in the first place, and allows not disclosing any value even if the information is purchased. Recent work that does consider an auction setting with a strategic broker, and in fact provides the underlying three-ply equilibrium analysis for this case [3, 33], limits the strategic behavior of the broker to price-setting only. In this paper we extend that work to include an additional strategic dimension for the broker, in the sense of anonymously disclosing some of the information for free. Furthermore, unlike this prior work, in this paper we deal with the computational aspects of extracting the broker's strategy.

Models where agents can disambiguate the uncertainty associated with the opportunities they consider exploiting through the purchase of information have been studied in several other multi-agent domains, e.g., in optimal stopping domains [27–30,38]. Here, the main questions studied were how much costly information it makes sense to acquire before making a decision [25,31], in particular when additional attributes can be revealed at certain costs along the search path [23,37]. Relaxation of the perfect signals assumption has also been explored in models of economic search [2,6]. Alas, mediators in such models usually take the form of matchmakers rather than information brokers. Those that do consider a self-interested information broker in these domains, e.g., Nahum et al. [26], focused on the way it should set the price for the information it provides and did not consider the option of free information disclosure.

Other related work can be found in the study of platforms that bring together different sides of the market (e.g., dating, or eCommerce platforms). Here, there is much work on the impact on selective information disclosure [15], strategic ordering of the disclosed information [16] and having the platform charging only one of the two participating sides [17] and even cases where consumers are in effect paid to use the platform were studied [32]. Our work can be viewed in a similar vein, especially in the context of the information broker subsidizing information provisioning, although the intuitions behind our results are quite different and grounded in the transition between different equilibria rather than in the profit of potentially increasing participation overall.

7   Conclusions and Future Work

Information brokers have become an integral part of many multi-agent systems. These range from individuals with specific expertise, offering their services for a fee (e.g., analysts), to large information services, such as Carfax.com or credit report companies. The model and analysis given in the paper adds an important strategic dimension to prior work in the form of influencing the auctioneer's and bidders' strategic interaction through the anonymous revelation of some of the information that is offered for sale. As discussed throughout the paper, this behavior may seem a bit unnatural. We show, however, that this strategy can actually be highly beneficial to the broker. In fact, as demonstrated in the paper, it can even lead to an overall improvement in the social welfare. Furthermore, if given the option to disclose the free information to both the bidders and the auctioneer or to the auctioneer only, the broker may benefit from choosing the first, despite the fact that the auctioneer is the one to decide about purchasing the information.

The paper presents two sequencing heuristics aiming to reduce the computation time of the broker's expected-profit maximizing strategy. The results of an extensive evaluation of these are quite encouraging - the generated sequences, with both heuristics, are quite effective, as the very few initial subsets placed first in the sequence offer expected profit very close to the expected-profit-maximizing one. Both methods use the variance as a measure for the profit in disclosing a given set, differing in the values based on which the variance is calculated—the bidder's private valuations and the expected second price bids. Interestingly, we find that while the use of the expected second-price produces a substantially more efficient sequence, it is better to rely on the raw values (i.e., bidders' valuations) as the execution time of generating the sequence using the latter method is substantially shorter, leading to better performance overall.

We note that, much like prior work, our model makes several assumptions that can be relaxed in future research. For example, one can think of settings where the information is provided to the bidders not just based on the auctioneer's decision to disclose it. Here, numerous variations can be considered. For example, the bidders can purchase the information, whether symmetrically or asymmetrically, either directly from the broker or indirectly from the auctioneer. These of course require extending the analysis to include all the different dynamics that will be formed. Another natural extension of our model would be one where the auctioneer and the bidders are aware to the fact that the broker is the one that disclosed the information for free (i.e., the free disclosure is not anonymous anymore) as discussed in the analysis section.

References

1. Akerlof, G.: The market for "lemons": quality uncertainty and the market mechanism. Q. J. Econ. **84**(3), 488–500 (1970)
2. Alkoby, S., Sarne, D., Das, S.: Strategic free information disclosure for search-based information platforms. In: Proceedings of the 2015 International Conference on Autonomous Agents and Multiagent Systems, pp. 635–643. International Foundation for Autonomous Agents and Multiagent Systems (2015)
3. Alkoby, S., Sarne, D., David, E.: Manipulating information providers access to information in auctions. In: Cheng, S.M., Day, M.Y. (eds.) TAAI 2014. LNCS, vol. 8916, pp. 14–25. Springer, Cham (2014)
4. Board, S.: Revealing information in auctions: the allocation effect. Econ. Theor. **38**(1), 125–135 (2009)
5. Bredin, J., Parkes, D., Duong, Q.: Chain: a dynamic double auction framework for matching patient agents. J. Artif. Intell. Res. (JAIR) **30**, 133–179 (2007)
6. Das, S., Kamenica, E.: Two-sided bandits and the dating market. In: Proceedings of the Nineteenth International Joint Conference on Artificial Intelligence, Edinburgh, UK, pp. 947–952, August 2005
7. Dobzinski, S., Nisan, N.: Mechanisms for multi-unit auctions. J. Artif. Intell. Res. (JAIR) **37**, 85–98 (2010)
8. Dufwenberg, M., Gneezyi, U.: Information disclosure in auctions: an experiment. J. Econ. Behav. Organ. **48**(4), 431–444 (2002)
9. Dughmi, S., Immorlica, N., Roth, A.: Constrained signaling for welfare and revenue maximization. CoRR, abs/1302.4713 (2013)
10. Emek, Y., Feldman, M., Gamzu, I., Leme, R., Tennenholtz, M.: Signaling schemes for revenue maximization. In: Proceedings of the 12th ACM Conference on Electronic Commerce (EC-12), pp. 514–531 (2012)
11. Eső, P., Szentes, B.: Optimal information disclosure in auctions and the handicap auction. Rev. Econ. Stud. **74**(3), 705–731 (2007)

12. Ganuza, J.J., Penalva, J.S.: Signal orderings based on dispersion and the supply of private information in auctions. Econometrica **78**(3), 1007–1030 (2010)
13. Goeree, J., Offerman, T.: Efficiency in auctions with private and common values: an experimental study. Am. Econ. Rev. **92**(3), 625–643 (2002)
14. Goeree, J., Offerman, T.: Competitive bidding in auctions with private and common values. Econ. J. **113**, 598–613 (2003)
15. Hajaj, C., Hazon, N., Sarne, D.: Improving comparison shopping agents' competence through selective price disclosure. Electron. Commer. Res. Appl. **14**(6), 563–581 (2015)
16. Hajaj, C., Hazon, N., Sarne, D.: Enhancing comparison shopping agents through ordering and gradual information disclosure. To Appear in Autonomous Agents and Multi-Agent Systems (2016)
17. Hajaj, C., Sarne, D.: Strategic information platforms: selective disclosure and the price of free. In: Proceedings of the Fifteenth ACM Conference on Economics and Computation, pp. 839–856. ACM (2014)
18. Hajiaghayi, M., Kleinberg, R., Mahdian, M., Parkes, D.: Online auctions with re-usable goods. In: Proceedings of the Sixth ACM Conference on Electronic Commerce (EC-2005), pp. 165–174 (2005)
19. Jewitt, I., Li, D.: Cheap-talk information disclosure in auctions. Technical report, Working paper (2012)
20. Johnson, J.P., Myatt, D.P.: On the simple economics of advertising, marketing, and product design. Am. Econ. Rev. **96**, 756–784 (2006)
21. Juda, A., Parkes, D.: An options-based solution to the sequential auction problem. Artif. Intell. **173**(7–8), 876–899 (2009)
22. Klemperer, P.: Auctions: Theory and Practice. Princeton University Press, New Jersey (2004)
23. Lim, C., Bearden, J.N., Smith, J.C.: Sequential search with multiattribute options. Decis. Anal. **3**(1), 3–15 (2006)
24. Miltersen, P., Sheffet, O.: Send mixed signals: earn more, work less. In: Proceedings of the 13th ACM Conference on Electronic Commerce (EC 2012), pp. 234–247 (2012)
25. Moscarini, G., Smith, L.: The optimal level of experimentation. Econometrica **69**(6), 1629–1644 (2003)
26. Nahum, Y., Sarne, D., Das, S., Shehory, O.: Two-sided search with experts. In: Proceedings of the 13th ACM Conference on Electronic Commerce, pp. 754–771. ACM (2012)
27. Rochlin, I., Aumann, Y., Sarne, D., Golosman, L.: Efficiency and fairness in team search with self-interested agents. Auton. Agent. Multi-Agent Syst. **30**(3), 526–552 (2016)
28. Rochlin, I., Sarne, D.: Utilizing costly coordination in multi-agent joint exploration. Multiagent Grid Syst. **10**(1), 23–49 (2014)
29. Rochlin, I., Sarne, D.: Constraining information sharing to improve cooperative information gathering. J. Artif. Intell. Res. (JAIR) **54**, 437–469 (2015)
30. Rochlin, I., Sarne, D., Mash, M.: Joint search with self-interested agents and the failure of cooperation enhancers. Artif. Intell. **214**, 45–65 (2014)
31. Rochlin, I., Sarne, D., Zussman, G.: Sequential multi-agent exploration for a common goal. Web Intell. Agent Syst. **11**(3), 221–244 (2013)
32. Rysman, M.: The economics of two-sided markets. J. Econ. Perspect. **23**, 125–143 (2009)
33. Sarne, D., Alkoby, S., David, E.: On the choice of obtaining and disclosing the common value in auctions. Artif. Intell. **215**, 24–54 (2014)

34. Stone, P., Schapire, R., Littman, M., Csirik, J., McAllester, D.: Decision-theoretic bidding based on learned density models in simultaneous, interacting auctions. J. Artif. Intell. Res. **19**(1), 209–242 (2003)
35. Tennenholtz, M.: Tractable combinatorial auctions and b-matching. Artif. Intell. **140**(1/2), 231–243 (2002)
36. Vickrey, W.: Counterspeculation, auctions, and competitive sealed tenders. J. Finance **16**(1), 8–37 (1961)
37. Wiegmann, D.D., Weinersmith, K.L., Seubert, S.M.: Multi-attribute mate choice decisions and uncertainty in the decision process: a generalized sequential search strategy. J. Math. Biol. **60**(4), 543–572 (2010)
38. Wilson, K.E., Szechtman, R., Atkinson, M.P.: A sequential perspective on searching for static targets. Eur. J. Oper. Res. **215**(1), 218–226 (2011)

On Revenue-Maximizing Walrasian Equilibria for Size-Interchangeable Bidders

Enrique Areyan Viqueira$^{(\boxtimes)}$, Amy Greenwald, Victor Naroditskiy,
and Daniels Collins

Brown University, Providence, RI 02912, USA
{eareyan,amy,daniel_collins}@brown.edu, vnarodit@gmail.com

Abstract. We study a market setting in which bidders are single-valued but size-interchangeable, and there exist multiple copies of heterogeneous goods. Our contributions are as follows: (1) providing polynomial-time algorithms for finding a *restricted* envy-free equilibrium with reserve prices (EFEr); (2) posing the problem of finding a revenue-maximizing EFEr, and running experiments to show that our algorithms perform well on the metrics of revenue, efficiency, and time, without incurring too many violations of the stronger Walrasian equilibrium with reserve (envy-free plus market clearance) conditions.

1   Introduction

In a **centralized combinatorial matching market (CCMM)**, a market maker offers a set of n heterogeneous **goods** to m consumers (or **bidders**), the latter of which are interested in acquiring certain combinations (or **bundles**) of goods. In general, there are multiple copies of each good i, but the total supply N_i of each good is finite. Bidder j's preferences are captured by a **valuation** function $v_j(\cdot)$ that describes how bidder j values each bundle.

In general, a bidder's valuation function can be an arbitrary function of the set of all bundles. We study a case where bidders are only interested in specific varieties of goods, and we model these interests as edges in a graph connecting bidders only to their goods of interest. Furthermore, in our model, bidder's valuations are **single-valued**, and depend only on the bundle's size, assuming the bundle is a match for the bidder. The value then is either a positive value R_j, if the size of the bundle is at least some threshold I_j, and 0 otherwise.

Our model is motivated by the Trading Agent Competition Ad Exchange game (TAC AdX) [15], which in turn models online ad exchanges in which agents face the challenge of bidding for display-ad impressions needed to fulfill advertisement contracts, after which they earn the amount the advertiser budgeted. Other settings captured by this model include the problem of how to allocate specialized workers to firms, and how to compensate the workers, where each firm requires a certain number of workers to produce an output (a new technology, for instance) that yields a certain revenue.

© Springer International Publishing AG 2017
S. Ceppi et al. (Eds.): AMEC/TADA 2015/2016, LNBIP 271, pp. 19–34, 2017.
DOI: 10.1007/978-3-319-54229-4_2

One well-studied special case of our model is that of (single-valued) **single-minded** consumers [11]. There, bidders are only interested in one particular bundle. Hence their valuation function can be understood as assigning value R_j to that bundle or any superset thereof, and 0 to all other bundles. We call our valuations (single-valued) **size-interchangeable**, because bidders can be satisfied (i.e., achieve value R_j) by any bundle of size I_j that consists of their desired goods. Like single-minded valuations, our interchangeable valuations model complements, since a bidder is not satisfied unless it receives a bundle of sufficient size. Furthermore, our interchangeable valuations model (perfect) substitutes, since any bundle of sufficient size that consists of suitable goods will do.

In this paper, we assume valuations are known to the market maker. Thus, our problem is one of equilibrium computation rather than traditional mechanism design (where values are private). A market **outcome** is an allocation-pricing pair (X, p), where X describes the assignment of goods to bidders, and p ascribes prices to goods. While X is a matrix, we assume p is a vector, which precludes any form of price discrimination (all copies of the same good must have the same price). Furthermore, we assume **item pricing**, not bundle pricing, so that the price of a bundle is the sum of the prices of all the goods (items) in the bundle. Both of these assumptions—no price discrimination and item pricing—are most natural.

Example 1 (CCMM and possible outcomes). Consider the CCMM in Figure (A). There are two goods, G and F, with 2 copies of good G and 3 copies of good F, and two bidders, Y and Z. Bidder Y wants two copies of good G (as indicated by the edge from G to Y) and values this bundle at 10, and bidder Z ascribes the value 5 to any bundle of size 2 comprised of any combination of Gs and Fs (also indicated by edges). Possible outcomes of this markets are depicted in Figures (B) and (C).

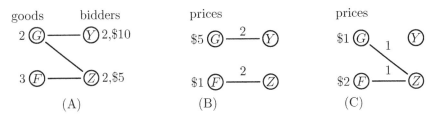

Outcome (B) allocates 2 copies of good G to bidder Y at a price of $5 per copy, and 2 copies of good F to bidder Z at a price of $1 per copy. This outcome results in the optimal social welfare ($15) and a revenue of $12.

Outcome (C) allocates to bidder Z only, 1 copy of good G at a price of $1, and 1 copy of good F at a price of $2. This outcome results in a social welfare of $5 and a revenue of $3.

In an important related setting, bidders have unit-demand valuations, meaning they are interested in at most one good, but may have different valuations for different goods. This is a well-studied setting [1,2,6,7], with important theoretical guarantees. In particular, there always exists a Walrasian equilibrium (WE) outcome [5] in which bidders are envy-free, meaning they all receive one of their favorite bundles at the set prices, and the market clears, meaning unallocated goods are priced at zero. It follows from this second condition, by the first welfare theorem of economics, that any allocation that is part of any WE outcome maximizes social welfare. In addition, it is possible to find a revenue-maximizing WE among all WE outcomes in polynomial-time (assuming unit demand) [6].

Building on Myerson's [10] intuition, Guruswami et al. [7] generalized the problem of searching for a revenue-maximizing WE to that of searching for a revenue-maximizing Walrasian equilibrium with reserve prices (WEr), where bidders are envy-free and the market clears up to the reserve price: i.e., unallocated goods are priced at the reserve. For bidders with unit-demand valuations a WE always exists [5]; likewise, a WEr always exists. In addition, for a fixed reserve price, we can find the revenue-maximizing WEr in polynomial-time (using the same approach as in [6]). With this more general solution concept in mind, Guruswami et al. pose the problem of finding a revenue-maximizing WEr, for which they propose a polynomial-time approximation algorithm that picks a particular set of candidate reserve prices, generates a revenue-maximizing WEr for each, and then returns the revenue-maximizing WEr among those considered.

For our model—single-valued, size-interchangeable bidders—we remind the reader that WE do not exist in general; in fact, they are not guaranteed to exist even for single-minded bidders. By relaxing the market clearance condition, we arrive at more general solution concept—an **Envy-Free Equilibirum (EFE)**— which insists only that bidders are envy-free, and which always exists. However, the first welfare theorem does not hold for EFE, so maximal social welfare is not guaranteed by this solution concept.

Departing from the social welfare concern, we instead tackle the competing problem of maximizing seller revenue. Since finding revenue-maximizing WEr is APX-hard in a CCMM assuming single-minded bidders [7], we propose a polynomial time heuristic for approximately solving for revenue-maximizing EFEr (an EFE in which unallocated goods are priced at a reserve), where we relax the envy-free condition to a **restricted envy-free** condition, which we are able to express as linear constraints. Building on the ideas of Guruswami et al., we then search over a space of carefully chosen reserve prices to find an approximately revenue-maximizing EFEr. In particular, whereas Guruswami et al. used this approach to find an approximately revenue-maximizing WEr for unit-demand bidders, we apply this same idea to the case of size-interchangeable (and hence, single-minded) bidders.

In sum, our contributions are: (1) providing polynomial-time algorithms for finding a *restricted* envy-free equilibrium with reserve prices (EFEr); (2) posing the problem of finding a revenue-maximizing EFEr, and running experiments to show that our algorithms perform well on the metrics of revenue, efficiency, and time, without incurring too many violations of the WEr (envy-free plus market clearance) conditions.

2   Model and Solution Concepts

We define a **centralized combinatorial matching market** (CCMM) to be
an augmented bipartite graph $(U, C, E, \boldsymbol{N}, \boldsymbol{I})$ with a set of n types of goods U,
a set of m bidders C, a set of edges E from bidders to goods indicating which
goods are of interest to which bidders, a supply vector $\boldsymbol{N} = (N_1, \ldots, N_n)$, and a
demand vector $\boldsymbol{I} = (I_1, \ldots, I_m)$. That is, there are $N_i > 0$ copies of good $i \in U$,
and $I_j > 0$ *total* goods are demanded by bidder $j \in C$. Note, however, that
bidder j only demands copies of goods it is connected to via an edge.

In other words, in a CCMM, bidders are interested in acquiring bundles of
goods of at least some fixed size. Note that this is a more general case of the well-
studied problem of single-minded consumers [11] where bidders are interested
only in one particular bundle of goods. For this reason, we call our valuation
function size-interchangeable. Formally:

Definition 1 *(Single-valued, Size-interchangeable valuations). Given a CCMM
$M = (U, C, E, \boldsymbol{N}, \boldsymbol{I})$, a bidder j is single-valued, size-interchangeable, if it
demands $I_j > 0$ goods among those to which it is connected, and values all
such bundles by the function: $v_j(X_j) = R_j > 0$, if $\sum_{i|(i,j)\in E} x_{ij} \geq I_j$, and 0
otherwise. We call R_j the reward attained by j in case its demand I_j is fulfilled.*

Definition 2 *(Market). We call a **market** M a pair consisting of a CCMM
$(U, C, E, \boldsymbol{N}, \boldsymbol{I})$ and a reward vector $\boldsymbol{R} = (R_1, \ldots, R_m)$.*

Given a market M, an **allocation** A is a labeling $x(i, j) \in \mathbb{Z}_{\geq 0}$ of E that
represents the number of copies of good i allocated to bidder j. Such an allocation
can be represented by a matrix $\boldsymbol{X} \in \mathbb{Z}_{\geq 0}^n \times \mathbb{Z}_{\geq 0}^m$ where entry $x_{ij} = x(i, j)$. The
jth column of an allocation matrix is the **bundle** of goods assigned to bidder j,
which we denote by $X_j \in B(\boldsymbol{N})$, where $B(\boldsymbol{N}) = \prod_i \{0, 1, \ldots, N_i\}$.

A market **outcome** is an allocation-pricing pair $(\boldsymbol{X}, \boldsymbol{p})$, assigning goods to
bidders and per-good prices $p_i \in \mathbb{R}_+$. Given such an outcome, the cost of bundle
X_j to bidder j is given by $P_j(X_j) = \sum_i x_{ij} p_i$.

An allocation is **feasible** if, for all i, the total number of goods assigned
across bidders is no more than i's supply: i.e., for all $i : \sum_{j=1}^m x_{ij} \leq N_i$. We use
$F \equiv F(M)$ to denote the set of all feasible allocations. In a **feasible outcome**
the allocation is feasible.

The **utility** of bidder j is defined as follows: $u_j(\boldsymbol{X}, \boldsymbol{p}) = v_j(X_j) - P_j(X_j)$. A
standard assumption is that all bidders are utility maximizers, and thus a bidder
prefers outcomes with higher utilities.

A fundamental market outcome studied in the literature is that of Walrasian
Equilibrium (WE) [14], which we define using our notation as follows.

Definition 3 *(Walrasian Equilibrium). A feasible outcome $(\boldsymbol{X}, \boldsymbol{p})$ is a **Walrasian Equilibrium** (WE) if the following two conditions hold:*

1. ***Envy-freeness** (EF): There is no bundle X_j' that any bidder j prefers to its
   assigned bundle X_j, i.e., for all j, $X_j \in \arg\max_{X_j' \in B(\boldsymbol{N})} \{v_j(X_j') - P_j(X_j')\}$.*

2. ***Market clearance** (MC): Every unallocated good is priced at zero.*

The EF condition is a fairness condition; it ensures that the outcome maximizes the utility of every bidder. Note that each bidder is individually rational i.e., $u_j(\boldsymbol{X}, \boldsymbol{p}) \geq 0$, since the null allocation is always a feasible allocation. The MC condition, together with EF, implies, by the first welfare theorem of economics, that any allocation that is part of a WE is also welfare-maximizing. However, a WE need not exist in the markets studied in this paper.

Example 2 (Non-existence of WE). Consider the market in Figure (A) with one good and two single-minded bidders. Good u_1 is supplied in $N_1 = 2$ copies, bidder c_1 demands $I_1 = 1$ good, and bidder c_2 demands $I_2 = 2$ goods. Rewards are $R_1 = 5$ and $R_2 = 7$.

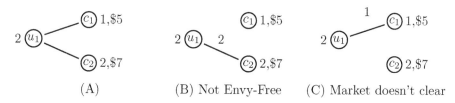

(A)   (B) Not Envy-Free   (C) Market doesn't clear

There are a total of 6 feasible allocations in this market and none of them are part of a Walrasian Equilibrium. Two such allocations are depicted in (B) and (C). In (B), there is no price p_1 for u_1 at which both bidders would be envy-free. In (C), we must have that $p_1 \geq 3.5$, or otherwise c_2 would have preferred 2 copies from u_1. But then the market does not clear since there is an unsold copy of u_1 with price greater than 0.

To address this existence problem, we drop the market clearance condition.

Definition 4 *(Envy-Free Equilibrium). A feasible outcome $(\boldsymbol{X}, \boldsymbol{p})$ is an **Envy-Free Equilibrium** (EFE) if envy-freeness holds.*

Note that, in outcome (C) of Example 2, at any price p_1 for u_1 such that $3.5 \leq p_1 \leq 5$, both bidders c_1 and c_2 are envy-free. It follows that this outcome is an EFE.

Unlike in the unit-demand case, where, by the first welfare theorem, a WE implies a welfare-maximizing allocation [12], an EFE (even for unit-demand bidders) does not guarantee a welfare-maximizing allocation. An outcome with a null allocation and prices high enough such that no bidder can afford even a single good is an EFE outcome with 0 welfare. But even for non-null allocations, an EFE outcome can yield low welfare.

Example 3 (An EFE does not imply an efficient allocation). Consider a market M with a single good that is supplied in $N_1 = m - 1$ copies and m bidders, where all bidders demand 1 good (i.e., $I_j = 1$, for all j). Rewards are defined as follow: for $1 \leq j < m : R_j = 1$ and $R_m = 2$.

Consider outcome $(\boldsymbol{X}, \boldsymbol{p})$, where bidder m is allocated one good at any price p_1 such that $1 < p_1 \leq 2$, and no other bidder is allocated any good. This outcome is an EFE since all bidders are envy-free. However, the welfare of this outcome is 2 for any $m > 1$, since we only satisfy bidder m.

A welfare maximizing allocation for this market is one that satisfies bidder m as well as many other bidders as possible, obtaining welfare $2 + \sum_{j=1}^{m-2} R_j = 2 + m - 2 = m$. Therefore, the welfare of the EFE $(\boldsymbol{X}, \boldsymbol{p})$, relative to the optimal welfare, approaches zero, as m approaches ∞.

Although at first glance it may seem disappointing the first welfare theorem does not hold for EFE, it is not a show stopper. Even in the unit-demand case, where the first welfare theorem does hold, there exists the competing, and incompatible goal, of maximizing seller revenue.

In a unit-demand CCMM, if we let $m(< r) = \{j \mid R_j < r\}$, then $|m(< r)|$ is the number of bidders with reward less than the reserve r. Assuming there exists an allocation that satisfies all bidders, by setting a reserve price r we lose at least $R_{\min}|m(< r)|$ welfare, where $R_{\min} = \min_j\{R_j\}$, while we are guaranteed revenue of at least $r|m(< r)^c|$. (Here A^c denotes the complement of set A.)

The following example further illustrate the tradeoff between welfare and revenue, in the case of single-minded bidders.

Example 4 (Welfare-Revenue Tradeoff). Consider the market in Figure (A) and the two different outcomes in Figures (B) and (C)

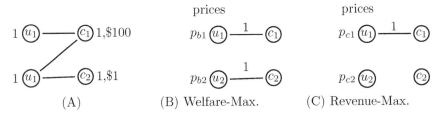

| (A) | (B) Welfare-Max. | (C) Revenue-Max. |

Outcome (B)'s allocation is welfare maximizing. To support an EFE we must have $0 \le p_{b2} \le 1$; otherwise c_2 would not be envy-free. Moreover, $p_{b1} \le p_{b2}$; otherwise c_1 would have preferred a copy of u_2. So prices can only be as high as $p_{b1} = p_{b2} = 1$, yielding revenue of 2. Outcome (C)'s allocation is not welfare maximizing. However, in this case, an EFE can be supported by higher prices than those in (B). In particular, $p_{c2} \ge 1$; otherwise c_2 would have preferred a copy of u_2. Again $p_{c1} \le p_{c2}$ for the same reasons as in (B). Prices could be as high as $p_{c1} = p_{c2} = 100$, yielding revenue of 100.

Example 4 motivates the introduction of reserve prices as a way to increase revenue while maintaining envy-freeness among market participants. In the previous example, we could set a reserve price of \$2 for u_2. Doing so would increase revenue from a maximum possible of \$2 (with no reserve price) to \$100. However, by setting reserve prices some bidders are effectively thrown out of the market, so welfare might not be maximized, because any value these bidders bring to the market is lost.

Motivated by this discussion, we generalize the definition of WE so that unallocated goods are priced at some, possibly non-zero, reserve price $r \in \mathbb{R}_+$.

Definition 5 *(Walrasian Equilibrium with reserve r). A feasible outcome* $(\boldsymbol{X}, \boldsymbol{p})$ *is a **Walrasian Equilibrium with reserve** r (WEr) if it is a WE with prices at least r, including unallocated goods, which must be priced at exactly r.*

Analogously, we augment the definition EFE to an EFE with reserve price r.

Definition 6 *(Envy-Free Equilibirum with reserve r). A feasible outcome* $(\boldsymbol{X}, \boldsymbol{p})$ *is an **Envy-Free Equilibirum with reserve** r (EFEr) if it is an EFE with prices at least r.*

3 Computation of Envy-Free Equilibria

Chen et al. [8] showed that deciding the existence of WE in a CCMM assuming single-minded bidders is NP-hard. Consequently, we propose a natural restriction on the envy-freeness condition, which lends itself to a polynomial-time computation. With it, we can find a *restricted* WE (outcomes that satisfy restricted EF and MC) in polynomial time in single-minded CCMMs. Furthermore, in size-interchangeable CCMMs, we can find a *restricted* EFE in polynomial time.

Before presenting our algorithm, we formally define **restricted envy-free prices**. Let $|X_j| = \sum_{i=1}^{n} x_{ij}$ be the size of the bundle assigned to bidder j.

Definition 7 *(Restricted Envy-Free). A price vector* $\boldsymbol{p}$ *is called **restricted envyfree** with respect to a feasible allocation* $\boldsymbol{X}$ *if, for all* J *such that* $|X_j| > 0$:

$$X_j \in arg \max_{X'_j \in B(\boldsymbol{N}_{|X_j|})} \{v_j(X'_j) - P_j(X'_j)\}$$

where $B(\boldsymbol{N}_{|X_j|}) = \{\boldsymbol{0}\} \cup \{X'_j \in B(\boldsymbol{N}) \mid |X'_j|x' = |X_j|\}$, *i.e., the set of all feasible bundles of size equal to* $|X_j|$.

This definition is "restricted" because it assumes an allocation, and then is only concerned with bidders that are allocated (non-zero) bundles in that allocation. Any envy felt by any other bidders is simply ignored.

Another seeming restriction is that even for a bidder j with $|X_j| > 0$, it does not require envy-freeness with respect to all bundles $X'_j \in B(\boldsymbol{N})$, but only with respect to bundles of the same size as X_j (i.e., $X'_j \in B(\boldsymbol{N}_{|X_j|})$), and the empty bundle $\boldsymbol{0}$. This definition might seem overly restrictive, but as we are focused on bidders with single-valued, size-interchangeable valuations, we are likewise concerned with all-or-none allocations, which either allocate to a bidder in full—meaning a bundle of size I_j—or does not allocate at all. Hence, for our purposes the size restriction is not restrictive at all.

Finally, note that restricted envy-free prices always exist. Given an allocation, we can simply set prices equal to zero, and the condition will be satisfied. No one who is allocated would have any envy at zero prices; and the restricted envy-free condition ignores bidders that are unallocated.

Theorem 1. *Given a market M and a feasible allocation* $\boldsymbol{X}$, *the following conditions are necessary and sufficient for* $\boldsymbol{p}$ *to be restricted envy-free.*

Individual Rationality: $\forall j \in C : P_j(X_j) \leq v_j(X_j)$.

Compact Condition: $\forall i \in U, j \in C : If\, x_{ij} > 0\, then$
$$\forall k \in U : If\, (k,j) \in E\, and\, x_{kj} < N_k\, then\, p_i \leq p_k.$$

Proof (Sketch): The Individual Rationality condition ensures that bidders do not pay more than their reward while the Compact Condition ensures that, among all goods assigned to a bidder, she first consumes cheaper goods before consuming more expensive ones. Equivalently, this condition states that prices of goods that are completely consumed are cheaper than those that are only partially consumed. □

The linear program shown in Algorithm 1, which uses seller revenue as the objective function and the linear conditions that characterize restricted envy-freeness as constraints, can be used to find a set of restricted envy-free prices that maximizes seller revenue.

Algorithm 1. LP *restricted* EFE

Input: Market $(U, C, E, \boldsymbol{N}, \boldsymbol{I}, \boldsymbol{R})$ and allocation $\boldsymbol{X}$
Output: A pricing $\boldsymbol{p}$
maximize $\sum_j \sum_i x_{ij} p_i$
subject to (1) $\forall j \in C$: If $|X_j| > 0$, then $p_j(X_j) \leq v_j(X_j)$
(2) $\forall i \in U, \forall j \in C$: If $x_{ij} > 0$ then
$\forall k \in U$: If $(k,j) \in E$ and $x_{kj} < N_k$ then $p_i \leq p_k$

---

4 Revenue Maximizing Prices

In the remainder of this paper, we will be concerned with finding prices that maximize seller revenue for different market outcomes. We start by defining what a revenue-maximizing problem means for different solution concepts and review algorithms found in the literature to compute these prices in the special case of unit-demand bidders. We then present our algorithm for finding revenue-maximizing EFEr in size-interchangeable CCMMs.

Definition 8. *The revenue-maximizing WE problem: Given a CCMM, find a revenue-maximizing WE.*

Gul and Stachetti [6] presented a VCG-inspired [13] polynomial-time algorithm that solves the revenue-maximizing WE problem in unit-demand CCMMs: let $V \in \mathbb{R}_+^n \times \mathbb{R}_+^m$ be the valuation matrix of a market with n items and m unit-demand bidders where entry v_{ij} denotes bidder j's valuation for good i. Let π denote a maximum weight matching of V, and let $w(V)$ denote the weight of π. Let V_{-i} denote the same valuation matrix, but with good i removed. For each good i, set $p_i = w(V) - w(V_{-i})$. We call this algorithm, which returns $(\pi, \boldsymbol{p})$, **MaxWE**.

Then, building on Myerson's [10] intuition that reserve prices can boost revenue, Guruswami et al. [7] went one step further, essentially generalizing the problem of searching for a revenue-maximizing WE to that of searching for a revenue-maximizing WEr.

Definition 9. *The revenue-maximizing **WEr** problem: Given a CCMM, find a revenue-maximizing WEr.*

Recall from Example 4 that different allocations can support different levels of seller revenue, while still maintaining the envy-freeness property. Algorithm 2 is a high-level strategy for searching among WEr for one that is revenue maximizing. The algorithm searches over different allocations X, computing WEr prices p for each, and then outputs a pair (X, p) among those seen with maximal seller revenue. The interesting choice, which governs the algorithm's success, is which allocations to search over. Generally speaking, based on some initial allocation, the algorithm determines a set of reserve prices, each of which corresponds to an alternative allocation, whose supporting envy-free prices may or may not yield higher revenue than the others seen.

Algorithm 2. Strategy for finding a revenue-maximizing WEr

Input: Market $M = (U, C, E, N, I, R)$
Output: A pricing p and an allocation X
1. Find an initial allocation X.
2. For all $x_{ij} > 0$:
    2.0 Set a reserve price r as a function of x_{ij}.
    2.1 Find a WEr (X, p).
Output a pair (X, p) among those seen with maximal seller revenue.

In the unit-demand case, Guruswami et al. [7], showed that the following instance of Algorithm 2 finds a revenue-maximizing WEr with revenue at least $\text{OPT}/(2 \ln m)$, where OPT is the revenue of a revenue-maximizing WEr. (Step 1.) Find a maximum weight matching X of V. (Step 2.) For each valuation r on the edges of X, compute a WEr as follows: for each good i augment the valuation matrix to include two dummy bidders, each with reward r. Run **MaxWE** on the new valuation matrix to obtain a WE (π, p), based on which a new matching π' can be inferred by reallocating goods from dummy bidders to real bidders.

As shown in Example 2, a WE might not exist for a CCMM; thus, a WEr might also not exist. But recall that an EFEr always exists. Hence, we define the following problem:

Definition 10. *The revenue-maximizing **EFEr** problem: Given a CCMM, find a revenue-maximizing EFEr.*

Like the algorithm of Guruswami et al. [7], our approach (Algorithm 3) to searching for a revenue-maximizing EFEr in a size-interchangeable CCMM follows the structure of Algorithm 2. That is, for various choices of r, corresponding to various allocations X_r, we find an EFEr, and then we output an EFEr which is revenue-maximizing among all those considered.

More specifically, we first find an allocation X (Step 1), and then for all $x_{ij} > 0$, we find a restricted EFEr (Step 2). Step 2.0 defines a reserve price, and Step 2.1 finds an allocation that respects this reserve price (see Definition 12).

Step 2.2 then invokes a subroutine we call *restricted* EFEr, which is a straightforward generalization of Algorithm 1 that finds a revenue-maximizing EFEr with restricted envy-free prices in polynomial time. The generalization is simply that this algorithm takes as input a reserve price r, and then includes the additional set of constraints: $\forall i \in U : p_i \geq r$.

Algorithm 3. Revenue-Maximizing EFEr (RM-EFEr)

Input: Market $M = (U, C, E, \boldsymbol{N}, \boldsymbol{I}, \boldsymbol{R})$
Output: A pricing $\boldsymbol{p}$ and an allocation $\boldsymbol{X}$
1. Find an initial allocation $\boldsymbol{X}$.
2. For all $x_{ij} > 0$:
    2.0 Set reserve price $r = R_j / x_{ij}$.
    2.1 Find an allocation $\boldsymbol{X}_r$ that respects reserve price r.
    2.2 Run restriced EFEr on M, reserve price r, and allocation $\boldsymbol{X}_r$.
Output the pair $(\boldsymbol{X}, \boldsymbol{p})$ with maximum seller revenue.

Allocations in Size-interchangeable CCMMs. Two steps in Algorithm 3 depend on an allocation. The natural place to look are among those of optimal value. A feasible allocation is *optimal* if it maximizes the total of all bidders' rewards.

Definition 11 *(Optimal Allocation). An optimal allocation is a solution to the following optimization problem:*

$$\max_{\boldsymbol{X}} \sum_{j=1}^{m} R_j y_j, \quad subject\ to: \quad \forall i : \sum_{j=1}^{m} x_{ij} \leq N_i, \quad \forall j : y_j \in \{0,1\}$$

In the Appendix we present an ILP to compute optimal allocations.

Definition 12 *(Optimal Allocation that respects a reserve price). An optimal allocation that respects a reserve price is a solution to the following optimization problem:*

$$\max_{\boldsymbol{X}} \sum_{j=1}^{m} (R_j - rI_j) y_j, \ subject\ to: \quad \forall i : \sum_{j=1}^{m} x_{ij} \leq N_i, \quad \forall j : y_j \in \{0,1\}$$

The following theorem implies that is unlikely that one can devise an Algorithm that optimizes welfare in size-interchangeable CCMMs in polynomial time.

Theorem 2. *Finding an optimal allocation is NP-hard. (Proof in Appendix)*

Since finding an optimal allocation is NP-Hard, we present a greedy heuristic (Algorithm 4) to find allocations. This algorithm can easily be adapted to produce an allocation that respects reserve price r as follows: given input market M, construct new market M' by removing any bidder j for which $R_j - rI_j < 0$, and setting the reward of the remaining bidders to be $R_j - rI_j$. Now run Algorithm 4 on input M' to obtain an allocation $\boldsymbol{X}'$, which we lift up to create an allocation, $\boldsymbol{X}_r$, in the original market M that respects reserve prices.

Algorithm 4. Greedy Approximation Algorithm

Input: Market $M = (U, C, E, \boldsymbol{N}, \boldsymbol{I}, \boldsymbol{R})$
Output: Allocation $\boldsymbol{X}$
For all i, j set $x_{ij} = 0$.
foreach $j \in C$ **do**
    Let $U_j = \{i \mid (i,j) \in E$ and $\sum_{j=1}^{m} x_{ij} < N_i\}$.
    if $\sum_{i \in U_j} N_i \geq I_j$ **then**
        foreach $i \in U_j$ **do**
            $x_{ij} = \min\{I_j - \sum_{i=1}^{n} x_{ij}, N_i - \sum_{j=1}^{m} x_{ij}\}$.

There are two sources of non-determinism in Algorithm 4: (1) the order in which to loop through bidders and (2) the order in which to loop through goods. One approach is to orders bidders in descending order by rewards per square root of goods demanded, i.e., $R_j/\sqrt{I_j}$, and goods in ascending order of remaining supply. We also experiment with other combinations, e.g., ordering goods in descending order of remaining supply.

5 Experiments

Experimental Setup. Given outcome $(\boldsymbol{X}, \boldsymbol{p})$, seller revenue $\rho = \sum_j \sum_i x_{ij} p_i$, and total welfare $W = \sum_j R_j y_j$, where $y_j = 1$ in case bidder j is a winner under $\boldsymbol{X}$ and 0 otherwise. Let OPT_W be the value of a welfare-maximizing allocation. Since we assume bidders are individually rational, seller revenue cannot exceed OPT_W. We thus report metrics of efficiency W/OPT_W, and seller revenue ρ/OPT_W. We also report metrics based on violations of the (unrestricted) envy-freeness and market clearing conditions. Given a market M and outcome $(\boldsymbol{X}, \boldsymbol{p})$, we define an envy-free violation (EF) as the ratio between the number of bidders that are not envy-free, and the total number of bidders in the market; and define a market clearance violation (MC) as the ratio between the number of goods completely unallocated whose price is greater than zero, and the total number of goods in the market.

All metrics are reported over random markets M drawn from a distribution we call *Random-k-Market*(n, m, p, k). Let $S = \sum_i N_i$ be the total supply of M, and let $D = \sum_j I_j$ be the total demand of M. The supply-to-demand ratio S/D, is a measure of how much over (or under) demanded a market is. A market is over demanded if $S/D < 1$ and under demanded if $S/D > 1$. A random market drawn from *Random-k-Market*(n, m, p, k) over CCMM has n goods and m bidders. The parameter p is the probability that an edge (i,j) is present in E, and thus, the expected number of edges is pnm. Both N_i and I_j are randomly and independently drawn integers between 1 and 10 such that the supply-to-demand ratio is k. Finally, each bidder's reward R_j is uniformly and independently drawn uniformly on $[1, 10]$. From *Random-k-Market*(n, m, p, k) we generate markets with $n, m = 1, \ldots, 20$, $p = 0.25, 0.5, 0.75, 1.0$ and $k = 0.25, 0.33, 0.5, 1, 2, 3, 4$. For each metric, we report the average across markets over 100 independent trials. Results are shown in Table 1.

Table 1. Results.

	Efficiency	Revenue	Time (ms)	EF	MC
Under-demanded Singleton CCMM					
CK	1.00	0.00	0.25	0.00	0.00
MaxWE	1.00	0.04	0.41	0.00	0.00
MaxWErApprox	0.85	0.67	12.94	0.00	0.64
LP Optimal	0.86	0.73	15.73	0.00	0.63
Over-demanded Singleton CCMM					
CK	1.00	0.49	4.57	0.00	0.00
MaxWE	1.00	0.80	0.24	0.00	0.00
MaxWErApprox	0.96	0.84	5.69	0.00	0.12
LP Optimal	0.95	0.86	11.47	0.00	0.13
Under-demanded CCMM, $k \in \{2, 3, 4\}$					
CK	0.97	0.08	4.22	0.00	0.07
LP Optimal	0.84	0.65	232.22	0.00	0.43
LP Greedy	0.84	0.65	12.87	0.00	0.49
Over-demanded CCMM, $k \in \{0.25, 0.33, 0.5\}$					
CK	0.79	0.41	2.50	0.00	0.21
LP Optimal	0.93	0.75	199.59	0.02	0.11
LP Greedy	0.89	0.72	9.08	0.02	0.15

Algorithms. Algorithms' names are abbreviated as follows: **CK** refers to the Crawford-Knoer ascending auction [5] (see the Appendix for details). **MaxWE** and **MaxWErApprox** refer to Guruswami et al.'s algorithms (see Sect. 4). **LP** refers to our revenue-maximizing EFEr algorithm. The algorithm **LP** is qualified by the type of allocation given as input: **LP Optimal** refers to the case when an optimal allocation is given as input, and **LP Greedy** refers to the case when the greedy allocation is given as input. We report results where the greedy approximation orders goods by descending order of remaining supply. We also experimented with ordering goods by ascending order of remaining supply, but saw no qualitative differences in the results.

Results. We report on two sets of experiments: singleton CCMMs, and general. In both cases, we take as a baseline the CK auction, which, in the case of unit-demand markets, like MaxWE, is guaranteed to produce an efficient outcome, but at the expense of low revenue. For singleton CCMMs, we compare our algorithm to MaxWErApprox as well.

As expected, the efficiency of CK and MaxWE in singleton CCMMs is perfect. Also, these algorithms yield zero violations, as they are known to generate Walrasian equilibria. However, their revenues are low, particularly in under-demanded markets, because there are more unallocated goods in these markets, each of which must be priced at zero, thereby limiting the price of allocated goods, in order to avoid envy. Our algorithm and MaxWErApprox both impose a reserve, enabling them to disregard some of these overly constraining goods, but ours obtains substantially more revenue than MaxWErApprox, with fewer (but not significantly fewer) violations. In over-demanded markets, the performance of our algorithm is comparable to that of MaxWErApprox, and both algorithms outperform MaxWE, which outperforms CK. Note that our algorithm produces *un*restricted envy-free outcomes in singleton CCMMs.

In general CCMMs, CK is nearly efficient in under-demanded markets, but much less so in the over-demanded case. But in neither case does it strike a good balance between efficiency and revenue. In contrast, our algorithm is able to accrue upwards of 72% revenue in over-demanded markets, while retaining an efficiency of 89%, and it does so with hardly any EF violations, compared to CK, which obtains an efficiency of only 79% and revenue of only 41%. As in the case of singleton CCMMs, our algorithm does not fare as well in the harder case of under-demanded markets, where once again there are more unallocated goods, although it again produces nearly-*un*restricted envy-free outcomes. These experiments suggest that while not perfect, finding revenue-maximizing restricted envy-free outcomes in polynomial time is a reasonable heuristic for maximizing revenue among nearly-*un*restricted envy-free outcomes.

6   Conclusion and Future Directions

CCMMs with unit-demand valuations have some important properties, e.g., a WE always exists and there are polynomial-time algorithms to find such outcomes. A WE outcome guarantees that all bidders are envy-free and that the market clears, and thus, by the first welfare theorem of economics, yields an allocation that maximizes social welfare. Guruswami et al. [7] proposed an algorithm for the unit-demand case, sacrificing social welfare in an attempt to maximize seller revenue, while maintaining the envy-freeness property. In this paper, we proposed an algorithm that generalize this well-known algorithm for the unit-demand case to the case of single valued, size-interchangeable CCMMs. In future work, we plan to look more closely at algorithms [3,4,7,9] that have been proposed for the more difficult case of single-minded bidders, and to perhaps generalize results about those algorithms to the single-valued, size-interchangeable bidder setting studied here. We will also explore alternative solution concepts where we combine the restricted EF condition with the objective of maximizing the number of allocated bidders.

Appendix

Mixed ILP to Find Optimal Allocations

Given a market $(U, C, E, \boldsymbol{N}, \boldsymbol{I}, \boldsymbol{R})$, Algorithm 5 is a mixed ILP that can be used to find an optimal allocation.

Algorithm 5. Mixed ILP Optimal Allocation

Input: Market $M = (U, C, E, \boldsymbol{N}, \boldsymbol{I}, \boldsymbol{R})$
Output: An optimal allocation $\boldsymbol{X}$

maximize $\sum_{j=1}^{m} R_j y_j$

subject to (1) $\forall i : \sum_{j=1}^{m} x_{ij} \leq N_i$
     (2) $\forall i, j :$ If $(i, j) \notin E$ then $x_{ij} = 0$
     (3) $\forall j : y_j \leq \frac{1}{I_j} \sum_{i=1}^{n} x_{ij} \leq y_j$
     (4) $y_j \in \{0, 1\}$
     (5) $\forall i, j : x_{ij} \in \mathbb{Z}^+$

Constraints (1), (2) and (5) imply that a solution to the Mixed-ILP is a feasible allocation. Constraints (3) and (4) imply that a bidder attains reward R_j if and only if it is completely fulfilled, and together with constraint (5), imply that if $y_j = 0$ then $x_{ij} = 0$ for all i. The objective of the mixed ILP implies that the solution maximizes bidders' rewards over all feasible allocations and thus, it is an optimal allocation. To obtain an allocation that respects reserve price r, change the objective of the mixed ILP to $\sum_{j=1}^{m} (R_j - rI_j) y_j$, where $r \in \mathbb{R}^+$ is the reserve price parameter.

Proof of Theorem 2

Finding an optimal allocation is NP-hard. To prove this, we reduce from the following version of set packing: Given a universe $\mathcal{U} = \{u_1, u_2, \ldots, u_n\}$ and a family of subsets $\mathcal{S} = S_1, S_2, \ldots, S_k \subseteq \mathcal{U}$, find the maximum number of pairwise disjoint sets in $\mathcal{S}$.

Consider an input $(\mathcal{U}, \mathcal{S})$ to the set packing problem as described above. Let us construct a market $(U, C, E, \boldsymbol{N}, \boldsymbol{I}, \boldsymbol{R})$ from $(\mathcal{U}, \mathcal{S})$ as an input to the optimal allocation problem. At a high level, the input market consists of n goods each offered in exactly 1 copy and k bidders where each bidder corresponds to a member $S_j \in \mathcal{S}$ that demand as many goods as elements in S_j and attains a reward of exactly 1. A goods is connected to a bidder only if the index of the good is contained in the set S_j associated with the bidder.

Formally, given $(\mathcal{U}, \mathcal{S})$ where $\mathcal{U} = \{1, 2, \ldots, n\}$ and $\mathcal{S} = \{S_1, S_2, \cdots, S_k\}$, construct $f(\mathcal{U}, \mathcal{S}) = (U, C, E, \boldsymbol{N}, \boldsymbol{I}, \boldsymbol{R})$ as follow: (1) let $U = \mathcal{U}$ and $N_i = 1$ for all $i = 1, 2, \ldots, n$. (2) let $C = \{1, 2, \ldots, k\}$, and associate each bidder $j \in C$ to $S_j \in \mathcal{S}$ so that $I_j = |S_j|$. Also, $R_j = 1$ for all $j = 1, 2, \ldots, k$. (3) add edge (i, j) to E only if $i \in S_j$. Clearly the transformation f is polynomial on the size of the input $(\mathcal{U}, \mathcal{S})$.

We now show that a set packing for $(\mathcal{U}, \mathcal{S})$ corresponds to an optimal allocation for $f(\mathcal{U}, \mathcal{S})$ and vice versa. Suppose that l is the maximum number of pairwise disjoint sets in $\mathcal{S}$ and that $S_1, S_2, \ldots, S_l \in \mathcal{S}$ are these sets. By our transformation f we know that each bidder j associated with a set S_j from the previous list is connected to as many goods as $|S_j|$. Since all these sets are pairwise disjoint, all bidders are connected to different goods. Therefore, each of these bidders can be fulfilled which means that the value of the optimal allocation is at least l. Moreover, we know that is not possible to fulfill more than l bidders since l is the maximum number of pairwise disjoint sets, and selecting more than l bidders would imply, by our transformation f, that at least one good has a supply greater than 1. Therefore, l is the value of the optimal allocation of $f(\mathcal{U}, \mathcal{S})$.

Suppose that l is the value of the optimal allocation of $f(\mathcal{U}, \mathcal{S})$. This means that l is the maximum number of bidders that can be fulfilled. Bidder j is fulfilled only if its allocation is at least $|S_j|$. By construction we know that a bidder is connected to exactly $|S_j|$ many goods. Therefore, each allocated bidder j is fulfilled by exactly $|S_j|$ goods. Moreover, none of these goods are allocated to different bidders since there is exactly 1 copy of each good. Therefore, the sets associated with the selected bidders must not overlap in any element, i.e., they must be pairwise disjoint. This shows that there are at least l pairwise disjoint sets in $(\mathcal{U}, \mathcal{S})$. We also know that there must be at most l pairwise disjoint sets or otherwise the value of the optimal allocation would have been more than l. Therefore, l is the maximum number of pairwise disjoint sets in $\mathcal{S}$.   □

Crawford and Knoer Ascending Auction

In the unit-demand setting, it is well known that Walrasian Equilibria exist [6]. Furthermore, Crawford and Knoer [5] proposed an ascending auction mechanism which, for price increment ϵ, yields an ϵWE.[1] We describe the workings of their mechanism in a unit-demand CCMM in Algorithm 6.[2]

Algorithm 6. Crawford-Knoer Ascending Auction (Unit-demand)

Input: Market $M = (U, C, E, \mathbf{N}, \mathbf{I}, \mathbf{R})$, where $\forall i : N_i \geq 1$ and $\forall j : I_j = 1$
Output: A pricing $\mathbf{p}$ and an allocation $\mathbf{X}$
For every i, set $p_i = 0$
For every i, j, set $x_{ij} = 0$
while *TRUE* **do**
    foreach *Unallocated bidder j* **do**
        Let $i^* \in \arg\max_{i \in U}\{R_j - (p_i + \epsilon)\}$.
        Add (i^*, j) to B.
    if $B = \emptyset$ **then**
        Halt with current allocation $\mathbf{X}$ and prices $\mathbf{p}$.
    else
        Choose $(i, j) \in B$.
        $x_{ij} = 1$.
        if $\sum_l x_{il} > N_i$ **then**
            $p_i = p_i + \epsilon$.
            Completely unallocate all bidders $j' \neq j$ such that $x_{ij'} > 0$.
Output the final pair $(\mathbf{X}, \mathbf{p})$.

---

[1] In an ϵWE, envy-free-ness is satisfied up to ϵ.
[2] The only difference between our presentation and the original one is that N_i may exceed 1, so in the final **if** statement, it may be necessary to unallocate goods from more than one bidder.

This algorithm, as stated, generalizes to size-interchangeable CCMMs, except that at each step of the algorithm we must query bidders for their favorite bundles at the current prices plus ϵ, rather than their favorite individual goods.

References

1. Briest, P.: Uniform budgets and the envy-free pricing problem. In: Aceto, L., Damgård, I., Goldberg, L.A., Halldórsson, M.M., Ingólfsdóttir, A., Walukiewicz, I. (eds.) ICALP 2008. LNCS, vol. 5125, pp. 808–819. Springer, Heidelberg (2008). doi:10.1007/978-3-540-70575-8_66
2. Chen, N., Deng, X.: Envy-free pricing in multi-item markets. In: Abramsky, S., Gavoille, C., Kirchner, C., Meyer auf der Heide, F., Spirakis, P.G. (eds.) ICALP 2010. LNCS, vol. 6199, pp. 418–429. Springer, Heidelberg (2010). doi:10.1007/978-3-642-14162-1_35
3. Chen, N., Deng, X., Goldberg, P.W., Zhang, J.: On revenue maximization with sharp multi-unit demands. J. Comb. Optim. **31**(3), 1174–1205 (2014)
4. Cheung, M., Swamy, C.: Approximation algorithms for single-minded envy-free profit-maximization problems with limited supply. In: IEEE 49th Annual IEEE Symposium on Foundations of Computer Science, FOCS 2008, pp. 35–44. IEEE (2008)
5. Crawford, V.P., Knoer, E.M.: Job matching with heterogeneous firms and workers. Econometrica J. Econometric Soc. **49**(2), 437–450 (1981)
6. Gul, F., Stacchetti, E.: Walrasian equilibrium with gross substitutes. J. Econ. Theory **87**(1), 95–124 (1999). http://EconPapers.repec.org/RePEc:eee:jetheo:v:87:y:1999:i:1:p:95-124
7. Guruswami, V., Hartline, J.D., Karlin, A.R., Kempe, D., Kenyon, C., McSherry, F.: On profit-maximizing envy-free pricing. In: Proceedings of the Sixteenth Annual ACM-SIAM Symposium on Discrete Algorithms, pp. 1164–1173. Society for Industrial and Applied Mathematics (2005)
8. Huang, L.S., Li, M., Zhang, B.: Approximation of Walrasian equilibrium in single-minded auctions. Theor. comput. sci. **337**(1), 390–398 (2005)
9. Monaco, G., Sankowski, P., Zhang, Q.: Revenue maximization envy-free pricing for homogeneous resources. In: Proceedings of the 24th International Conference on Artificial Intelligence, pp. 90–96. AAAI Press (2015)
10. Myerson, R.B.: Optimal auction design. Math. Oper. Res. **6**(1), 58–73 (1981)
11. Nisan, N., Roughgarden, T., Tardos, E., Vazirani, V.V.: Algorithmic Game Theory. Cambridge University Press, New York (2007)
12. Tan, K.T.K.: The first fundamental theorem of welfare economics (2008) (Unpublished)
13. Vickrey, W.: Counterspeculation, auctions, and competitive sealed tenders. J. Finan. **16**(1), 8–37 (1961)
14. Walras, L.: Elements of Pure Economics: Or the Theory of Social Wealth. Elements of Pure Economics, Or the Theory of Social Wealth, Routledge (2003). https://books.google.com/books?id=hwjRD3z0Qy4C
15. Wellman, M., Wurman, P.R.: A trading agent competition for the research community. In: IJCAI-99 Workshop on Agent-Mediated Electronic Trading (1999)

Electricity Trading Agent
for EV-enabled Parking Lots

Jurica Babic[1]([⊠]), Arthur Carvalho[2], Wolfgang Ketter[3], and Vedran Podobnik[1]

[1] Faculty of Electrical Engineering and Computing,
University of Zagreb, Zagreb, Croatia
{jurica.babic,vedran.podobnik}@fer.hr
[2] Farmer School of Business, Miami University, Oxford, OH, USA
arthur.carvalho@miamioh.edu
[3] Rotterdam School of Management,
Erasmus University Rotterdam, Rotterdam, Netherlands
wketter@rsm.nl

Abstract. The reduction of greenhouse gas emissions is seen as an important step towards environmental sustainability. Perhaps not surprising, many governments all around the world are providing incentives for consumers to buy electric vehicles (EVs). A positive response from consumers means that the demand for the charging infrastructure increases as well. We investigate how an existing traditional parking lot, upgraded with chargers, can suit the present demand for charging stations. In particular, a resulting *EV-enabled parking lot* is an electricity trading agent (i.e., broker) which acts as an energy retailer and as a player on a target electricity market. In this paper, we use agent-based simulation to present the EV-enabled parking lot ecosystem in order to model the underlying dynamics and uncertainties regarding parking lots with electricity trading agent functionalities. We instantiate our agent-based simulations using real-life data in order to perform the what-if analysis. Several key performance indicators (KPIs), including parking utilization, charging utilization and electricity utilization, are proposed. We also illustrate how those KPIs can be used to choose the effective investment strategy with respect to the number and speed of chargers.

Keywords: Trading agents · Agent-based simulation · EV-enabled parking lot · Electric vehicles

1   Introduction

Recent years have seen a steady growth in the sales of electric vehicles (EV). For example, a recent report by McKinsey & Company [14] estimates that the

---

This paper extends the paper "Extending Parking Lots with Electricity Trading Agent Functionalities" presented at the "Workshop on Agent-Mediated Electronic Commerce and Trading Agent Design and Analysis (AMEC/TADA 2015) @ AAMAS 2015".

© Springer International Publishing AG 2017
S. Ceppi et al. (Eds.): AMEC/TADA 2015/2016, LNBIP 271, pp. 35–49, 2017.
DOI: 10.1007/978-3-319-54229-4_3

share of EVs in new sales reached 12% in Norway, 4% in the Netherlands, and growth rates of 50% in France, Germany, and the UK. As a consequence of the increasing number of EVs on the road, there is a growing need for charging stations [19] as well.

A potential solution to address the need for charging stations is to transform traditional parking lots into EV-enabled parking lots, in a sense that EV-enabled parking lots provide not only *parking services*, but also the possibility for EV owners to charge and discharge their cars for a price [3], *i.e.*, to take advantage of the *electricity service* [2,7,18]. Within this perspective, the parking lot's smartness comes from the possibility to act as an electricity retailer and a player on a target electricity market.

A single EV is, to a certain degree, a prosumer, in a sense that it can procure electricity from its battery (discharge) as well as consume electricity (charge) [9]. A single EV, however, is not able to actively participate in an electricity market on its own due to the fact that it only has a modest amount of electricity available to buy or sell. Our proposed model tackles this issue by putting the parking lot owner in the role of an electricity broker [17] which trades electricity between EVs and the target electricity market, thus behaving as an "aggregator" [12].

Due to the inherently complex and dynamic environment, a potential obstacle, from a business perspective, to the process of transforming parking lots into EV-enabled parking lots is the complexity of estimating the utilization of the electricity service and its profit [1]. The information about electricity service utilization is valuable to the EV-enabled parking lot's owner because it provides guidelines on how many traditional parking spots need to be upgraded with electricity chargers, while the information about profits enables one to calculate the amount of time required to recover the cost of the initial investment.

In this paper, we suggest an agent-based simulation approach [5,11,13] for studying the economic benefits of EV-enabled parking lots. In particular, our main contribution is a computational technique that allows one to estimate the parking lot's electricity service utilization and profitability given a period of time. We illustrate the application of our approach using data derived from a real-world parking lot and electricity market. To the best of our knowledge, our work is the first to suggest a computational tool to study the economic feasibility of EV-enabled parking lots.

The paper is organized as follows. Section 2 presents the EV-enabled parking lot ecosystem through the definition of entities and relationships among them. The agent-based simulation set-up, as well as simulation scenarios, are presented in Sect. 3. Section 4 elaborates upon simulation results. Section 5 concludes the paper and presents ideas for future work.

2   EV-enabled Parking Lot Ecosystem

Figure 1 presents the EV-enabled parking lot ecosystem, which consists of 3 *entities*, namely the *EV-enabled Parking Lot*, the *Electric Vehicles*, and the *Electricity Market*, and 2 *relationships*, namely the "EV-enabled Parking Lot - Electric

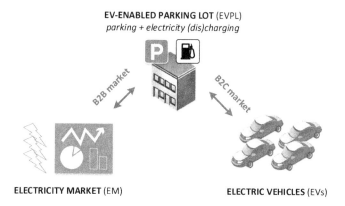

Fig. 1. Entities and relationships in an EV-enabled parking lot ecosystem

Vehicles" relationship and the "EV-enabled Parking Lot - Electricity Market" relationship. We model entities and relationships through, respectively, *agents* and *markets*. The EV-enabled Parking Lot acts as a broker connecting both markets, as we detail later. Table 1 describes all the parameters and values in the EV-enabled Parking Lot ecosystem.

2.1 EV-enabled Parking Lot Agent

As shown in Table 1, the EV-enabled Parking Lot agent (EVPL) is defined according to the tuple:

$$EVPL = (EVPL^{spots}, EVPL^{qs}, EVPL^{mrg}, EVPL^{pp},$$
$$EVPL^{(d)cr}, EVPL^{cuc}, EVPL^{ic}) \tag{1}$$

The EVPL agent model is shown in Fig. 2. Furthermore, the EVPL agent implements 3 activities, which we describe next.

Calculation of free parking spots and queue size. This activity is *event-based* and triggered after an Electric Vehicle agent (EV) wants to either enter or leave the EVPL. If the EV wants to enter the EVPL, the EVPL will provide the EV with a free parking spot from its pool of free parking spots (if the pool is not empty) or the EV will be put in the EVPL queue (if there is space, i.e., if the current number of EVs in the queue $EVPL^q$ is smaller than a queue size $EVPL^{qs}$).

Calculation of electricity price. This activity is *time-based* and regularly occurs with an hourly frequency. In the beginning of every time-slot (hour), the EVPL fetches the current electricity price (ep^{EM}) from the Electricity Market agent (EM) and uses its profit margin $(EVPL^{mrg})$ to calculate its selling $(EVPL_{ep}^{sell})$ and buying $(EVPL_{ep}^{buy})$ electricity prices as follows:

Table 1. EV-enabled parking lot ecosystem model parameters.

Parameter (unit)	Description	Notation	Value
EVPL parking spots	Number of parking spots	$EVPL^{spots}$	30, 60, 90
EVPL queue size	Number of spaces in a queue	$EVPL^{qs}$	0
EVPL margin	EVPL profit margin relative to the electricity market price	$EVPL^{mrg}$	0.1
EVPL parking price (€/h)	Price EV pays for each parking hour	$EVPL^{pp}$	3
EVPL (dis)charge rate (kW)	Maximum rate at which electricity is charged or discharged	$EVPL^{(d)cr}$	5, 10, 20
EVPL charger unit cost (€/charger)	Cost for one charger	$EVPL^{cuc}$	2,000, 10,000, 30,000
EVPL investment cost (€)	Investment cost for chargers	$EVPL^{ic}$	$EVPL^{ps} \cdot EVPL^{cuc}$
EV home supplier margin	Home supplier profit margin relative to electricity market price	EV^{mrg}	N{$\mu = 0.2$, $\sigma = 0.1$, a=0, b=1}
EV (dis)charge quantity (kWh)	Amount of electricity an EV is willing to charge or discharge	$EV^{(d)cq}$	N{$\mu = 15$, $\sigma = 10$, a=-30, b=30}
EV charge sensitivity	Probability an EV will be subjected to a price matching mechanism for a charging service	EV^{cs}	0.8
EV discharge sensitivity	Probability an EV will be subjected to a price matching mechanism for a discharging service	EV^{dcs}	1
EV stay longer	Probability an EV will stay parked longer to fully complete the electricity service	EV^{sl}	0.2
EV parked home time (h)	Amount of hours potentially spent by an EV (dis)charging at home	EV^{pht}	U{a=1, b=12}
EV arrival rate (EV/h)	Hourly arrival rates. Derived from the work by Ferreira et al. [6]	EV^{ar}	2, 1, 2, 1, 1, 1, 2, 2, 24, 43, 18, 7, 15, 14, 22, 18, 14, 8, 10, 7, 6, 3, 1, 3
EV service rate (EV/h)	Hourly service rates. The mean number of hours an EV will stay parked is given by $1/EV^{pr}$. Derived from the work by Ferreira et al. [6]	EV^{pr}	0.15, 0.85, 3.85, 0.35, 0.35, 0.35, 0.07, 0.18, 0.16, 0.16, 0.28, 0.30, 0.33, 0.36, 0.38, 0.45, 0.66, 0.44, 0.62, 0.45, 0.51, 4.76, 4.35, 3.85
Simulation steps (h)	Simulation duration in time slots	t	8,760
Electricity market prices (€/kWh)	Real-world electricity prices from the day-ahead Nord Pool Elspot market (2014)	ep^{EM}	Hourly electricity prices during one year period

$$EVPL_{ep}^{sell} = ep^{EM} \cdot (1 + EVPL^{pm}) \tag{2}$$

$$EVPL_{ep}^{buy} = ep^{EM} \cdot \frac{1}{(1 + EVPL^{pm})} \tag{3}$$

Thereafter, EVs charge energy at the EVPL at a price $EVPL_{ep}^{sell}$ and they discharge energy at a price $EVPL_{ep}^{buy}$.

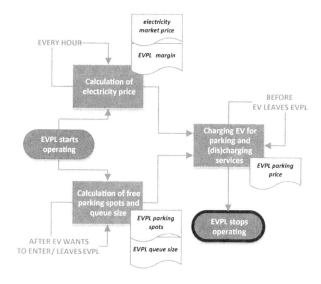

Fig. 2. The model of a EV-enabled parking lot agent

Payment for parking and (dis)charging services. This activity is *event-based* and triggered before an EV leaves the EVPL. The EV needs to pay to the EVPL agent for both parking and the electricity service provided. Therefore, the EVPL revenue from an electric vehicle EV is calculated as follows:

$$EVPL^{rev} = EVPL^{ps} + EVPL^{ets} \qquad (4)$$

where $EVPL^{ps} = \lceil timeParked(EV) \rceil \cdot EVPL^{pp}$ is the revenue from parking service, and $EVPL^{ets} = EV^{(d)cq} \cdot EVPL_{ep}^{trade}$ is the revenue from electricity service, where:

$$EVPL_{ep}^{trade} = \begin{cases} EVPL_{ep}^{sell} & \text{if } EV^{(d)cq} \geq 0 \\ EVPL_{ep}^{buy} & \text{if } EV^{(d)cq} < 0 \end{cases} \qquad (5)$$

The $timeParked(EV)$ is the parking duration of the electric vehicle agent EV. We note that the EVPL rounds up $timeParked(EV)$ to the nearest larger integer to mimic real-world practices regarding parking service payment. We also note that EV's (dis)charge quantity, $EV^{(d)cq}$, is a positive value in case EV is charging its battery at the EVPL, and a negative value in case EV is discharging its battery.

2.2   Electric Vehicle Agent

As shown in Table 1, the Electric Vehicle agent (EV) is defined according to the tuple:

$$EV = (EV^{mrg}, EV^{(d)cq}, EV^{cs}, EV^{dcs}, EV^{sl}, EV^{pht}, EV^{ar}, EV^{pr}) \qquad (6)$$

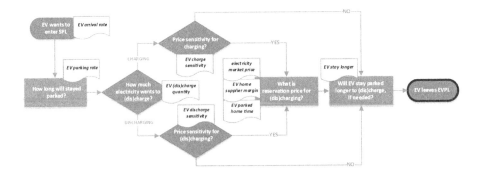

Fig. 3. The model of electric vehicle agent

The EV life cycle is described with a flowchart in Fig. 3. In particular, the EV agent implements 5 activities, which we describe next.

Calculation of parking duration. We model arrivals and staying at the parking lot using a M/M/c/0 queue with time varying parameters, allowing different timeslots (hours) to have different arrival rates (EV^{ar}) and service rates (EV^{pr}). This activity is *event-based* and triggered after an EV wants to enter the EVPL, which is defined by the arrival rate EV^{ar}. The calculation of parking duration for a specific EV (EV^{ipd}) is based on the service rate EV^{pr}.

Calculation of the amount of electricity an EV is willing to (dis)charge. This activity is *event-based* and triggered after an EV enters the EVPL. We assume that the amount of electricity an EV is willing to (dis)charge, $EV^{(d)cq}$, follows a normal distribution with mean equal to 15 kWh, truncated at ± 30 kWh, the standard deviation being equal to 10. A positive value of the EV's (dis)charge quantity means that EV is willing to charge its battery at the EVPL, whereas a negative value means that it is willing to discharge, *i.e.*, sell electricity. By setting the mean value to 15 kWh, we mimic the real-world situation where more cars want to charge their batteries rather than discharge. The truncation is set to mimic the maximum capacity of today's mid-size EVs (*e.g.*, Nissan Leaf).

Determining whether the EV is willing to (dis)charge regardless of price. This activity is *event-based* and triggered after an EV enters the EVPL and wants to charge or discharge a certain amount of electricity. This activity decides whether EV will take into account the electricity price when deciding whether to engage in (dis)charging. The electric vehicle EV will engage in charging, regardless of the current electricity price $EVPL_{ep}^{sell}$, with the probability $1 - EV^{cs}$. On the other hand, EV will engage in discharging, regardless of the current electricity price ($EVPL_{ep}^{buy}$), with the probability $1 - EV^{dcs}$.

Through the probabilities EV^{cs} and EV^{dcs}, we mimic the real-world situation where a car arrives at a charging station and needs to charge its battery regardless of the price, *e.g.*, because the battery is almost empty or because there is no other charging station nearby. In our simulation, EV^{dcs} is always set to 1 because it would be irrational for EV to discharge at a price lower than what was previously paid for charging.

Calculation of the reserve price for (dis)charging. This activity is *event-based* and triggered after an EV enters the EVPL, and the same wants to (dis)charge a certain amount of electricity while taking into account the profitability aspect of such a transaction. In case of charging, the electric vehicle EV decides to proceed with the transaction only if the EV's reserve price, $EV^{buy(res)}$, is higher than the current electricity price offered by the EVPL, $EVPL_{ep}^{sell}$. In case of discharging, the EV decides to proceed with the transaction only if the EV's reserve price, $EV^{sell(res)}$, is lower than the current electricity price offered by the EVPL, $EVPL_{ep}^{buy}$.

For the calculation of EV's reservation prices, we assume that EV has the alternative choice of (dis)charging at home, where its home supplier forms an electricity price analogously to the EVPL, but with different profit margin EV^{mrg}. We assume that EV^{mrg} follows a normal distribution with mean equal to 0.2, standard deviation equal to 0.1, and truncated at $[0, 1]$. Further, we assume that EV was parked at home for EV^{pht} hours before entering the EVPL in case of discharging or, in case of charging, that EV will be parked at home for EV^{pht} hours after leaving the EVPL. The value EV^{pht} follows a uniform distribution with range $[1, 12]$.

Determining whether the EV will stay parked longer to fully complete the electricity service. This activity is *event-based* and triggered after an EV enters the EVPL and decides to (dis)charge a certain amount of electricity. The EVPL's (dis)charging rate is defined by parameter $EVPL^{(d)cr}$, and the EV's initial parking duration, EV^{ipd}, is defined according to the hourly service rate EV^{pr}.

A priori, the maximum amount of electricity an EV is able to (dis)charge is $EVPL^{(d)cr} \cdot EV^{ipd}$. If the amount of electricity demanded/offered by EV is less than or equal to $EVPL^{(d)cr} \cdot EV^{ipd}$, *i.e.*, $EV^{(d)cq} \leq EVPL^{(d)cr} \cdot EV^{ipd}$, then there is enough time for the EV to fully (dis)charge its battery during its parking time. On the other hand, if $EV^{(d)cq} > EVPL^{(d)cr} \cdot EV^{ipd}$, then it means that there is not enough time for the EV to fully (dis)charge its battery during its initial parking period. In the latter situation, the EV has two options: (i) to partially (dis)charge $EVPL^{(d)cr} \cdot EV^{ipd}$; or (ii) to prolong its parking time until the full (dis)charging is complete, which means that the EV will stay parked longer, *i.e.*, for a total of $EV^{(d)cq}/EVPL^{(d)cr}$ hours. We assume that the EV will go for option (iii) with probability EV^{sl}.

2.3 Electricity Market Agent

The role of the Electricity Market agent (EM) is to provide electricity for the EVPL agent. The underlying electricity price, ep^{EM}, is available with an hourly granularity for the whole calendar year. In our simulations, we use real-world

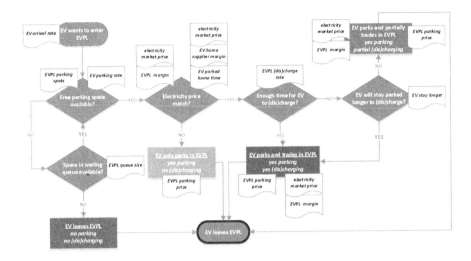

Fig. 4. EV-enabled parking lot transaction model

electricity prices from the day-ahead Nord Pool Elspot market[1], where the price volatility is not as high as in real-world intra-day markets. Consequently, the EM agent provides conservative, stable electricity prices.

2.4 EV-enabled Parking Lot B2C Market

The EV-enabled Parking Lot B2C (Business-to-Consumer) market models the "EV-enabled Parking Lot - Electric Vehicles" relationship. Activities in this market are defined through the EVPL transaction model shown in Fig. 4, which has 4 major steps as we detail next.

Entering the EVPL by the EV. Every EVPL transaction begins with an *EV* entering the EVPL. The occurrence of this event is modeled with the arrival rate EV^{ar}.

Determining whether there is a free parking space available at the EVPL. The *EV* can enter the EVPL only if there is an available parking spot. If there is no parking space available at the time of the *EV*'s arrival, the *EV* will be put in the EVPL queue in case there is space, i.e., current number of *EV*s in the queue $EVPL^q$ is smaller than a queue size $EVPL^{qs}$. If there is no space available in the queue as well, the *EV* leaves the EVPL without parking and without (dis)charging. Consequently, the *EV* does not pay any money to the EVPL.

Matching EVPL electricity price with EV's reserve price. In case of charging, the *EV* will proceed with the electricity transaction only if the *EV*'s

---

[1] Available at: www.nordpoolspot.com/historical-market-data.

reserve price, $EV^{buy(res)}$, is higher than the current electricity price at the EVPL, $EVPL_{ep}^{sell}$. In case of discharging, the EV will proceed with the electricity transaction only if the EV's reserve price, $EV^{sell(res)}$, is lower than the current electricity price at the EVPL, $EVPL_{ep}^{buy}$. Nevertheless, even if the electricity price matchmaking fails, the EV will still park at the EVPL for EV^{ipd} hours, and leave the EVPL after paying $EVPL^{ps} = \lceil timeParked(EV) \rceil \cdot EVPL^{pp}$ for using EVPL's parking service.

Determining whether there is enough time for the EV to fully complete (dis)charge service. After the EV decides to (dis)charge a certain amount of electricity, some calculation should be made regarding whether there is enough time for the EV to fully (dis)charge. Such a calculation must take into account the EVPL charging rate, $EVPL^{(d)cr}$, and the EV's initial parking duration EV^{ipd}.

If there is enough time for the EV to fully (dis)charge, then the EV will park at the EVPL for EV^{ipd} hours, (dis)charge $EV^{(d)cq}$ amount of electricity, and leave the EVPL after paying $EVPL^{rev}$ (see Eq. (4)) for using both the EVPL's parking and electricity services. If there is not enough time for the EV to fully (dis)charge, i.e., $EV^{(d)cq} > EVPL^{(d)cr} \cdot EV^{ipd}$, then, as mentioned before, the EV has two options, which are determined according to the probability EV^{sl}:

- (i) to partially (dis)charge $EVPL^{(d)cr} \cdot EV^{ipd}$ of electricity; or
- (ii) to prolong its parking time until the full (dis)charging is complete, i.e., the EV will stay parked for a total of $EV^{(d)cq}/EVPL^{(d)cr}$ hours.

When option (i) is activated, then the EV will park at the EVPL for EV^{ipd} hours, (dis)charge $EVPL^{(d)cr} \cdot EV^{ipd}$ amount of electricity, and leave the EVPL after paying $EVPL^{rev}$ for using both the EVPL's parking and electricity services. If option (ii) is activated, the EV will park at the EVPL for a total of $EV^{(d)cq}/EVPL^{(d)cr}$ hours, (dis)charge $EV^{(d)cq}$ of electricity, and leave the EVPL after paying $EVPL^{rev}$ for using both EVPL's parking and electricity services. Clearly, the EVPL's profit is higher when option (ii) is activated.

2.5   EV-enabled Parking Lot B2B Market

The EV-enabled Parking Lot B2B (Business-to-Business) market models the "EV-enabled Parking Lot - Electricity Market" relationship. This relationship is an important prerequisite for the EVPL ecosystem because it procures the necessary amount of electricity for charging services as well as it liquidates discharged electricity from parked EVs to the EM. It is important to note that our present model assumes perfect information about prices from both EVs and EVPL's point-of-view. Also, a transaction between the EVPL and the EM is presumed to have perfect liquidity.

3   EV-enabled Parking Lot Simulation Set-Up

Due to the high stakes and complexity of the interactions within the EVPL ecosystem, the real-life applicability of our proposed model needs to be first considered in a risk-free and feature-packed simulation environment. Such an environment allows one to determine whether EVPLs can deal with uncertainties imposed by EV owners in a profitable way.

At the core of our model is a $M/M/c/0$ queue with time varying arrival and service rates. In such settings, traditional closed-form equations offered by queueing theory are often invalid [8,16]. Hence, we opted to represent our model as an agent-based simulation[2], which allows for a rich analysis under dynamic and highly volatile settings [10]. Table 2 shows the values of the simulation parameters. These values reflect three different sizes of EVPLs (*small*, *medium*, and *large*) and three different types of chargers: (i) *slow* and *cheap*, (ii) *moderately fast* and *reasonably priced*, and (iii) *fast* and *expensive*. Consequently, different parking lot sizes and charger infrastructures equates to the total of nine possible scenarios that might happen in the real-world and are therefore incorporated in our analysis.

Table 2. Scenario-dependent parameter values and results.

Scenario (*(dis)charge rate-parking size*)	EVPL (dis)charge rate (kW)	Charger unit cost (€/charger)	EVPL parking spots	Profits from electricity trading (€)	Profits from extended parking (€)	Aggregate profits $EVPL_{agg}^{prof}$ (€)	Mean parking util. (%)	Mean charger util. (%)	Mean electricity util. (%)
SLOW-SMALL	5	2,000	30	1,769.09	47,332.42	49,101.51	61.4	36.5	21.3
SLOW-MEDIUM	5	2,000	60	2,785.62	69,738.83	72,524.45	50.7	33.3	16.7
SLOW-LARGE	5	2,000	90	3,172.07	80,304.99	83,477.06	37.7	33.8	12.7
STEADY-SMALL	10	10,000	30	1,810.53	16,778.21	18,588.74	58.5	21.9	12.4
STEADY-MEDIUM	10	10,000	60	2,825.14	23,359.06	26,184.2	48.2	19.3	9.4
STEADY-LARGE	10	10,000	90	3,104.85	25,252.31	28,357.16	35.0	19.2	6.9
FAST-SMALL	20	30,000	30	1,907.26	5,548.62	7,455.88	58.2	12.1	6.8
FAST-MEDIUM	20	30,000	60	2,920.72	7,204.47	10,125.19	48.1	10.5	5.1
FAST-LARGE	20	30,000	90	3,216.65	8,123.31	11,339.96	34.5	10.6	3.8

4   Results and Discussion

Our analysis of the EVPL ecosystem identifies potential consequences for the EVPL business by considering different investment pathways. In particular, under the model assumptions and parameter values, we scrutinize the 9 different EVPLs from the perspectives of both *electricity trading* and *extended parking* due to the provision of electricity service. Furthermore, we discuss the EVPL utilization, which is an important key performance indicator (KPI) that provides insights on the usage of the parking and electricity services.

---

[2] Our simulation is implemented using R, a free software environment for statistical computing and graphics. It takes around three minutes to simulate one year scenario on a system with 4-core CPU and 8 GB RAM. Please note R does not utilize multithreading and therefore a computer with less CPU cores will produce similar running times.

4.1   Benefits from Electricity Trading

The fifth column (i.e., *profits from electricity trading*) in Table 2 presents how much money the EVPL earned under different scenarios. It can be noticed that profits from electricity trading increase with parking size and charger speed. Although this outcome is intuitive and somewhat expected, the low absolute values, including low profit discrepancies between the nine scenarios, might make one question about the profitability of the EVPL business. For example, given that in the best case scenario the EVPL makes a profit of just over 3,200 € per year, it would take decades for the parking lot's owner to obtain the invested money back. However, the overall benefit from the energy service is not only measured in terms of electricity trading profits, but also from the extra time an EV was parked in order to fully complete the (dis)charging operation, a point that we discuss next.

4.2   Benefits from Extended Parking

The sixth column (i.e., *profits from extended parking*) in Table 2 presents how much money the EVPL earned due to the prolonged parking in each scenario. Recall that prolonged parking may occur when the (dis)charging operation cannot be fully completed during the EV's initial parking period. In that case, there is the probability EV^{sl} that an EV will prolong its parking duration to fully (dis)charge. Otherwise, the EV will settle for the amount of electricity that is feasible during the initial parking duration. The probability EV^{sl} encodes real-world examples of behavioral patterns of EV owners. For instance, an EV owner that frequently travels to distant locations might suffer from *range anxiety* [15]. Also, an EV owner may not be able to charge at home due to a lack of the required infrastructure, thus the same has to resort to a EVPL.

Interestingly, the results show that the most profitable investment option is to buy the slowest type of charger. The rationale behind this result is that, in comparison to other charger types, the slowest charger increases the chance that the requested amount of electricity $EV^{(d)cq}$ cannot be transferred between the EV and the EVPL within the initial parking duration. Another interesting point is that the results in Table 2 show that the EVPL's main source of income is due to the extended parking service. In our simulations, the parking service has a fixed price $EVPL^{pp}$ set at 3 €/h. As for the electricity service, assuming the discharge rate $EVPL^{(d)cr}$ of 5 kW, the ep^{EM} price set at reasonable 0.035 €/kWh, and the EVPL's profit margin $EVPL^{mrg}$ to be 10%, then the EVPL can expect the maximum profit of 0.0175 € for a single parking space in one hour. Hence, the parking service can bring as much as 170 times more profit than the electricity service alone.

4.3   EV-enabled Parking Lot Utilization

We introduce three types of KPIs that explain how well a particular EVPL is utilized:

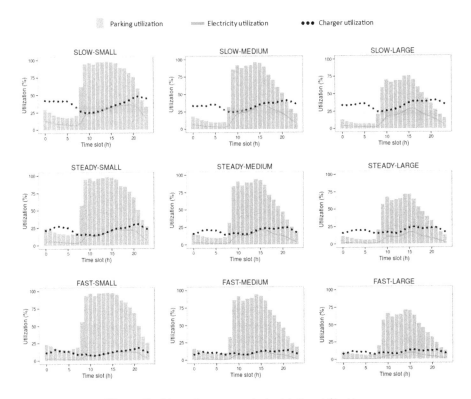

Fig. 5. Parking, charger, and electricity utilizations

– *parking utilization*;
– *charger utilization*; and
– *electricity utilization*.

Parking utilization measures how many EVs were parked at the EVPL. *Charger utilization* is defined as the ratio between the amount of electricity EVs (dis)charged and the maximum amount of electricity that could be (dis)charged in case chargers from occupied parking spots ran at 100% rate while EVs were parked. *Electricity utilization* is defined as the ratio between the amount of electricity EVs (dis)charged and the potential amount of electricity that could be (dis)charged in case all chargers ran at 100% rate all the time. Figure 5 shows the hourly mean values for the three KPIs in each scenario.

Figure 5 shows that the peak hours are between 9 AM and 5 PM, which is in accordance with the arrival rates EV^{ar} and service rates EV^{pr}. Small EVPLs have higher parking utilizations than medium and high EVPLs. Also, large EVPLs have the lowest levels of parking utilization throughout the whole day, which implies that the number of parking spots in large EVPLs in our simulation is indeed too high. Although the arrival rates are lower during night hours (at most three cars per hour), the corresponding parking utilization values from Fig. 5 shows that the amount of time an EV stays parked is prolonged due to the introduction of electricity service.

The KPI charger utilization explains how efficient the chargers of occupied parking spots operate and, thus, it effectively minimizes the impact of the EVPL's size on our analysis. Notably, the results in Fig. 5 show that the charger utilization is higher during off-peak hours than during on-peak hours. The reason for this lies in the fact that parking durations, defined by EV^{pr}, are significantly lower during off-peak hours than during on-peak hours, thus promoting the overall mean charger utilization for off-peak hours.

In contrast to the charger utilization, the electricity utilization KPI indicates the overall performance regarding the EVPL's electricity trading. Figure 5 shows that the electricity utilization correlates with the parking utilization. It also shows that the difference between electricity and charger utilization is lower during on-peak hours and higher during off-peak hours.

The mean values of electricity utilizations are 16.92%, 9.59% and 5.25% for slow, steady and fast charger scenarios, respectively. Furthermore, the maximum values of electricity utilizations are 35.86%, 22.77%, and 12.89% for, respectively, slow, steady, and fast chargers. These numbers can be very helpful for the EVPL when deciding how many traditional parking spots need to be upgraded with electricity chargers. First, from Table 2, one can conclude that the most profitable scenarios are those with slow chargers, due to increased profits from extended parking. Furthermore, from Table 1, one can see that the price of such a charger is $EVPL_{slow}^{cuc} = 2,000€^3$. The payback period (PB) for transforming traditional parking lots into EV-enabled parking lots, assuming that the transformation is implemented by upgrading all parking spots with slow chargers, are:

$$PB_{small}^{full(slow)} = \frac{EVPL_{small}^{ps} \cdot EVPL_{slow}^{cuc}}{EVPL_{agg}^{prof}} = 1.22 \tag{7}$$

$$PB_{medium}^{full(slow)} = \frac{EVPL_{medium}^{ps} \cdot EVPL_{medium}^{cuc}}{EVPL_{agg}^{prof}} = 1.65 \tag{8}$$

$$PB_{large}^{full(slow)} = \frac{EVPL_{large}^{ps} \cdot EVPL_{medium}^{cuc}}{EVPL_{agg}^{prof}} = 2.15 \tag{9}$$

It is noteworthy that the above calculation is conservative due to fact that the EVPL investment costs could be smaller in practice due to economy of scale. Nevertheless, the payback numbers are even more impressive if the EVPL owner decides, based on the data on electricity utilizations shown in Fig. 5, to optimize the number of traditional parking spaces which will be upgraded with chargers. From Fig. 5, one can conclude that only around 36% of parking spots need to be upgraded with electricity chargers in order to maintain the EVPL electricity service. Therefore, the PB in the case of optimal charger installation is the following:

$$PB_{small}^{optimal(slow)} = 36\% \cdot PB_{small}^{full(slow)} \approx 0.44 \tag{10}$$

---

[3] Available at: http://www.greenbiz.com/blog/2014/05/07/rmi-whats-true-cost-ev-charging-stations.

Similar calculations show that $PB_{medium}^{optimal(slow)} \approx 0.59$ and $PB_{large}^{optimal(slow)} \approx$ 0.77. In words, it would take less than one year for an investor to get the invested money back, thus showing that the economic benefits of investing in EV-enabled parking lots are quite significant.

5   Conclusion and Future Work

EV-enabled parking lots provide a natural solution to address the current need for charging stations due to the increased number of electric vehicles on the road. From a business perspective, two potential obstacles to the process of transforming parking lots into EV-enabled parking lots are the complexity of estimating the utilization of the electricity service and the profitability of the resulting EV-enabled parking lot. In this paper, we proposed an agent-based simulation approach that tackles the above problems. Using real-life data, we showed how one can use our approach to study the economic benefits of EV-enabled parking lots. In particular, we illustrated how to estimate the EV-enabled parking lot's profit due to the trade of electricity and extended parking service, how to estimate the number of needed chargers using the electricity utilization KPI, and how to estimate the payback period concerning the invested money.

When using our approach, one must tailor the parameter values in Table 1 to the underlying parking lot setting. One exciting research direction is to perform a case study where one estimates *a priori* the metrics previously discussed using our approach and, then, measures *a posteriori* the accuracy of such estimations. Another research direction relevant to the computational sustainability community is on how to integrate our simulation approach with broader, energy-related simulators, such as Power TAC [4,10]. This would allow one to use competitive benchmarking in order to study the impact of more elaborate trading strategies by the EVPL.

Acknowledgements. The authors acknowledge the support of the research project "Managing Trust and Coordinating Interactions in Smart Networks of People, Machines and Organizations", funded by the Croatian Science Foundation under the project UIP-11-2013-8813 and COST Action IC1404 on Multi-Paradigm Modelling for Cyber-Physical Systems, funded by European Union.

References

1. Babic, J., Carvalho, A., Ketter, W., Podobnik, V.: Economic benefits of smart parking lots. In: Proceedings of the Erasmus Energy Forum 2015 Science Day: Energy Informatics & Management (EIM 2015), pp. 1–8 (2015)
2. Babic, J., Carvalho, A., Ketter, W., Podobnik, V.: Extending parking lots with electricity trading agent functionalities. In: Workshop on Agent-Mediated Electronic Commerce and Trading Agent Design and Analysis (AMEC/TADA 2015)@ AAMAS 2015 (2015)

3. Babic, J., Carvalho, A., Ketter, W., Podobnik, V.: Modelling electric vehicle owners' willingness to pay for a charging service. In: Proceedings of the Erasmus Energy Forum 2016 Science Day: Energy Informatics & Management (EIM 2016), pp. 1–8 (2016)
4. Babic, J., Podobnik, V.: An analysis of power trading agent competition 2014. In: Ceppi, S., David, E., Podobnik, V., Robu, V., Shehory, O., Stein, S., Vetsikas, I.A. (eds.) AMEC/TADA 2013-2014. LNBIP, vol. 187, pp. 1–15. Springer, Cham (2014). doi:10.1007/978-3-319-13218-1_1
5. Babic, J., Podobnik, V.: A review of agent-based modelling of electricity markets in future energy eco-systems. In: International Multidisciplinary Conference on Computer and Energy Science (SpliTech), pp. 1–9. University of Split, FESB (2016)
6. Ferreira, M., Damas, L., Conceicao, H., D'Orey, P.M., Fernandes, R., Steenkiste, P., Gomes, P.: Self-automated parking lots for autonomous vehicles based on vehicular ad hoc networking. In 2014 IEEE IEEE Intelligent Vehicles Symposium Proceedings, pp. 472–479. IEEE, June 2014
7. Gerding, E., Stein, S., Robu, V., Zhao, D., Jennings, N.R.: Two-sided online markets for electric vehicle charging. In: Proceedings of 12th International Conference on Autonomous Agents and Multi-Agent Systems, pp. 989–996 (2013)
8. Hasofer, A.: On the single-server queue with non-homogeneous poisson input and general service time. J. Appl. Probab. $\mathbf{1}$(2), 369–384 (1964)
9. Hosseini, S.S., Badri, A., Parvania, M.: A survey on mobile energy storage systems (MESS): applications, challenges and solutions. Renew. Sustain. Energy Rev. $\mathbf{40}$, 161–170 (2014)
10. Ketter, W., Collins, J., Reddy, P.: Power TAC: a competitive economic simulation of the smart grid. Energy Econ. $\mathbf{39}$, 262–270 (2013)
11. Ketter, W., Peters, M., Collins, J., Gupta, A.: A multiagent competitive gaming platform to address societal challenges. Mis Q. $\mathbf{40}$(2), 447–460 (2016)
12. Khalen, M., Ketter, W., van Dalen, J.: Balancing with electric vehicles: a profitable business model. In: Proceedings of European Conference on Information Systems 2014, Tel Aviv, Israel, pp. 1–15 (2014)
13. Macal, C.M., North, M.J.: Tutorial on agent-based modelling and simulation. J. Simul. $\mathbf{4}$(3), 151–162 (2010)
14. McKinsey & Company. Electric vehicles in Europe: Gearing up for a new phase? (2015)
15. Neubauer, J., Wood, E.: The impact of range anxiety and home, workplace, and public charging infrastructure on simulated battery electric vehicle lifetime utility. J. Power Sources $\mathbf{257}$, 12–20 (2014)
16. Rothkopf, M.H., Oren, S.S.: A closure approximation for the nonstationary M/M/s queue. Manage. Sci. $\mathbf{25}$(6), 522–534 (1979)
17. Urieli, D., Stone, P.: Tactex'13: a champion adaptive power trading agent. In: Proceedings of the Twenty-Eighth AAAI Conference on Artificial Intelligence (2014)
18. Valogianni, K., Ketter, W., Collins, J., Zhdanov, D.: Effective management of electric vehicle storage using smart charging. In: Proceedings of the Twenty-Eighth AAAI Conference on Artificial Intelligence (2014)
19. Zhang, L., Brown, T., Samuelsen, S.: Evaluation of charging infrastructure requirements and operating costs for plug-in electric vehicles. J. Power Sources $\mathbf{240}$, 515–524 (2013)

Auction Based Mechanisms for Dynamic Task Assignments in Expert Crowdsourcing

Sujit Gujar[1,2](✉) and Boi Faltings[1,2]

[1] International Institute of Information Technology, Hyderabad, India
sujit.gujar@iiit.ac.in
[2] Artifitial Intelligence Laboratory, EPFL, Lausanne, Switzerland
boi.faltings@epfl.ch

Abstract. Crowdsourcing marketplaces link large populations of workers to an even larger number of tasks. Thus, it is necessary to have mechanisms for matching workers with interesting and suitable tasks. Earlier work has addressed the problem of finding optimal workers for a given set of tasks. However, workers also have preferences and will stay with a platform only if it gives them interesting tasks. We therefore analyze several matching mechanisms that take into account workers' preferences as well. We propose that the workers pay premiums to get preferred matches and auction-based models where preferences are expressed through variations of the payment for a task. We analyze the properties of two matching different mechanisms: Split Dynamic VCG (SDV) and e-Auction. We compare both the mechanisms with Arrival Priority Serial Dictatorship (APSD) empirically for efficiency.

1 Introduction

Crowdsourcing has emerged as a new paradigm in getting work done, where human agents solve tasks that are difficult to solve by software agents. Crowdsourcing is used in numerous applications. For example, hand written character recognition is easy for humans, but it is difficult for software. Real-time applications like VizWiz [3] leverage crowdsourcing to gather specific information from an image.

In the crowdsourcing market, there are two types of users of the platform, a *requester*, the one who posts and a *worker*, the one who seeks to work on the tasks. Typically, the term crowdsourcing refers to settings where the requesters post simple microtasks which can be performed quickly by human workers. With the success in crowdsourcing, it is becoming prevalent to crowdsource complex macro tasks which is referred to as *expert crowdsourcing* [22]. For example, oDesk, topcoder are expert crowdsourcing platforms. Consider the following scenario of an expert crowdsourcing as shown in Fig. 1.

This work was carried out when the first author was a post-doctoral researcher at EPFL.

S. Ceppi et al. (Eds.): AMEC/TADA 2015/2016, LNBIP 271, pp. 50–65, 2017.
DOI: 10.1007/978-3-319-54229-4_4

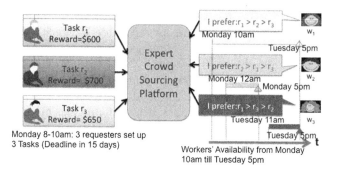

Fig. 1. An expert crowdsourcing scenario with three tasks and three workers

Example 1. On a Monday morning three requesters login to a crowdsourcing platform with their tasks. These tasks are to develop software modules and are having deadlines in two weeks. w_1, w_2 and w_3 are eligible and interested workers for these tasks. The worker w_3 prefers to work on r_1 then r_2, r_3. Similarly the other workers have preferences over the tasks, as shown in Fig. 1. w_1 is available from Monday morning till Tuesday evening for the task assignment, where as w_2 and w_3 are present only on Monday and Tuesday respectively. The goal is to optimally assign the tasks to the dynamic workers.

The prior work for the task assignments in crowdsourcing is mainly focused on catering to the requesters needs, i.e., addresses concerns with quality of the workers and the answer aggregation. It takes into account the workers' reputation and the requesters' requirements and budgets. However, one of the important advantages for the workers to work on the platform is to select tasks of their own choice. As seen from the above example, workers have preferences over the tasks they are assigned. In this paper, we address the task assignment problem in crowdsourcing catering to the workers' preferences.

Task Assignments with the Workers' Preferences. Difallah *et al.* [5] proposed to push the tasks to the workers based on their preferences. These are only categorical preferences and not the workers' preferences for the requesters. The authors do not address strategic nature of the workers. Gujar and Faltings [9] addressed the strategic and dynamic workers. The authors model the problem as a two sided matching without money to achieve stability. In this paper, we consider task assignment to dynamically arriving workers. The dynamic workers are of two types, namely *exogenous* and *endogenous*. (i) The exogenous workers do not lie about their arrival-departure. (ii) The endogenous workers can report late arrival or early departure if its beneficial for them.[1] The goal in this paper is to improve *efficiency*, the valuation that workers assign to their assigned tasks, in task assignments to dynamic workers of an expert crowdsourcing platform.

---

[1] The workers has to be logged into the system for his availability and hence cannot report early arrival or late departure.

We propose that workers pay the platform a *premium* to obtain a preferable match. We refer to such task assignment with side payments as a *matching mechanism*. A matching mechanism is designed to induce a truthful behaviour among the workers and achieve efficiency.

To validate the hypothesis about side payments in task assignments, we conducted a survey with crowd workers. 92.6% of the workers were positive about the tasks assignments with side payments. Section 6 provides more details about the survey.

With such side payments, we design auction based matching mechanisms for the task assignment problem in an expert crowdsourcing platform. As users of these mechanisms may not be experts in game theory/mechanism design, the goal is to design mechanisms that are simple and avoid any complex models such as dynamic optimization using Markov Decision Processes and prior on the workers preferences. Secretary problem [1] based solutions are useful. However, the difference between classical secretary problem and the settings addressed here is, ours is a combinatorial problem with multiple recruiters interested in the workers who have high valuation for their tasks and ensuring truthfulness of reported preferences. Our contributions are as follows.

Contributions. We allow the workers to pay a premium to obtain a better match. We propose two dynamic matching mechanisms for the task assignment problem. For exogenous settings, we first develop a matching mechanism generalizing Vickrey-Clarke-Groves (VCG) mechanism, namely *Split Dynamic VCG* (SDV). We prove that SDV is strategyproof and k-competitive where k is the number of tasks. We show empirically that in SDV, the efficiency of matching improves by 5–10% over Arrival Priority Serial Dictatorship (APSD). In endogenous settings, we propose a strategyproof matching mechanism, e-Auction. It is adapted from e-competitive, single item dynamic auction proposed in [19]. The workers cannot manipulate their arrival departure periods in e-Auction. We prove that it is e^2-competitive for efficiency, as against SDV and Arrival Priority Serial Dictatorship (APSD) are k-competitive. However, empirically APSD and SDV perform better than e-Auction.

Organization. In the next section, we review the related literature. We describe our model, notation and assumptions in Sect. 3. We explain how to design matching mechanisms based on auctions in Sect. 4. With simulations, we analyze empirical efficiency of all the mechanisms in Sect. 5. In Sect. 6, we compare SDV, e-Auctionand APSD mechanisms and discuss how to relax the assumptions made in the paper. We conclude the paper in Sect. 7.

2   Related Work

The term *crowdsourcing* was introduced by Howe [13]. Since then it has attracted researchers, practitioners, entrepreneurs, industrialists etc. Currently there are thousands of websites available for crowdsourcing.[2] It is a pull model of work where workers decide what to work on and when to work as against the traditional push model where management distributes the work among employees and monitors the progress. As it is an uncontrolled manner of getting work done, there is always a concern about the quality of the work done. Lots of research has been carried out to ensure the quality of the received answer [2,4,11,12,15–17,20,22]. Most of them use machine learning for the task assignments. For example, [15,20] proposed EM based algorithms for quality management in the crowdsourcing. [22] proposed the multi-armed-bandit based algorithm to learn the qualities of the workers and analyzed it for regret. [14] discussed how to design the tasks so as to improve the quality of answers. Note that all this work is focused mainly for the requesters.

Kittur *et al.* [18] studied worker's perspective on crowdsourcing. The authors conducted user studies on AMT and proposed different techniques to improve performance of the workers on the tasks by intelligent task design. [8,16] considered bidding based task allocation, to elicit the costs incurred by the workers. Our paper is different from all the above as focus is on the task assignments catering to the qualified but strategic, dynamically arriving workers' preferences over the tasks and the bids are not for the costs incurred by the workers.

If side payments are not feasible and workers are static with ordinal preferences, the task assignment problem is same as assignment problem studied in economics. Sönmez and Ünver [21] is a survey that summarizes the results for the static assignment problem. For the dynamic endogenous workers with ordinal preferences, APSD is the only strategyproof mechanism [23]. In this paper, we use side payments to increase efficiency of the task assignment and address the problem as a mechanism design problem in auctions. For more about mechanism design theory, the interested readers are referred to [6,7] and the references cite therein.

3 The Model and Notation

In this paper our focus is on the task assignments in an *expert crowdsourcing* market where workers are skilled, tasks are complex and rewards are relatively high as seen in Example (1). For designing matching mechanisms in this setting, we make the following assumptions.[3]

Assumptions

– The number of tasks and the corresponding qualified workers is not so large that the workers will have difficulty in reporting their preferences. For example, on oDesk, on a particular day only a small portion of the tasks may be relevant for a software professional with specific skills.

---

[2] http://crowdsourcing.org.

[3] It should be noted that, the settings of expert crowdsourcing are different than microtasking where the workers finish the task quickly and move on to a next task immediately.

- All the workers satisfy pre-qualification for the tasks.
- We focus on a time window during which each worker takes up only one task. We discuss how to relax this assumption in Sect. 6.
- The workers may strategize their preferences to get preferable tasks.

There are k tasks with i^{th} task denoted as r_i. $W = \{w_1, \ldots, w_k\}$ are eligible aspirants for these tasks who arrive dynamically to the market. Upon arrival in the time slot arr_j, a worker w_j observes the tasks in the system and reports his preferences over the tasks and a deadline dep_j until when he can accept a task. If an impatient worker needs a task immediately, he can indicate $dep_j = arr_j$. We capture the preferences of a worker by a valuation he assigns to the task he receives. Let b_{ij} be the value that w_j assigns to the matching where he is matched with the task r_i. We also interpret these numbers as a *bid*, maximum premium a worker is willing to pay, for the task. If a worker does not have any preferences over the tasks, he can set the preference to be a zero vector. The notation used in the paper is described in Table 1. With this notation, we now define matching mechanism and desirable properties.

Table 1. Notation

k	Total number of tasks (workers)
R	The set of tasks
r_i	i^{th} Task
w_j	j^{th} worker
arr_j, dep_j	Arrival time and departure time for w_j
$R(t)$	The tasks not assigned till t
$W(t)$	$\{w_j \ni arr_j \leq t \leq dep_j \text{ and} w_j \text{ is not been assigned any task.}\}$
$AW(t)$	$\{w_j | arr_j = t\}$. Set of workers arriving in time slot t
$DW(t)$	$\{w_j | dep_j = t\}$. Set of workers departing in time slot t
$\mathbf{b_j}$	$= (b_{ij})$ Preference of w_j over the tasks
μ	Matching algorithm
p_j	Payment made by worker w_j to the platform for the matching
$\mathbf{p}$	$= (p_j)_{j \in W}$

Matching Mechanisms. The task assignment problem is divided into two parts: (i) *A matching algorithm* (μ) - It produces (w, r) pairs, where the worker w is assigned with the task r[4]. A task should be assigned to a worker before he leaves the system. (ii) *Payment*: It decides a payment to be paid by the users for receiving preferable matches. We refer to a matching algorithm along with payments as a *matching mechanism*.

---

[4] μ takes $\mathbf{b_j}$s, arr_j, dep_j as inputs and produces a bipartite matching. However to simplify notation, we just refer to μ as a bipartite matching.

Desirable Game Theoretic Properties of Matching Mechanisms. Let $\mathcal{M} = (\mu, \mathbf{p})$ be a given mechanism.

Strategyproof. Let $\mathbf{b}_{-j} = (\mathbf{b}_1, \ldots, \mathbf{b}_{j-1}, \mathbf{b}_{j+1}, \ldots, \mathbf{b}_k)$ and w_j be assigned with $r_{i_1} = \mu(w_j)$ with payment p_j when he reports his preference as $\mathbf{b}_j$ and remaining workers report $\mathbf{b}_{-j}$. Let $r_{i_2} = \mu(w_j)$ when he reports $\mathbf{b}'_j$ while remaining workers report $\mathbf{b}_{-j}$ and his payment be p'_j. We say $\mathcal{M}$ is strategyproof, if $\forall w_j$,

$$b_{i_1 j} - p_j \geq b_{i_2 j} - p'_j \qquad \forall \mathbf{b}_{-j}.$$

That is, by misreporting the preferences over matching, the workers cannot gain.

Efficiency. Let V^μ be the valuation that all the workers assign to their match. I.e., $V^\mu = \sum_j b_{\mu(w_j)j}$. We say μ is efficient if μ selects a matching that maximizes V^μ. If all the preferences are known before-hand, we can always find an optimal matching. This is called as off-line optimal (OFF-OPT) solution and $V^{OFF-OPT}$ is valuation of the off-line optimal solution.

Competitive Ratio. No matching mechanism can predict preferences of the workers yet to arrive and make perfect decisions for the departing workers. Hence in dynamic (on-line) settings, it is impossible to achieve efficiency. The *Competitive ratio* is a widely used measure of the performance of on-line algorithms. It measures how bad the solution found by the algorithm can be as compared to an optimal solution. An on-line algorithm is c-competitive if,

$$\mathbb{E}[V^\mu] \geq \frac{1}{c} \mathbb{E}[V^{OFF-OPT}] \quad \forall (\mathbf{b}_1, \ldots, \mathbf{b}_k)$$

The expectation is with respect to random orderings of the workers. Instead of expectation if we consider this ratio for each instance, in adversarial settings, it will be arbitrarily bad. Hence we measure it under a random hypothesis where all orders in which the workers arrive are equally likely.

We model task assignment as a dynamic auction. In the next section, we propose two matching mechanisms having different competitive ratios. We refer to the first matching mechanism, which is VCG based, as *SDV*. We also propose a matching mechanism e-Auctionto improve efficiency. In both the mechanisms, matching algorithms are induced by the underlying auction's allocation rules.

4   Matching Mechanisms: Dynamic Auctions

In this section, we first describe APSD. We then propose our mechanisms.

4.1   Arrival Priority Serial Dictatorship (APSD)

Zou *et al.* [23] proved that in endogenous settings, APSD is the only strategyproof mechanism for assignment problem when the preferences are ordinal. In this mechanism, the workers are assigned a priority based on their arrival time and the tasks are assigned according to the priority of the workers. It is k-competitive for efficiency and in general, it can lead to inefficient task assignments.

4.2   SDV: Dynamic VCG AUCTION

Let the system have tick events which are a collection of time slots. We say a tick event occurs when the system time matches with one of the time given in the list. Whenever a tick event occurs, the matching of the unassigned and available workers happens. At tick events, the platform solves an optimization problem described in (1). Let $\{t'\}$ be the tick events defined by the system, x_{ij} be an indicator variable indicating whether the task r_i is assigned to w_j or not, and $\alpha_{ij} = b_{ij}$.

$$
\begin{aligned}
\max \quad & \sum_{i \in R(t'), j \in W(t')} \alpha_{ij} x_{ij} \\
s.t. \quad & \sum_i x_{ij} \le 1 \ \forall i \in R(t') \\
& \sum_j x_{ij} \le 1 \ \forall j \in W(t') \\
& x_{ij} \in \{0, 1\}
\end{aligned}
\tag{1}
$$

For the matching mechanism SDV $= (\mu^{SDV}, P^{SDV})$, μ^{SDV} is defined in Algorithm 1.

Algorithm 1. Matching Algorithm μ^{SDV}

Input: Workers' preferences (b_js)
Output: A matching
1 $t = 1$, $R(1) = R, W(1) = AW(1)$
2 **if** $t \in \{t'\}$ **then**
3 $\quad$ | Solve Optimization Problem (1)
4 $\quad$ | **if** $x_{ij} = 1$ **then**
5 $\quad$ | $\quad$ | $\mu(w_j) = r_i$ and $\mu(r_i) = w_j$.
6 $\quad$ | $\quad$ | Determine p_j^{SDV}

7 $t \leftarrow t + 1$
8 $R(t) \leftarrow R(t-1)\backslash\{r_i : \exists j \ni x_{ij} = 1\}$;
$\quad$ $W(t) \leftarrow \{W(t-1)\backslash\{w_j : \exists i \ni x_{ij} = 1\}\} \cup AW(t)$
9 **if** $W(t) == \emptyset$ OR $R(t) == \emptyset$ **then**
10 $\quad$ | STOP.

11 **else**
12 $\quad$ | Go to Step 2

Payment P^{SDV}: At the tick event t', let $OPT^{t'}$ be the value of the above optimization problem (1). VCG payment for w_j who is matched at t':

$$
p_j^{SDV} = V_{-j}^* - OPT_{-j}^{t'}
\tag{2}
$$

where, $V_{-j}^* = OPT^{t'} - b_{i^*j}$. $OPT_{-j}^{t'}$ is the optimal value obtained by solving the above optimization problem with workers $W(t)\backslash w_j$. $\qquad\square$

Note that (i) the duration between two consecutive tick events is chosen indepen-dent of the users' preferences. (ii) It can be a minute or can be hours depending upon the task complexity. While defining tick events, the system ensures that every worker is present at least for one tick event. For example, the system can add all the departure periods of the workers in the list of tick events.

Even though integer programs are NP-hard, this particular optimization problem can be solved in polynomial time as this is a maximum weight bipartite matching between the tasks and the workers having edges from each task r_i to each worker w_j with weight $\alpha_{ij} = b_{ij}$. We illustrate SDV mechanism with an example.

Table 2. SDV: Example Preferences

w_1	$r_1 \succ r_2 \succ r_3$	$\mathbf{b_1} = (10, 9, 0)$
w_2	$r_2 \succ r_1 \succ r_3$	$\mathbf{b_2} = (5, 12, 1)$
w_3	$r_1 \succ r_3 \succ r_2$	$\mathbf{b_3} = (15, 5, 10)$

Example 2. Consider the same scenario as depicted in Fig. 1 with bids as indi-cated in Table 2. Let the tick events t' be Monday evening 5pm ($t = 1$) and Tuesday evening 5pm ($t = 2$). At $t = 1$, the platform solves a maximum weight bipartite matching and assigns r_1 to w_1 and r_2 to w_2. VCG payments are 0 for both of them. At $t = 2$, r_3 is assigned to w_3 and his payment is also 0. Instead of $(5, 12, 1)$ if w_2 has preference $(12, 5, 1)$, he is assigned to task r_1 and needs to pay 1 whereas w_1 gets r_2 at no cost.

From the above example, it is clear that the workers may not have to pay if their interests are not conflicting. As our goal is not to make money out of such matching mechanisms, low payments are acceptable. We now see the analysis of SDV.

Proposition 1. *SDV is strategyproof when workers are exogenous.*

Proof: We partition the workers using tick events such that in each subgroup, all the workers are available simultaneously and treat each of the subgroups as an independent problem. Each sub-problem is solved using VCG auction. No worker can manipulate SDV because, his preference cannot choose which VCG auction to be part of and each VCG auction is strategyproof. Thus, SDV is strategyproof. □

Proposition 2. *SDV is k-competitive for efficiency of the matching.*

Proof: Let $V^{\mu^{SDV}}$ be the total valuation of the matching in SDV. For a given preference profile, let r_{i^*} be a task of a worker w_j in an optimal assignment and let r_i be a task assigned to him by SDV. The expected valuation of the matching to him be $\mathbb{E}[b_{ij}]$ where expectation is with respect to orderings of the workers. With the random ordering hypothesis, each agent is first to arrive with probability $\frac{1}{k}$.

$$\Rightarrow \quad b_{ij} \geq b_{i^*j} \quad \text{with probability} \frac{1}{k}$$
$$\Rightarrow \quad \mathbb{E}[b_{ij}] \geq \frac{1}{k}b_{i^*j}$$
$$\Rightarrow \quad \sum_{w_j} \mathbb{E}[b_{ij}] \geq \sum_{w_j} \frac{1}{k}b_{i^*j}$$
$$\Rightarrow \quad \mathbb{E}[V^{\mu^{SDV}}] \geq \frac{1}{k}V^{OFF-OPT}$$

The above holds true for any preference profile and hence SDV is k-competitive.

This bound is tight up to an additive constant 1 from the following preference. w_1 has valuation $\mathbf{b_1} = (k^2, 0, \ldots, 0)$. All the other workers have valuation $(\epsilon, 0, \ldots, 0)$, where is ϵ is very small positive real number. The optimal solution has value k^2 and SDV will achieve this with probability $\frac{1}{k}$. For all the instances where w_1 does not arrive before the first tick event where matching happens, SDV has valuation of ϵ leading to competitive ratio arbitrarily close to k. □

This efficiency is based on the valuations that the workers assign to the matching and not based on payments or costs incurred by workers. To improve on the high competitive ratio of SDV, we propose e-Auctionmatching mechanism.

4.3   e-Auction

In [19], the following strategyproof auction was proposed for selling a single item to dynamically arriving k agents. We explain this for single task, k workers settings.

Single Task Dynamic Auction. The platform waits until it receives $\frac{k}{e}$ bids. p, q be the two highest bids received so far. If the worker with bid p is available, allocate the task to him at price q. Otherwise, whenever a worker with bid higher than p arrives, allocate the task to that agent at price p. It is shown that the above auction is e-competitive for efficiency.

Multi Task Dynamic Auction. We adopt the above auction to our setting which is combinatorial. We have k tasks to be assigned to the k workers each requiring only one. We call the new matching mechanism e-$Auction = (\mu^{eA}, P^{eA})$. The algorithm μ^{eA} is described in Algorithm 2. Recall that the workers not having preferences for a task(s), put a bid of '0' and k being the number of workers, step 1 of the above algorithm will not wait indefinitely.

Payment P^{eA}: Each worker who wins the task in the first $\frac{k}{e}$ bids, has to pay the second highest bid received up to the first $\frac{k}{e}$ bids for the task. Other workers, if they receive a task, pay the highest bid received up to the first $\frac{k}{e}$ bids for that task.

Proposition 3. e-Auctionis strategyproof.

Algorithm 2. Matching Algorithm μ^{eA}

Input: Users Preferences ($\mathbf{b}_j s$)
Output: A Matching
1 Wait until $\frac{k}{e}$ bids for each task have been received.
2 After this, for each task, if the highest bidder is present, and not assigned any
  task, allocate him the task at second highest bid received so far for the task.
3 If a worker is winner at more than one task, he is assigned with the task having
  highest pay-off (his bid $-$ payment).
4 This worker is marked as absent.
5 For all the tasks which are not assigned in the above step, the highest bid
  received for the task is marked as a reserve price.
6 The first worker who submits a bid higher than the reserve price and is not
  assigned to any of the other tasks is assigned the task.

Proof: In e-Auctionpayment, for all $w_j \in W$, p_j is independent of $\mathbf{b}_j$ and if a
worker is winner in multiple tasks, he is assigned a task with the highest $b_{ij} - p_j$.
Hence no worker has any incentive to misreport his bid. If an worker reports the
late arrival than true arrival, it does not increase his chance of winning on any of
the tasks. If the worker tries to report departure before $\frac{k}{e}$ workers have arrived,
he will not get the task. After that, does not matter when is his departure. Thus,
no worker can gain anything by late-arrival or early departure.   □

Proposition 4. e-Auctionis at-most e^2-competitive for efficiency of the
matching.

Proof: Let R' be the set of tasks assigned to the workers by e-Auctionand W'
be the set of workers who receive a task. Let $r_i = \mu^{eA}(w_j)$. $V^{\mu^{eA}} = \sum_{j \in W'} b_{ij} = \sum_{i \in R'} b_{ij}$.

For a single task case, from the classic secretary problem analysis, with probability $\frac{1}{e}$, each task will be assigned to the worker having highest valuation for
that task. Say $\mu^{eA}(r_{i*}) = w_{j*}$. With probability $\frac{1}{e}$, $b_{i*j*} \geq b_{i*j}$, In particular,
$b_{i*j*} \geq b_{i*j'}$ where $w_{j'}$ is the OFF-OPT assignment of the task r_{i*}.

In our settings, each worker can take up only one task. Say for the task
r_{i*}, w_{j*} is the highest bidder. It may happen that a worker w_{j*} is the highest
bidder at multiple tasks, and this may lead to the task r_{i*} being not assigned.
If a winner for r_{i*} is not a winner at any other task, then definitely, the task
assigned. If the valuations of the workers are independent and are identically
distributed, each worker is equally likely to be winner at all the tasks. Hence,
probability that a worker is winner exactly at on task is $(1 - \frac{1}{k})^{k-1}$ which is $\frac{1}{e}$
for large k.

$$\Rightarrow \text{Probability that a task is assigned } \geq \frac{1}{e}$$
$$\mathbf{E}[V^{\mu^{eA}}] = \sum_{i \in R'} \mathbf{E}[b_{ij}]$$
$$\Rightarrow \mathbf{E}[V^{\mu^{eA}}] \geq \sum_{i \in R} \frac{1}{e} \mathbf{E}[b_{ij}]$$
$$\Rightarrow \mathbf{E}[V^{\mu^{eA}}] \geq \sum_{i \in R} \frac{1}{e^2} \max_j b_{ij}$$
$$\Rightarrow \mathbf{E}[V^{\mu^{eA}}] \geq \sum_{i \in R} \frac{1}{e^2} V^{OFF-OPT}$$

This proves the claim.[5]   □

e-Auctionis an interesting auction as on worst case analysis, it has a much lower competitive ratio as compared to SDV. The disadvantage of e-Auctionis that some tasks may not get assigned in e-Auction.

5   Evaluation of the Mechanisms

The proposed mechanisms in this paper inherently hypothesize that workers will participate in bidding for the tasks. To evaluate this hypothesis, we conducted a survey with crowd workers.

5.1   Survey: Bidding Based Task Assignments

We conducted the survey on Amazon Mechanical Turk (AMT).[6] To safeguard against spammers, only workers with high acceptance over at least 5000 HITs were allowed to participate in the survey. The survey included java questions to ensure that the participant has java programming knowledge. We told workers that there are java programming tasks having a reward of $200[7] and we are researching about possibility of bidding based task allocation for high paying tasks. We asked the workers whether they had worked on crowdsourced programming tasks and will they be willing to bid to the platform in such task assignments and how much. The workers were paid $0.1 for participation and bonus of $0.9 to those who did well on java questions. 56 different workers participated. 75% of the participants claimed that they had worked on crowdsourced programming tasks. 45% were proficient in Java. 92.8% of all the participants and all of the java proficient responded positively for participating in the bidding based task assignments. We observed that the workers are interested in bidding aggressively on a task where their chance of getting the task is higher over the task they actually prefer.

This survey supports the notion of premium to be charged in the form of bids for the task-assignments in expert crowdsourcing environment. With this positive feedback from the workers, we further evaluate the mechanisms for empirical efficiency. We perform the empirical analysis by simulations.

5.2   Empirical Evaluation

We simulated the mechanisms by generating random preference profiles and arrival-departure for the users. For arrival of the workers, we assume the workers arrive in the system according to a Poisson process with mean λ and wait in the system according to an exponential distribution with mean $\mu = 2$. We used the following three generative models for the preferences of the workers.

---

[5] Note that this is upper bound on competitive ratio.

[6] http://mturk.com.

[7] Note that we are referring to expert crowdsourcing tasks and not the microtasks. Hence, such rewards are feasible.

- I *Uniform*: For each task, all the workers' bids are generated uniformly at random from interval [0,1].
- II *Single Peaked*: Each worker's ordinal preference over the tasks is generated using uniform distribution. His bid for the most desirable task is drawn uniformly at random from [1,2]. However, his bid for i^{th} ranked tasks is $\frac{1}{i}$ of his the most desirable task.
- III *Single Peaked with Popularity* In this model, we assume certain tasks are more desirable than the others. Here, the workers ordinal preferences are drawn according to the popularity. And these preferences are converted to bids in the same manner as in Single Peaked case. The ordinal preferences with popularity $(\phi_1, \phi_2, \ldots, \phi_k)$ are generated as described below.
  - $R_1 = \{1, 2, \ldots, k\}$ A task r_i is selected as the most preferred tasks from R_1 with probability $\frac{\phi_i}{\sum_{l \in R_1} \phi_l}$. Let it be, r_{j_1}
  - $R_2 = R_1 \backslash \{r_{j_1}\}$. Now the next best task is sampled from R_2 with probabilities proportional to $\frac{\phi_i}{\sum_{l \in R_2} \phi_l}$ and so on.

For each of these three generative models, with $k = 30$, we generated 10,000 different preference profiles and studied empirical efficiency by considering the average valuation of the matching per worker per task by varying λ. In SDV, we

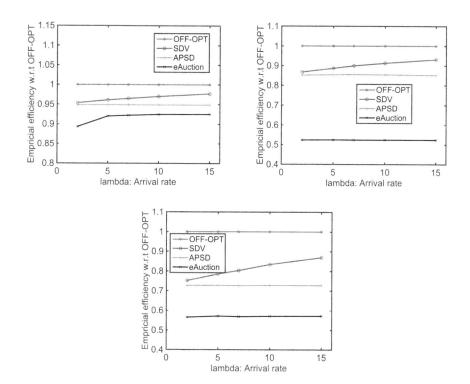

Fig. 2. Empirical Comparison of SDV, *e*-Auction, APSD and OFF-OPT for efficiency

used tick events generated by workers arrival. That is, every worker is assigned a task as soon as he arrives.

Figure 2 shows empirical efficiency SDV, APSD, e-Auctionand OFF-OPT. It is the average valuation of a matching per work normalized to OFF-OPT $= 1$. Clearly, SDV improves over APSD by 2–3% for $\lambda \in (\frac{k}{6}, \frac{k}{4})$ when the workers are of type I. For workers of type II and III, this improvement is 5% and 10% respectively. This arrival rate matches on average λ workers together. Hence, if on average all the workers are willing to wait till λ workers to arrive, they clearly see an improvement in quality of matching by SDV. From simulations, it is clear that, though e-Auctionhas better worst case guarantees, it is within only 2-competitive (50% of the off-line optimal) where as SDV is 1.25-competitive (that is, within 80% of the off-line optimal).

In the next section, we provide a unified comparison of the mechanisms discussed in the paper. We also describe how to relax some of the assumptions.

6   Discussion

The crowdsourcing platform needs to propose/assign tasks to the workers. To keep users interested in the platform, it needs to achieve efficiency in such task assignments. Strategic workers may manipulate the task assignment by misreporting their preferences. So we need strategyproofness. Towards this, we focused on expert crowdsourcing and proposed two matching mechanisms namely, SDV and e-Auction. Table 3 compares both the proposed mechanisms for strategyproofness, efficiency and empirical efficiency for type III workers described in the previous Section.

Table 3. Comparison of mechanisms SDV, e-Auctionand APSD

	SDV	eA	APSD
StrategyProofness	Y	Y	Y
Endogenous	N	Y	Y
Competitive Ratio	k	e^2	k
Expected Competitive Ratio	1.25	1.76	1.38
Is market cleared?	Y	N	Y

APSD does not need any side payments as well as works in endogenous settings. SDV assumes exogenous settings. Both the mechanisms have same guarantee on competitive ratio. However, empirically SDV performs better than APSD.

– In endogenous settings, we proposed e-Auctionwhich has better competitive ratio. However, we observe in experiments, it performs poor for average case efficiency.

Thus, if we can assume exogenous settings, we propose to use SDV. If side payments are not desired or in endogenous settings, one can use APSD proposed by Zou *et al.* [23]. If stronger worst case guarantee on competitive ratio is needed, we propose to use e-Auction. However, empirically, we observe that e-Auction does not perform that well.

Note that, typically to best of our knowledge there is no prior work in online mechanism with competitive ratio guarantees when private information is multi-dimensional.

e-Auction: Empirical Analysis. In APSD, the mechanism does not wait to gather any information about the valuations of the workers yet to arrive, but assigns the best possible task to the worker upon arrival. In worst case, such mechanism can lead to a very poor performance. In SDV, the mechanism waits certain duration defined by tick events and optimizes the sum of valuations of the workers present in the system at tick events. This improves the efficiency, but still on worst case, it may lead to poor performance. As opposed to these two matching mechanisms, e-Auction is designed to improve guarantees on the worst performance. It waits for $\frac{k}{e}$ workers to arrive and learns about valuations of the workers and then matches workers and tasks. This improves the worst case guarantees. However, typically it loses opportunity to assign some tasks to the initial workers who might have left the platform before the assignments happen. This leads to a poor performance on average case analysis, as observed in the experiments (Table 3). To overcome this, in follow up work, we proposed Online Ranked Competition Auction (ORCA) [10]. ORCA waits for different thresholds for each task rather than uniform $\frac{k}{e}$ that of e-Auction before matching the task to a worker. This should improve worst case performance further. Such analysis is still open. We observed, empirically ORCA improves over e-Auction. For more details, please refer to [10].

The Expert Crowdsourcing Model. Note that the expert crowdsourcing settings in this paper are different from the widely referred crowdsourcing of micro tasks. Hence the assumptions made in the paper, may not model the microtasking environment well. We demonstrate how to relax some of the assumptions.

(a) If the workers want the tasks without waiting, all the mechanisms are valid. Either workers can set, $arr_j = dep_j$ or the tick events can occur at faster rates. As the analysis is for worst case, it is still valid. However, in the long run, users may realize that quality of matching is better if everybody is patient.

(b) If a worker is unable to determine preferences or is not interested in reporting preferences, he can indicate it by $b_{ij} = 0$. However, if workers indicate a preference, they get preferable tasks as compared to not indicating preferences.

(c) The tasks in expert crowdsourcing are typically complex and require more time to finish them. We focus on a time-window during which only one such task can be performed. Hence, we make the assumption that each worker takes up one task. If we relax that, all mechanisms can adopt with the claimed properties. Say each worker takes up l tasks:

- For e-Auction, we can still set prices with the same rule and let the worker select up to l most preferred tasks if he is winner at multiple tasks. In fact, the competitive ratio improves with increased competition. For example, if workers can take up to k tasks, the competitive ratio will be e.
- For, SDV, each instance being static VCG, the strategyproofness will hold true. (The optimization problem will change accordingly).

(d) All the mechanisms are valid even of the number of tasks is not same as the number of workers. However the competitive analysis will change.

7   Conclusion

In this paper, we addressed task assignments to dynamic workers in expert crowdsourcing platforms through matching mechanisms. We introduced the notion of a premium to be paid by the workers to get preferable matches. The monetary transfers help in achieving strategyproofness and efficiency. We proposed two dynamic matching mechanisms, SDV for exogenous workers and e-Auctionfor endogenous workers. We proved various properties of these mechanisms and in the previous section we summarized our results.

References

1. Babaioff, M., Immorlica, N., Kempe, D., Kleinberg, R.: Online auctions and generalized secretary problems. ACM SIGecom Exchanges **7**(2), 7 (2008)
2. Bhat, S., Nath, S., Zoeter, O., Gujar, S., Narahari, Y., Dance, C.: A mechanism to optimally balance cost and quality of labeling tasks outsourced to strategic agents. In: Thirtheenth International Conference on Autonomous Agents and Multiagent Systems, pp. 917–924 (2014)
3. Bigham, J.P., Jayant, C., Ji, H., Little, G., Miller, A., Miller, R.C., Miller, R., Tatarowicz, A., White, B., White, S., et al.: Vizwiz: nearly real-time answers to visual questions. In: Proceedings of the 23nd Annual ACM Symposium on User Interface Software and Technology, pp. 333–342. ACM (2010)
4. Chen, X., Lin, Q., Zhou, D.: Optimistic knowledge gradient policy for optimal budget allocation in crowdsourcing. In: Proceedings of the 30th International Conference on Machine Learning (ICML-2013), pp. 64–72 (2013)
5. Difallah, D.E., Demartini, G., Cudré-Mauroux, P.: Pick-a-crowd: tell me what you like, and i'll tell you what to do. In: Proceedings of the 22nd International Conference on World Wide Web, pp. 367–374 (2013)
6. Garg, D., Narahari, Y., Gujar, S.: Foundations of mechanism design: a tutorial - part 1: key concepts and classical results. In: Sadhana - Indian Academy Proceedings in Engineering Sciences, vol. 33(Part 2), pp. 83–130, April 2008
7. Garg, D., Narahari, Y., Gujar, S.: Foundations of mechanism design: a tutorial - part 2: advanced concepts and results. In: Sadhana - Indian Academy Proceedings in Engineering Sciences, vol. 33(Part 2), pp. 131–174, April 2008

8. Goel, G., Nikzad, A., Singla, A.: Allocating tasks to workers with matching constraints: truthful mechanisms for crowdsourcing markets. In: Proceedings of the Companion Publication of the 23rd International Conference on World Wide Web Companion, pp. 279–280 (2014)

9. Gujar, S., Faltings, B.: Dynamic task assignments: an online two sided matching approach. In: 3rd International Workshop on Matching Under Preferences, MATCHUP (2015)

10. Gujar, S., Faltings, B.: Online auctions for dynamic assignment: theory and empirical evaluation. In: ECAI 2016–22nd European Conference on Artificial Intelligence, 29 August-2 September 2016, The Hague, The Netherlands - Including Prestigious Applications of Artificial Intelligence (PAIS 2016), pp. 1035–1043 (2016)

11. Ho, C.J., Jabbari, S., Vaughan, J.W.: Adaptive task assignment for crowdsourced classification. In: Proceedings of the 30th International Conference on Machine Learning (ICML-2013), pp. 534–542 (2013)

12. Ho, C.J., Vaughan, J.W.: Online task assignment in crowdsourcing markets. In: AAAI (2012)

13. Howe, J.: The rise of crowdsourcing. Wired Mag. **14**(6), 1–4 (2006)

14. Huang, E., Zhang, H., Parkes, D.C., Gajos, K.Z., Chen, Y.: Toward automatic task design: a progress report. In: Proceedings of the ACM SIGKDD Workshop on Human Computation, pp. 77–85. ACM (2010)

15. Ipeirotis, P.G., Provost, F., Wang, J.: Quality management on Amazon mechanical turk. In: Proceedings of the ACM SIGKDD Workshop on Human Computation, HCOMP 2010, pp. 64–67. ACM, New York (2010)

16. Jain, S., Gujar, S., Zoeter, O., Narahari, Y.: A quality assuring multi-armed bandit crowdsourcing mechanism with incentive compatible learning. In: Thirtheenth International Conference on Autonomous Agents and Multiagent Systems, pp. 1609–1610 (2014)

17. Karger, D.R., Oh, S., Shah, D.: Budget-optimal crowdsourcing using low-rank matrix approximations. In: 49th Annual Allerton Conference on Communication, Control, and Computing (Allerton), pp. 284–291. IEEE (2011)

18. Kittur, A., Chi, E.H., Suh, B.: Crowdsourcing user studies with mechanical turk. In: Proceedings of the SIGCHI Conference on Human Factors in Computing Systems, CHI 2008, pp. 453–456. ACM, New York (2008)

19. Parkes, D.C.: Online mechanisms (2007)

20. Raykar, V.C., Yu, S., Zhao, L.H., Valadez, G.H., Florin, C., Bogoni, L., Moy, L.: Learning from crowds. J. Mach. Learn. Res. **11**, 1297–1322 (2010)

21. Sönmez, T., Ünver, M.U.: Matching, allocation, and exchange of discrete resources. Handbook Soc. Econ. **1**, 781–852 (2011)

22. Tran-Thanh, L., Stein, S., Rogers, A., Jennings, N.R.: Efficient crowdsourcing of unknown experts using multi-armed bandits. In: European Conference on Artificial Intelligence, pp. 768–773 (2012)

23. Zou, J.Y., Gujar, S., Parkes, D.C.: Tolerable manipulability in dynamic assignment without money. In: AAAI (2010)

An Effective Broker for the Power TAC 2014

Jasper Hoogland[1(✉)] and Han La Poutré[1,2]

[1] Centrum Wiskunde & Informatica (CWI), Amsterdam, The Netherlands
{J.Hoogland,Han.La.Poutre}@cwi.nl
[2] Delft University of Technology, Delft, The Netherlands

Abstract. The Power TAC is a competition-based simulation of an electricity market. The goal of the competition is to test retailer (broker) strategies in a competitive environment. Participants create broker agents that trade electricity. In this paper we describe our broker, which we created as a participant of the 2014 Power TAC competition. We describe the strategies for two main components of the game: the tariff market and the wholesale market. We also discuss the performance of our broker in the competition, where we were second in the final ranking.

1 Introduction

Computer simulations have often been used to examine the dynamics of electricity markets [7]. Simulations may consist of components like producers, consumers, and retailers. The number of potential strategies for each component is huge, however. Therefore, in the design of a simulation it is very difficult to anticipate on the wide range of strategies possibly employed by these components. The Power TAC project [3] aims to overcome this problem by providing a competition environment based on an open platform of a smart grid electricity market. On the other hand, participants of the competition can thus create and test retailer agents (brokers) that trade electricity in the simulation. Retailer agents make money by trading electricity. The winner of the competition is the agent that makes the most money.

In the Power TAC simulation, broker agents trade electricity by interacting with producers, consumers, and each other in three different markets: the wholesale market, the tariff market, and the balancing market. The wholesale market is a double-sided sequential auction, of which the participants are brokers and large generation companies. In this market, brokers mostly buy energy, though they may also sell it. In the tariff market, brokers sell energy to consumers, such as offices and households. Since the Power TAC platform simulates a smart grid electricity market, there is also decentralized production, such as wind farms and owners of solar panels. Brokers can buy energy from these small producers in the tariff market. Brokers trade in this market by publishing consumption and production tariffs, in which they set a unit price structure and other features (see below). A feature of electricity markets is that demand and supply must be balanced real-time. In the Power TAC, imbalances in the wholesale market and

S. Ceppi et al. (Eds.): AMEC/TADA 2015/2016, LNBIP 271, pp. 66–80, 2017.
DOI: 10.1007/978-3-319-54229-4_5

tariff market are resolved in the balancing market. Trading in this market is usually less favorable for brokers, so they are encouraged to balance their demand and supply themselves [5].

In this paper we describe the broker agent that we created for the 2014 competition. The objective in the competition was to create an agent that makes as much profit as possible. Our broker consists of two main components: a tariff market component and a wholesale market component. For the tariff market, we have developed an approach to determine the next retail price, based on the market share of the broker and the competing tariffs. For the wholesale market, we have developed a strategy that aims to acquire its entire demand in the first round of the sequential auction, when it is expected to be the cheapest. The broker does that by estimating the required limit price based on historical data of past auctions. In the 2014 competition, our broker was second in the final ranking. Based on this result, our paper provides useful insights for participants of future Power TAC competitions.

The rest of this paper is organized as follows. In Sect. 2 we discuss related work. Section 3 provides a description of the Power TAC game. In particular, we describe aspects of the game that are relevant to our broker. Next, we give an overview of our broker agent in Sect. 4. We give a detailed description of our broker's strategies for trading in the wholesale market (Sect. 5) and trading in the tariff market (Sect. 6). In Sect. 7, we discuss the performance of these strategies in the 2014 competition. Finally, we draw conclusions in Sect. 8.

2   Related Work

An extensive description of the Power TAC simulation server can be found in the game specification [4]. An analysis of the performance of all brokers in the 2014 competition is provided in [2]. Furthermore, several participants of previous tournaments have published work about their own broker agents. AstonTAC, who participated in 2012, uses a wholesale market strategy based on Markov Decision Processes. TacTex [8], who won the competition in 2013, use reinforcement learning (RL) to find the optimal actions in the wholesale market and tariff market. For the 2013 competition we also created a broker [6], which was the runner-up in this competition. This broker uses a tariff publication strategy inspired by Tit-for-Tat in the tariff market and a trading technique related to equilibria in continuous auctions in the wholesale market. CrocodileAgent [1] uses RL to choose among different strategies in the wholesale market. Most brokers aim to maximize a performance measure, such as utility or cumulative reward. Our approach, however, does not directly use a performance measure. Instead, we have developed heuristics based on domain knowledge that yield successful behavior.

3   The Power TAC Game

Here we provide a description of the Power TAC game [4]. In the Power TAC simulation, producers, consumers, and retailers interact in three different markets: the wholesale market, the tariff market, and the balancing market. In the simulation, time is divided into one hour intervals, referred to as timeslots.

The wholesale market is a double-sided sequential auction. Participants in this market are large producers of electricity and broker agents. Producers only supply electricity, while broker agents may buy or sell electricity. Electricity is traded in this market by submitting buy and sell orders, which specify a limit price and a quantity. For each timeslot there are 24 separate auctions, which we refer to as auction rounds.

In the tariff market, broker agents trade electricity with consumers (e.g. households and offices) and small producers (e.g. owners of solar panels and wind farms). Consumption and production is collectively referred to as prosumption. Brokers trade energy by publishing tariffs, in which they set a structure for the unit price and other features. Prosumers evaluate the available tariffs and subscribe to the tariff they prefer. They trade energy with the broker according to the conditions set by the tariff they are subscribed to.

In electricity grids, demand and supply must be balanced in real-time. In the Power TAC this is simulated by balancing demand and supply for each timeslot. The network operator achieves this by trading in the balancing market on behalf of each broker. The prices in this market are usually not favorable to the broker. Therefore, brokers are encouraged to balance supply and demand themselves, which means their net prosumption in the tariff market and wholesale market must be zero in each timeslot.

Agents pay a fixed fee per unit of electricity for using the electricity grid. This fee is called the distribution fee, and is announced to brokers in the beginning of a simulation. Also, agents pay a fixed fee for every tariff they publish.

In the 2014 competition there were 6 participants. There were three game categories: games with two players, with four players, and with all players.

4   Our Broker Agent

Here we describe our Power TAC broker agent. Brokers can trade in three markets: the tariff market, the wholesale market, and the balancing market. Since trading in the balancing market is usually not favorable to a broker, our broker aims to avoid this by balancing its demand and supply in each timeslot. Therefore, our broker has to know the prosumption in the tariff market for each timeslot. However, the quantity for a timeslot is unknown to the broker when it is trading for that timeslot, so our broker has to predict its customers' prosumption ahead of time. The approach is as follows.

To estimate its customers' prosumption, our broker uses a linear regression model, which takes into account weather factors, such as temperature, wind speed, and cloud coverage, all of which affect the consumption and production. Historical prosumption data and weather data are used to train the model. The approach is similar to the prosumption estimator of our broker in the 2013 competition. For more details on this approach, see [6].

Apart from the prosumption estimator, our broker consists of two main components: the tariff market component and the wholesale market component. We describe the parts of these components that have the main contribution to the performance of our broker.

5   Wholesale Market Strategy

In this section we discuss trading in the wholesale market. First, we describe how a wholesale auction works. Then we describe our broker's strategy in this market.

5.1   The Sequential Double-Sided Auction

The wholesale market is a sequential double-sided auction. For each timeslot, the auction is cleared 24 times, i.e. there are 24 auction rounds per timeslot. Participants in this market can buy and sell electricity by submitting buy offers (bids) and sell offers (asks). See Fig. 1 for examples of auction rounds. An offer (buy or sell) consists of a limit price and a (demanded or supplied) quantity. The limit price of a buy offer is the maximum unit price a buyer is willing to pay for its demanded quantity. Buy offers are sorted in decreasing order according to their limit price, which means that buy offers with a higher limit price have a higher priority to be cleared (executed). The limit price of a sell offer is the minimum unit price a seller is willing to accept for its supplied quantity. Sell offers are sorted in increasing order according to their limit price, which means that sell offers with a lower limit price have a higher priority to be cleared. Offers are cleared, as long as the limit price of the buy order is higher than the limit price of the sell order. Often, either a bid or an ask is cleared partially. The sum of the cleared bids (or asks) is referred to as the clearing quantity or execution quantity. All cleared orders result in transactions. All transactions of an auction

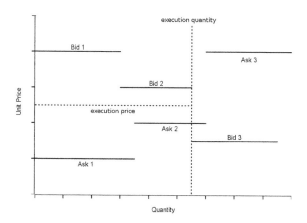

Fig. 1. An auction round diagram. Buy and sell orders are represented by horizontal bars, of which the vertical position indicates the limit price, and the length of the bar indicates the quantity. The execution price and quantity are indicated by dotted lines.

round have the same unit price. This price is the mean of the limit prices of the last bid and ask, and is referred to as the clearing price or execution price.

After every auction round, brokers receive the following public information on this round: the uncleared orders, the execution price, and the execution quantity. Brokers do not receive information on the cleared orders of past auctions rounds. This information is private and only known to the broker that submitted the order. Furthermore, the names of the owners of cleared orders are also private information. This allows us to define the known and unknown auction round data for each timeslot and auction round.

Definition 1. *Let R be an auction round and let t be a timeslot. Let $o_1^{buy}, \ldots, o_M^{buy}$ be the buy orders of round R and timeslot t, of which the first $m \leq M$ are cleared. Let $o_1^{sell}, \ldots, o_N^{sell}$ be the sell orders of round R and timeslot t, of which the first $n \leq N$ are cleared. In case an order is partially cleared order, it is treated as two separate orders: a cleared one and an uncleared one. If a buy order is partially cleared, then o_m^{buy} is the part that is cleared and o_{m+1}^{buy} is the part that is not cleared. Similarly, if a sell order is partially cleared, then o_n^{sell} is the part that is cleared and o_{n+1}^{sell} is the part that is not cleared. Let $Q_a \in [0, Q]$ be the quantity of the broker's bid that is (partially) cleared. Let p_e be the execution price and let Q_e be the execution quantity of R. Then, the **unknown auction round data** $X_{R,t}$ of auction round R and timeslot t consists of the buy orders $o_1^{buy}, \ldots, o_m^{buy}$ and the sell orders $o_1^{sell}, \ldots, o_n^{sell}$, with the exception of the broker's own bid o_j^{buy} if it was (partially) cleared. Furthermore, the **known auction round data** $Y_{R,t}$ of auction round R and timeslot t consists of the buy orders $o_{m+1}^{buy}, \ldots, o_M^{buy}$, the sell orders $o_{n+1}^{sell}, \ldots, o_N^{sell}$, the execution price p_e, the execution quantity Q_e, the broker's cleared quantity Q_a, and its own (partially) cleared bid o_j^{buy} if it exists.*

Thus, a broker's unknown auction round data is the private information of all the other brokers, and a broker's known auction round data is the public information and its own private information. For a more extensive description of the wholesale market, we refer to [4].

5.2   Wholesale Trading Strategy

The participants of the wholesale market are generation companies and broker agents. Generation companies only sell energy, while broker agents may buy or sell. In order to avoid costly trading in the balancing market, brokers must aim for a balance between their demand and supply in each timeslot. Since the total consumption in the tariff market is much bigger than the total production in the tariff market, we expect most brokers to buy energy in the wholesale market. Indeed, our broker only buys energy, because it only publishes consumption tariffs (see Sect. 6).

We expect that energy is the cheapest in the first auction round, and gets more expensive in consecutive rounds. The reason is that generation companies offer their energy in the first auction round, and keep offering their energy for the same limit price until their offer is cleared. Whereas generation companies are predictable, brokers may submit sell orders in a less predictable way. However, we expect their impact to be negligible, since brokers are more likely to submit buy offers. Thus, in order to acquire its demand for the lowest possible price, our broker aims to acquire its demand as quick as possible. Therefore, our broker bids its entire estimated demand (see Sect. 4) in the first auction round. In the remaining auction rounds it bids the estimated demand it has not yet acquired in the previous auction rounds.

Having determined the quantity to bid for, we now focus on choosing the limit price. Ideally, our broker bids the lowest limit price such that its bid will be cleared. However, this depends on the orders from all other players in the market, and the broker does not have this information at the time of bidding. Instead, for each auction round R and each timeslot t, the broker computes a limit price from the known auction round data $Y_{R,s}$ of past timeslots $s < t$. For the unknown auction round data $X_{R,s}$, the broker assumes the worst case scenario of all potential values of $X_{R,s}$ given $Y_{R,s}$ (see Definition 2 below).

Definition 2. *Let $Y_{R,t}$ be the known auction data of auction round R and timeslot t. Given $Y_{R,t}$, we call $X_{R,t}$ a **potential value** of the unknown auction data if and only if $X_{R,t}$ and $Y_{R,t}$ are compatible, i.e. the limit prices of the buy orders of $X_{R,t}$ are higher than the limit prices of the buy orders of $Y_{R,t}$, the limit prices of the sell orders of $X_{R,t}$ are lower than the limit prices of the sell orders of $Y_{R,t}$, and the orders of $X_{R,t}$ and $Y_{R,t}$ together result in execution price p_e and execution quantity Q_e.*

One cannot infer the actual value $X_{R,t}$ of the unknown auction round data given the known data $Y_{R,t}$ of an auction round, but it is possible to infer some properties. For example, both the sum of the quantities of the buy orders in $X_{R,t}$ and the sum of the quantities of the sell orders in $X_{R,t}$ are equal to the execution quantity Q_e. Furthermore, the limit prices of the buy orders in $X_{R,t}$ are higher than or equal to the execution price p_e, while the limit prices of the sell orders in $X_{R,t}$ are lower than or equal to p_e. Given the known data $Y_{R,t}$, we now define the worst case limit price that would have resulted in the acquisition of a quantity in a past auction round. We write $o = \langle p, Q \rangle$ to denote a (buy or sell) order with limit price p and quantity Q.

Definition 3. *Let $o^{buy} = \langle p, Q \rangle$ be the bid of the broker for timeslot t in auction round R, and let $Y_{R,t}$ be the known data of t and R. The **worst case limit price** $p_{R,t}^w$ to have acquired quantity Q for timeslot t in round R given $Y_{R,t}$ is the lowest limit price p' that would have resulted in an fully cleared bid $o_w^{buy} = \langle p', Q \rangle$ for all potential values $X_{R,t}$ of unknown data given $Y_{R,t}$, if it had bid o_w^{buy} instead of o^{buy} in auction round R.*

Note that the worst case limit price applies to the hypothetical situation where a broker's actual bid is replaced by a new bid in that past auction round. The value of the worst case limit price depends on whether the broker's actual bid was (partially) cleared, as we will see. We now show how to compute the worst case limit price for the situation where the broker's actual bid was *not* fully cleared (Lemma 1), and then we do the same for the situation where it was fully cleared (Lemma 2). Later, we show how the broker computes its limit price for future auction rounds, based on the worst case limit prices of past auction rounds. First we define the sell order book price.

Definition 4. *Let $Y_{R,t}$ be the known auction data of an auction round R and timeslot t, of which $o_{n+1}^{sell}, \ldots, o_N^{sell}$ are the uncleared sell orders, $o_i^{sell} = \langle p_i, Q_i \rangle$. Let $Q < \sum_{i=n+1}^N Q_i$ be an energy quantity. Then, the* **sell order book price** *$p_{Y_{R,t}}(Q)$ of quantity Q for sell orders $o_{n+1}^{sell}, \ldots, o_N^{sell}$ is defined as the limit price p_k of the unique sell order o_k such that $\sum_{i=n+1}^{k-1} Q_i < Q \leq \sum_{i=n+1}^k Q_i$.*

The following lemma specifies the worst case limit price for the case where the broker's actual bid was not fully cleared.

Lemma 1. *Let $o^{buy} = \langle p, Q \rangle$ be a broker's bid for timeslot t in auction round R. Let Q_a be the quantity acquired by the broker. Let $Y_{R,t}$ be the known auction information after R. If the broker did not acquire its entire demand ($Q_a < Q$), then the worst case limit price to have acquired Q given $Y_{R,t}$ is the sell order book price $p' = s_{Y_{R,t}}(Q - Q_a)$ of the remaining demand $Q - Q_a$.*

Proof. Let o_c^{sell} be the cleared sell orders and let o_u^{sell} be the uncleared sell orders in the actual auction. The broker's actual bid o^{buy} resulted in the acquisition of Q_a (though Q_a may be zero), so limit price p was high enough to match Q_a of its bid to o_c^{sell}. Since $p' > p$, this would also have been the case if it had bid $\langle p', Q \rangle$ instead of o^{buy}. Moreover, bidding p' would have been enough to match the remaining demand $Q - Q_a$ to o_u^{sell}. Thus, if the broker had bid $\langle p', Q \rangle$ instead of o^{buy}, the bid would have been fully cleared. A bid $\langle p'', Q \rangle$ with a limit price $p'' < p'$, however, may not have been enough for some potential values of X. Limit price p'' is not high enough to match all of $Q - Q_a$ to o_u^{sell}. This means that a quantity Q' that is larger than Q_a, has to be matched to o_c^{sell}. It may be that the quantity Q_m^{buy} of the last cleared buy order is less than Q', and the limit price p_{m-1}^{buy} of the second last cleared buy order is greater than p''. In that case, a bid $\langle p'', Q \rangle$ would not have been fully cleared, so $p' = s_{Y_{R,t}}(Q - Q_a)$ is the worst case limit price to have acquired Q. $\square$

We now examine the case where the broker's actual bid was fully cleared. First, we define $p^*(Y_{R,t})$.

Definition 5. *Let $Y_{R,t}$ be the known auction round data for timeslot t and auction round R. Then*

$$p^*(Y_{R,t}) = \begin{cases} p_{m+1}^{buy} & if \ p_e \leq p_{m+1}^{buy} \\ p_e & if \ p_{m+1}^{buy} \leq p_e \leq p_{n+1}^{sell} \\ p_{n+1}^{sell} & if \ p_{n+1}^{sell} \leq p_e \end{cases} \tag{1}$$

Lemma 2. *Let $o^{buy} = \langle p, Q \rangle$ be the broker's bid for timeslot t in auction round R. Let Q_a be the quantity acquired by the broker. Let $Y_{R,t}$ be the known auction* *data of R and t. If the broker acquired its entire demand ($Q_a = Q$), then $p' = p^*(Y_{R,t})$ is the worst case limit price to have acquired Q given $Y_{R,t}$, assuming that ties are decided in the broker's advantage.*

Proof. To prove this lemma, we reason about the hypothetical situation where the broker's actual bid $o^{\text{buy}} = \langle p, Q \rangle$ is replaced by bid $\langle p', Q \rangle$ in R. Due to this replacement, p' does not have to be higher than the limit prices of any of the other cleared bids in order to be fully cleared, as long as it is not lower than the limit prices of the uncleared bids (Condition I). Note that ties are decided in the broker's advantage, so $p' = p^{\text{buy}}_{m+1}$ is sufficient. Furthermore, the limit price of the new bid has to be higher than the limit prices of the cleared sell orders (Condition II). Condition I holds by Definition 5 and the property that bids are sorted in descending order. We now show that Condition II holds for cases $p^{\text{sell}}_{n+1} \geq p_e$ and $p^{\text{sell}}_{n+1} \leq p_e$ separately. If $p^{\text{sell}}_{n+1} \geq p_e$, then $p' \geq p_e$ and p_e in turn is higher than or equal to all of the cleared sell orders. Condition II also holds if $p^{\text{sell}}_{n+1} \leq p_e$. In that case $p' = p^{\text{sell}}_{n+1}$, which is higher than all of the cleared sell orders. Thus, Conditions I and II both hold, so bid $\langle p', Q \rangle$ would have been fully cleared in R. Bidding a limit price $p'' < p'$, however, may not have been enough for some potential values of $X_{R,t}$. We show this for cases $p^{\text{buy}}_{m+1} \geq p_e$ and $p_e \geq p^{\text{buy}}_{m+1}$ separately. If $p^{\text{buy}}_{m+1} \geq p_e$, then $p' = p^{\text{buy}}_{m+1}$. In that case o^{buy}_{m+1} would have been cleared before $\langle p'', Q \rangle$. Therefore, in order for $\langle p'', Q \rangle$ to be fully cleared, it has to be matched with the uncleared sell orders. However, their limit prices are higher than p'', so it will not be fully cleared. If $p_e \geq p^{\text{buy}}_{m+1}$, then $p' \leq p_e$ and consequently $p'' < p_e$. In that case there would have been potential $X_{R,t}$ such that $p'' < p^{\text{sell}}_1, \dots, p^{\text{sell}}_n$. This is the case, for example, if $n = 1$ and $p^{\text{sell}}_1 = p'$. Thus, $p' = p^*(Y_{R,t})$ is the worst case limit price to have acquired Q. $\square$

Lemmas 1 and 2 provide in hindsight the worst case limit price that would have been sufficient to acquire the broker's demand, given the known auction round data. This is expressed by the following theorem.

Theorem 1. *Let $Y_{R,t}$ be the known auction data of timeslot t and auction round R. Let Q_a be the broker's acquired energy of its demand Q. Then the worst case limit price $p^w_{R,t}$ for timeslot t in round R is*

$$p^w_{R,t} = \begin{cases} s_{Y_{R,t}}(Q - Q_a) & \text{if } Q_a < Q \\ p^*(Y_{R,t}) & \text{if } Q_a = Q \end{cases} \qquad (2)$$

Proof. This follows from Lemmas 1 and 2

Based on this analysis, we now give our broker's heuristic to compute its limit price in the wholesale market. For each auction round R, the limit price $p_{R,t+1}$ for the next timeslot $t + 1$ is computed from the worst case limit price $p^w_{R,t}$ in the most recent timeslot t using the following update rule:

$$p_{R,t+1} \leftarrow (1 - \lambda)p_{R,t} + \lambda p^w_{R,t} \qquad (3)$$

where λ is some manually chosen $\lambda \in (0, 1)$. Note that the best bid may depend on the time of the day or the day of the week, where consecutive timeslots are likely to be similar. The weighted update rule implicitly incorporates this dependency by assigning higher weights to more recent timeslots. λ is chosen such that the limit price is mostly determined by the most recent timeslots. The update rule also allows the broker to adapt to strategy changes of other brokers.

6 Tariff Market Strategy

In this section we describe our broker's strategy in the tariff market. First we describe the tariff market itself. Then we introduce the concept of competition price, which captures relevant information on the opponent's tariffs in a single value. Finally, we describe how the competition price is used to compute the next tariff price.

6.1 Tariff Market

In the tariff market, broker agents trade electricity with consumers (e.g. households and offices) and small producers (e.g. owners of solar panels and wind farms). Broker agents sell energy to consumers by publishing consumption tariffs, which are structures that specify the unit price and other features. From the set of available tariffs published by all brokers, the consumers choose to which tariff they subscribe. Consumers buy energy under the conditions set by the tariff they are subscribed to.

Since the Power TAC simulates a smart grid electricity market, there is also decentralized production, such as wind farms and solar panels. Broker agents can buy electricity from them in the tariff market by publishing production tariffs. Production tariffs are similar to consumption tariffs, except that the directions of the cash flow and the electricity flow are reversed. Even though decentralized production may offer potentially cheap supply, our broker agent does not publish any production tariffs. The decentralized production supplied in the tariff market is significantly smaller than both the consumption in the tariff market and the centralized production in the wholesale market. Therefore, the most important aspects of a broker agent are a consumption strategy for the tariff market and a buying strategy for the wholesale market. The implementation of a production tariff strategy is not a main priority. From now on, in this section we focus on consumption tariffs only.

A tariff is a complex structure that contains one or more rates (i.e. unit prices). A rate specifies the unit price of energy per kWh under a set of conditions. Conditions may specify the time to which a rate applies: A tariff can have different rates for different times of the day or different days of the week. Furthermore, tariffs may specify tiered rates, which means the unit price of energy depends on the quantity consumed by the customer in a single day. Also, rates may be fixed or dynamic. In the latter case the tariff specifies a minimum and

maximum value. The broker announces the actual value to its customers a prede-
termined number of timeslots ahead. Furthermore, tariffs may specify the option
of interruptible consumption.

Given a tariff τ a timeslot t and the quantity Q, we use $p_t(\tau, Q)$ to denote
the unit price of energy specified by tariff τ in timeslot t, if Q is the quantity
consumed in a day. In addition to one or more rates, tariffs can also have other
features. One of these features is a periodic fee, which allows brokers to specify
two-part tariffs. Given a tariff τ, we denote the periodic fee by $p_{\text{periodic}}(\tau)$. Furthermore, tariffs may specify a sign up fee or bonus, and/or an early-exit fee.
Brokers can publish as many tariffs as they want, but they pay a fixed publication fee for every tariff they publish. This fee is announced to the brokers in the
beginning of every simulation. Brokers can also revoke tariffs or supersede old
tariffs with new tariffs. The tariff structures (including rates, and periodic fees,
etc.) published by a broker are public information and hence known to all other
brokers. The number of subscriptions to a tariff, though, is private information
and only known to the owner of the tariff. In the simulation there are multiple
types of customers, including several types of households, offices, hospitals, etc.
Brokers know the number of subscriptions to their tariffs for each customer type.

6.2   The Competition Price

In the tariff market, brokers have to compete with each other for customers.
Therefore, the best choice of tariffs to publish depends on the tariffs published
by the other brokers. Due to the complexity of tariff structures and the unrestricted number of competitors' tariffs, it is difficult to determine the best set of
tariffs to publish. In order to reduce the information of all available tariffs, we
define the competition price, which captures relevant information on the tariffs
of all brokers. First, we define the integral unit price for a tariff τ, which is an
estimation of the cost per kWh given the estimated behavior of the consumers
in the simulation. The integral unit price is a measure of how expensive a tariff
is, and takes into account multiple features of a tariff, such as different rates and
the periodic fee. The reduction of a tariff to a single score allows comparison of
complex tariff structures.

Definition 6. *Let C be the set of customer types. Let $\hat{Q}_t^c$ be the estimated consumption per customer of type $c \in C$ in timeslot t. Let $d(t)$ be the set of timeslots
on the same day as timeslot t. Let N_c be the number of customers of type $c \in C$
in the simulation. Let $p_t(\tau, Q)$ be the unit price of tariff τ for a consumer in
timeslot t if quantity Q is the consumption of the consumer on the day of timeslot t up to and including timeslot t itself. Let $p_{periodic}(\tau)$ be the fixed daily fee of
tariff τ. Then, the* **integral unit price** *$p(\tau)$ of tariff τ is*

$$p(\tau) = \frac{7 \cdot p_{periodic}(\tau) + \sum_{t=1}^{168} \sum_{c \in C} p_t(\tau, \sum_{s \in d(t)} \hat{Q}_s^c) N_c \hat{Q}_t^c}{\sum_{t=1}^{168} \sum_{c \in C} N_c \hat{Q}_t^c}$$

The integral unit price is the revenue of this tariff divided by the consumption if
all customers in the simulation were subscribed to this tariff. It is an estimation of

the actual revenue per kWh for the tariff, which depends on the number of tariff subscriptions for each customer type, and their actual consumption. However, this is private information and therefore only known to the owner of the tariff. The integral unit price, on the other hand, is computed from public information available to the broker. This includes the customer types C as well as the number of customers N_c of every type $c \in C$, an estimation $\hat{Q}_t^c$ of customer consumption based on the bootstrap data of every simulation, and tariff features such as rates and periodic fees. The tariff unit price $p_t(\tau, Q)$ incorporates time-of-use tariffs and tiered rates tariffs. If the rate is fixed, then its actual value is used, in case it is dynamic, then an estimation of its value is used based on past prices.

Whereas the integral unit price deals with the complexity of tariff structures, the competition price deals with the potentially large number of published tariffs. Since customers prefer cheap tariffs, the most relevant competitor's tariff is the cheapest one. Therefore, we define the competition price to be the minimum of the integral unit price of all published tariffs.

Definition 7. *Let Tariffs be set of the tariffs published by all brokers. Then, the* **competition price** *is*

$$p_{comp}(\mathit{Tariffs}) = \min_{\tau \in \mathit{Tariffs}} p(\tau)$$

Defined as the estimated unit price of the cheapest tariff in the game, the competition price is a measure of the competitiveness in the tariff market. If the competition price is high, then our broker can publish expensive tariffs and still attract customers, but if the competition price is low, then it must also publish tariffs in order to get customers.

6.3 The Tariff Strategy

Our agent's tariff policy is competitive. This means our agent publishes tariffs with an energy unit price lower than the competition price, provided that the unit price is higher than an estimation of the cost price. Apart from the competition price and the estimated cost price, the broker's tariff prices also depend on its market share, which is the consumption of the broker's customers divided by the consumption of all consumers in the simulation.

Definition 8. *Let Q_{broker} be the consumption of all consumers subscribed to one of our broker's tariffs and let Q_{total} be the consumption of all consumers in the simulation. The* **market share** MS *of our broker is defined as*

$$MS = \frac{Q_{broker}}{Q_{total}}$$

If the broker's market share is close to one, then it has almost all the customers, so there is less need to compete for more. This would only cause the tariff price to decrease unnecessarily, which reduces the broker's profit. If the market share is close to zero, on the other hand, then the broker hardly makes any profit, so it decreases its tariff price faster, in order to get more customers.

Since our broker mostly decreases its tariff price, there is no need to revoke or supersede old tariffs. Our broker has a higher profit if customers stay with more expensive tariffs as long as possible. Our broker publishes only simple tariffs, i.e. its tariffs have no periodic payments, sign-up fees or bonuses, or early-exit fees. Although brokers may benefit from these additional features, we did not expect it to be a main priority. In the 2013 competition, the two best brokers (TacTex [8] and cwiBroker [6]) only published simple tariffs. Our broker publishes multiple new tariffs during a simulation. In several tournaments including the 2013 competition, the most successful brokers published a large number of tariffs.

A new tariff price is computed in the following way. First it computes p_0 from the competition price p_{comp} and the estimated energy cost price $\hat{p}_{cost}$.

$$p_0 = \max(r \cdot p_{\mathrm{comp}}, \hat{p}_{cost} + \varepsilon)$$

where $r \in (0,1]$ and $\varepsilon > 0$ are manually chosen parameters. The estimated energy cost price estimation $\hat{p}_{cost}$ is based on the distribution fee and historical data of the wholesale market. Our broker takes it into account, because it is never favorable to a broker to publish tariffs lower than the cost price. The parameter ε sets the minimal marginal profit that our broker aims for. The parameter $r \in (0,1]$ ensures p_0 is less than the competition price, provided p_0 is not less than $\hat{p}_{cost} + \varepsilon$; It controls the speed by which our broker decreases its tariff price. Given our broker's previous tariff price p', the new tariff price p is computed as a weighted average of p_0 and p'. The weights of p_0 and p' are respectively $(1 - MS)$ and MS. Thus, the new tariff price p is given by

$$p = (1 - MS) \cdot p_0 + MS \cdot p'$$

As the market share is lower, it will be closer to p_0, so the tariff price decreases faster. In this case our broker needs to compete harder in order to get more customers. On the other hand, if the market share is high, then it will be closer to the current tariff price p'. In this case our broker does not decrease its tariff price unnecessarily, because it already has a lot of customers.

7   Results of the 2014 Competition

Here we discuss our agent's performance in the Power TAC 2014. We analyze the wholesale market and the tariff market separately.

7.1   Wholesale Market

Here we discuss our agent's performance in the wholesale market in the competition. In the wholesale market we expected that the wholesale unit price is the lowest in the first auction round, and increases in consecutive auction rounds. Figure 2 shows the average clearing price for each auction round of all games in the competition. Indeed, we see that the average price per MWh is lower in the first auction round (21.0 €/MWh) than in the other rounds. Furthermore,

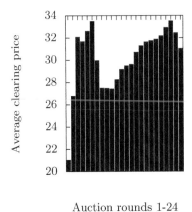

Auction rounds 1-24

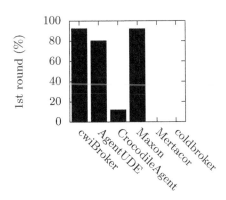

Fig. 2. Average clearing price (€/MWh) for each auction round of all games in the competition.

Fig. 3. Percentage of the demand that brokers acquired in the first auction round.

in the second auction round the average price per MWh is 26.8 €/MWh, which makes it the second cheapest auction round. The hypothesis that energy gets more expensive in consecutive auctions is not entirely correct, due to the peak between rounds 3 and 7. However, if our broker has already acquired its demand by then, then the remaining auction rounds are no longer relevant.

Based on our confirmed expectation that energy is the cheapest in the first auction round, our broker attempted to acquire its demand as quick as possible. Here, we evaluate the percentage of its demand that our broker acquired in the first auction round, and we compare this to the other brokers. The results are shown in Fig. 3. Our broker acquired 92% of its demand in the first auction round, which is the highest percentage together with Maxon. Note that other brokers do not necessarily aim to acquire their demand in the first round, but based on the results shown here, we argue that they should.

We now compare the performances of all brokers in the wholesale market. The goal of each broker in the wholesale market is to acquire its demand as cheap as possible. However, each broker has a different demand, so we cannot simply compare their wholesale costs. Instead, for each broker we computed the mean and standard deviation over the wholesale costs divided by the purchased quantities in the wholesale market. We only considered timeslots for a broker for which its net quantity was positive, because we measure buying performance rather than selling performance. The net quantity is the total quantity bought by a broker in all auction rounds for a timeslot. Transactions for an individual auction round can be negative, because it may be part of a broker's buying policy to buy more than its demand in early rounds, and sell excess energy in the later rounds [6]. The scores of all brokers are shown in Fig. 4. On average, our broker had the best performance of all brokers in the wholesale market.

Agent	Avg. price
cwiBroker	21.0 ± 3.0
AgentUDE	22.0 ± 2.3
CrocodileAgent	50.9 ± 7.6
Maxon	22.2 ± 2.2
Mertacor	25.4 ± 2.4
coldbroker	24.4 ± 5.8

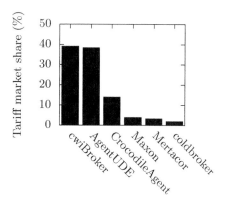

Fig. 4. The average unit prices that agents paid for energy in the wholesale market and their standard deviations.

Fig. 5. Average tariff market share of the games with all players.

7.2 Tariff Market

In the tariff market, the broker computes the competition price, which captures relevant information on the competitors' tariffs. From the competition price and the broker's market share, the broker computes its next tariff price. If the market share is lower, the broker decreases its tariff price faster in order to attract more customers. On the other hand, if the market share is higher, then it decreases its tariff price slower in order to keep the tariff price high. Figure 5 shows the average market share of all agents in the 6 player games. Due to our broker's competitive strategy, it had the highest market share (39%) in these games, only followed by AgentUDE with a slightly lower market share (38%).

8 Conclusions

In this paper, we presented our broker, which participated in the Power TAC competition of 2014. We described its strategies in the wholesale market and tariff market. In the wholesale market, we showed that energy is the cheapest in the first auction rounds of each timeslot, and gets more expensive in consecutive rounds. We have developed an estimator of the limit price that a broker must bid in order to acquire its demand as quick as possible for each timeslot. Our broker performed better than any other broker in acquiring its demand in the first auction round, and it had the lowest costs per MWh in the wholesale market. In the tariff market, our broker had the highest market share, though this was at the expense of a lower integral unit price. Out of six participants, our broker was second in the final ranking. Based on this result, we conclude that our broker's strategies were based on correct assumptions and approaches.

References

1. Babic, J., Podobnik, V.: Adaptive bidding for electricity wholesale markets in a smart grid. In: Proceedings of the Workshop on Agent-Mediated Electronic Commerce and Trading Agent Design and Analysis (AMEC/TADA 2014) @AAMAS 2014, pp. 1–14. International Foundation for Autonomous Agents and Multiagent Systems (IFAAMAS), Paris, France (2014)
2. Babic, J., Podobnik, V.: An analysis of power trading agent competition 2014. In: Ceppi, S., David, E., Podobnik, V., Robu, V., Shehory, O., Stein, S., Vetsikas, I.A. (eds.) AMEC/TADA 2013-2014. LNBIP, vol. 187, pp. 1–15. Springer, Cham (2014). doi:10.1007/978-3-319-13218-1_1
3. Ketter, W., Collins, J., Reddy, P.P., Weerdt, M.D.: The 2013 power trading agent competition. ERIM Report Series Reference No. ERS-2013-006-LIS (2013)
4. Ketter, W., Collins, J., Reddy, P.P., Weerdt, M.D.: The 2014 power trading agent competition. ERIM Report Series Reference No. ERS-2014-004-LIS, March 2014
5. Ketter, W., Peters, M., Collins, J.: Autonomous agents in future energy markets: the power trading agent competition. In: AAAI 2013 (2012)
6. Liefers, B., Hoogland, J., La Poutré, H.: A successful broker agent for power tac. In: Proceedings of the Workshop on Agent-Mediated Electronic Commerce and Trading Agent Design and Analysis (AMEC/TADA 2014) @AAMAS 2014, pp. 1–14. International Foundation for Autonomous Agents and Multiagent Systems (IFAAMAS), Paris, France (2014)
7. Somani, A., Tesfatsion, L.: An agent-based test bed study of wholesale power market performance measures. IEEE Comput. Intell. Mag. 3(4), 56–72 (2008)
8. Urieli, D., Stone, P.: TacTex'13: a champion adaptive power trading agent. In: Proceedings of the 2014 International Conference on Autonomous Agents and Multiagent Systems (2014)

Now, Later, or Both: A Closed-Form Optimal Decision for a Risk-Averse Buyer

Jasper Hoogland[1(✉)], Mathijs de Weerdt[2], and Han La Poutré[1,2]

[1] Centrum Wiskunde & Informatica (CWI), Amsterdam, The Netherlands
{J.Hoogland,Han.La.Poutre}@cwi.nl
[2] Delft University of Technology, Delft, The Netherlands
{M.M.deWeerdt,J.A.laPoutre}@tudelft.nl

Abstract. Motivated by the energy domain, we examine a risk-averse buyer that has to purchase a fixed quantity of a continuous good. The buyer has two opportunities to buy: now or later. The buyer can spread the quantity over the two timeslots in any way, as long as the total quantity remains the same. The current price is known, but the future price is not. It is well known that risk neutral buyers purchase in whichever timeslot they expect to be the cheapest, regardless of the uncertainty of the future price. Research suggests, however, that most people may in fact be risk-averse. If the future price is expected to be lower than the current price, but very uncertain, then they may prefer to purchase in the present, or spread the quantity over both timeslots. We describe a formal model with a uniform price distribution and a piecewise linear risk aversion function. We provide a theorem that states the optimal behavior as a closed-form expression, and we give a proof of this theorem.

1 Introduction

Sometimes a continuous good can be bought in two different timeslots, where the price in one timeslot is known while the price in the other timeslot is not. This paper analyses a buyer that must acquire a fixed quantity in this setting.

An example of such a case is the trading of electricity in a day ahead market and a balancing market (e.g. [7]). The price in the day ahead market is more certain than the price in the balancing market. Another example is the charging of electric vehicles (EVs). Owners may have several options where to charge their EV. For example, an owner may be able to charge his vehicle at home or at a local charging station. The price at home is known to the owner, but the current price at the charging station is not.

In these settings, the way a buyer spreads his consumption over the two timeslots depends on his preferences. For risk-neutral buyers this problem is well understood. They aim to minimize their expected cost, and do not care about the risk of bad outcomes. They buy the entire quantity either in the present or the future, depending on which timeslot they expect to be the cheapest.

However, in reality buyers are likely to care not only about expected cost minimization, but also about reducing the risk of bad outcomes. If the expected

© Springer International Publishing AG 2017
S. Ceppi et al. (Eds.): AMEC/TADA 2015/2016, LNBIP 271, pp. 81–95, 2017.
DOI: 10.1007/978-3-319-54259-4_6

future price is slightly lower than the current price, but very uncertain (i.e. it has a high standard deviation), then most buyers would still prefer to buy in the present. Even though their expected cost is higher this way, the uncertainty of the cost is lower. This type of behavior is called risk-aversion [1]. Unlike risk-neutral buyers, risk-averse buyers may spread their demanded quantity over both timeslots.

A sufficient property for risk aversion is concavity of the buyer's utility function. In the literature there is a large variation among types of utility functions. The choice for a specific form is often made based on mathematical convenience, rather than empirical evidence. In this paper we examine the case of a risk-averse buyer who has to buy a fixed quantity of a continuous good in two timeslots. To our knowledge no closed-form solution to this problem has been given for any concave utility function until now. We derive a closed-form solution for a two-segment piecewise linear utility function. We show that if the current price is slightly higher than the expected future price, then a risk-averse buyer may spread his consumption over both timeslots. This gives insight into risk averse buying with two timeslots. Moreover, our solution may open further research and development in finding closed-form solutions for other classes of this problem.

The remainder of this paper is as follows. In the next section we discuss previous work related to this topic. We then analyze the problem and give a formal problem description. Furthermore, we state a theorem that expresses the solution to this problem, and we provide a proof of this theorem. Also, we describe how the two-segment piecewise linear utility function can be extended to a multi-segment piecewise linear utility function. Finally, we conclude and discuss future work.

2   Related Work

Risk aversion has been considered an important research topic since the work of Arrow and Pratt [1]. This is supported by evidence for risk averse behavior in humans [13]. Risk aversion has been studied in economics [9]. Risk aversion has also been studied in the agent literature, and has been applied to task scheduling [2], multi-unit sealed-bid auctions [15], continuous double-sided auctions [16], and sequential auctions [14]. Liu et al. [10] provide a closed-form expression for the optimal bidding function of a risk averse agent in a one-shot auction.

Risk-aversion can be modeled by any concave utility function. Various utility functions are found in the literature, such as exponential functions [10,14], polynomial functions [17] and piecewise linear functions. The latter have been used in e.g. Prospect Theory [9] to model loss-aversion [3,6]. Thus, the variation on different forms of utility functions is large, and the choice of a specific form is often based on mathematical convenience, rather than empirical evidence. We use two-segment piecewise linear utility functions. This gives insight into risk averse buying with two timeslots. Moreover, our solution may open further research towards finding closed-form solutions for other classes of this problem.

An other line of research is the risk-sensitive Markov Decision Process (MDP) [4,8,11,12]. Most of this research, however, concerns discrete state and action spaces. In [5] the existence of closed-form solutions is shown for a class of risk-averse MDPs with continuous state and action spaces. However, no closed-form solution is provided for instances of this class.

3   Problem Description

We examine a buyer that must purchase a fixed quantity Q of a continuous good. There are two timeslots to buy this good: in the present or in the future, respectively at unit price p_1 or p_2. Buyers have to decide how to spread the total quantity Q over the two timeslots. This decision is expressed as the quantity $Q_1 \in [0, Q]$ purchased in the present. The quantity $Q_2 = Q - Q_1$ to be purchased in the future is then simply the remaining quantity. The buyer can choose to buy the entire quantity in the present ($Q_1 = Q$), to buy the entire quantity in to the future ($Q_1 = 0$), or to spread the quantity over both timeslots ($Q_1 \in (0, Q)$).

We assume the buyer does not prefer one timeslot over the other, except for the difference in cost. Thus, the most important variable to be evaluated is the total cost made in both timeslots. The following definition expresses the total cost made by the buyer in terms of the decision variable Q_1.

Definition 1. *Let Q be the total quantity to be purchased, let p_1, p_2 respectively be the prices in the present and the future, and let $Q_1 \in [0, Q]$ be the quantity purchased in the present. Then, the* **cost function** *$Z(Q_1)$ is defined as*

$$Z(Q_1) = p_1 Q_1 + p_2(Q - Q_1).$$

The cost function expresses a preference order over the set of possible decisions $[0, Q]$. If the buyer knew both prices p_1, p_2, then according to this preference order he would buy the entire quantity in whichever timeslot is the cheapest.

However, at the time of the decision, the buyer does not know the future price p_2. Fortunately, the buyer may have some information on what p_2 may be. To incorporate this knowledge, we model p_2 as a stochastic variable, of which the buyer knows the distribution. Due to the stochasticity of p_2, the cost function yields a probability distribution over the cost, rather than a deterministic value. This means the optimal decision now depends on his attitude towards risk.

The most common attitude towards risk in the literature is risk neutral behavior. Risk-neutral buyers minimize their expected total cost. They are indifferent towards the variance of the cost. For the setting above, the decision of a risk neutral buyer is trivial. He simply buys the entire quantity in whichever timeslot has the lowest expected price. Thus, this situation is the same as the deterministic case, except that p_2 is replaced by $\mathbb{E}p_2$. For risk neutral consumers, spreading the purchase over two timeslots is never strictly better than buying the entire quantity in the cheapest timeslot.

Though risk neutral buyers are common in the literature, there is evidence that buyers are in fact risk averse [1,14] rather than risk neutral. Risk averse buyers do not only prefer low costs, but they also want to reduce the risk of bad outcomes. In case of two actions that yield equal expected costs, the buyer prefers the one with the least uncertain cost. Furthermore, a risk averse buyer may prefer an action that yields a higher expected cost, if the cost is less uncertain.

Risk aversion is usually modeled as maximization of the expected utility. The utility is a monotonic, concave transformation of the pay-off. Our problem, though, is formulated in terms of the cost rather than pay-off. Therefore, we would like to express risk aversion in terms of the cost. We do this by introducing the notion of disutility. The disutility is a monotonic, convex transformation of the cost. If the cost is equal to minus the pay-off, then expected utility maximization is equivalent to expected disutility minimization.

For any decision Q_1 the disutility is obtained by applying the disutility function $u(Z)$ to the total cost $Z(Q_1)$. Risk averse behavior is then characterized as minimization of the expected disutility $\mathbb{E}[u(Z(Q_1))]$. The buyer's preference for low costs follows from the monotonicity of the disutility function. His risk aversion follows from the convexity of the disutility function. The optimal decision will be denoted by Q_1^* and is defined as follows.

Definition 2. *The **optimal consumption** Q_1^* in timeslot 1 is given by*

$$Q_1^* = \underset{Q_1 \in [0,Q]}{argmin} \; \mathbb{E}[u(Z(Q_1))].$$

The minimization of expected disutility results in risk averse behavior, for any disutility function, provided that it is monotonic and convex. The exact specification of the (dis)utility function differs per application. Common examples are exponential utility functions [14] and the piecewise linear utility functions [3]. The theoretical analysis in this paper is done for buyers with piecewise linear disutility functions. These are defined as follows:

Definition 3. *The piecewise linear disutility function $u(Z)$ is defined as*

$$u(Z) = \begin{cases} Z & \text{if } Z \leq \alpha \\ \alpha + \beta(Z - \alpha) & \text{if } Z \geq \alpha \end{cases}$$

where $\alpha > 0$ and $\beta > 1$ are the parameters of the disutility function.

A possible application of a piecewise linear disutility function is to describe the preferences of a buyer with a certain budget, who has to pay interest over the portion of the cost that exceeds this budget. All outcomes up to threshold α yield a disutility equal to the total cost, while all outcomes beyond α yield a disutility higher than the cost. Hence, outcomes exceeding α are penalized more than they would have been if the buyer were risk neutral.

In our analysis, we use a uniform distribution to model the uncertain price:

$$p_2 \sim U[a, b]$$

where $0 < a < b$. The buyer knows the values of the parameters a and b, which respectively specify the minimum and maximum values of p_2.

The choices for a piecewise linear disutility function and a uniform distribution for the uncertain price are sufficient to show how risk aversion influences the decision of a buyer under uncertainty, and how an optimal decision can be derived. In the next section we derive expressions for $\mathbb{E}[u(Z(Q_1))]$ and Q_1^*. Furthermore, for both expressions we give formal proofs.

4   The Solution

In this section we give a closed-form expression for the optimal action Q_1^*. We show that if the current price p_1 is lower than the expected future price $\mathbb{E}p_2$, then the optimal action is to buy the entire load immediately at price p_1. Furthermore, if p_1 is sufficiently higher than $\mathbb{E}p_2$, then the optimal action is to delay the purchase of the entire load. If p_1 is only slightly higher than $\mathbb{E}p_2$, though, then the optimal action may be to spread the quantity over both timeslots. A necessary condition for spreading to be optimal is that delaying the purchase leads to uncertainty on whether the total cost $Z(Q_1)$ will be less or greater than the risk aversion threshold α. In this section we give an exact specification on when the buyer will purchase right away, delay, or spread the quantity over the two timeslots. In case of spreading, we specify exactly how much will be purchased immediately (and thus how much will be delayed).

For this purpose we first derive an expression for the expected disutility $\mathbb{E}[u(Z(Q_1))]$. The form of the disutility $u(Z(Q_1))$ depends on whether the total cost $Z(Q_1)$ is less then risk aversion threshold α (by Definitions 1 and 3). The expected disutility $\mathbb{E}[u(Z(Q_1))]$ consequently has three different forms or segments, corresponding to the probability of $Z(Q_1) \leq \alpha$ being one, zero, or otherwise. We refer to them as segment I, II, and III respectively.

For actions Q_1 in segment I or II (i.e. $\mathbb{P}_{p_2}(Z(Q_1) \leq \alpha)$ is zero or one), the expected disutility is linear with respect to Q_1. For actions Q_1 in segment III (i.e. $\mathbb{P}_{p_2}(Z(Q_1) \leq \alpha)$ is neither zero nor one), though, the expected disutility is non-linear. This segment of the expected disutility function may or may not have a local minimum. If a local minimum exists, then it also minimizes $\mathbb{E}[u(Z(Q_1))]$ for any $Q_1 \in [0, Q]$, because $\mathbb{E}[u(Z(Q_1))]$ is continuous and differentiable (as we show later) and the other segments are linear. If a local minimum does not exist, then $\mathbb{E}[u(Z(Q_1))]$ is minimized by one of the extreme values: $Q_1 = 0$ or $Q_1 = Q$. Examples of the expected disutility are shown in Fig. 1.

The theorem below that states an expression for the expected disutility for all cases $\mathbb{P}_{p_2}(Z(Q_1) \leq \alpha) = 1$, $\mathbb{P}_{p_2}(Z(Q_1) \leq \alpha) = 0$ and $\mathbb{P}_{p_2}(Z(Q_1) \leq \alpha) \in (0, Q)$. First we define the risk aversion threshold price $\pi(Q_1)$, which expresses the future price p_2 for which the costs $Z(Q_1)$ are lower than threshold α for some $Q_1 < Q$:

$$Z(Q_1) \leq \alpha \iff p_2 \leq \pi(Q_1).$$

If the entire quantity is purchased in the present ($Q_1 = Q$), then the risk aversion threshold is not defined, because in that case the cost does not depend on the future price p_2.

Definition 4. *For $Q_1 \in [0, Q)$, the **risk aversion threshold price** $\pi(Q_1)$ is*

$$\pi(Q_1) = \frac{\alpha - p_1 Q_1}{Q - Q_1}.$$

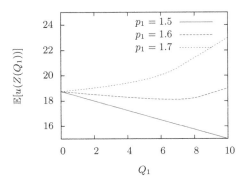

Fig. 1. Expected disutility with $\alpha = 15, \beta = 4, p_2 \sim U[1.0, 2.0], Q = 10$ for low, medium, and high current prices $p_1 = 1.5, 1.6, 1.7$.

The following theorem specifies the expected disutility.

Theorem 1. *Let $Q_1 \in [0, Q]$ be an arbitrary action. $\mathbb{P}_{p_2}(Z(Q_1) \leq \alpha) = 1$ if and only if*

$$p_1 Q_1 + b(Q - Q_1) \leq \alpha. \tag{1}$$

We call this segment I, and in this case the expected disutility has the form

$$\mathbb{E}[u(Z(Q_1))] = p_1 Q_1 + \frac{a+b}{2}(Q - Q_1). \tag{2}$$

Furthermore, $\mathbb{P}_{p_2}(Z(Q_1) \leq \alpha) = 0$ if and only if

$$p_1 Q_1 + a(Q - Q_1) \geq \alpha. \tag{3}$$

We call this segment II, and in this case the expected disutility has the form

$$\mathbb{E}[u(Z(Q_1))] = \alpha + \beta(p_1 Q_1 + \frac{a+b}{2}(Q - Q_1) - \alpha). \tag{4}$$

Finally, $\mathbb{P}_{p_2}(Z(Q_1) \leq \alpha) \in (0, 1)$ if and only if

$$p_1 Q_1 + a(Q - Q_1) < \alpha < p_1 Q_1 + b(Q - Q_1). \tag{5}$$

We call this segment III, and in this case the expected disutility has the form

$$\mathbb{E}[u(Z(Q_1))]$$
$$= \alpha + \frac{(Q - Q_1)}{2(b - a)}\left[\beta(b - \pi(Q_1))^2 - (\pi(Q_1) - a)^2\right]. \tag{6}$$

Later in this paper we give a proof of this theorem. First we provide a theorem that gives a closed-form expression for Q_1^*, which minimizes the expected disutility $\mathbb{E}[u(Z(Q_1))]$ for Q_1. If the current price p_1 is lower than the expected future price $\mathbb{E}p_2$, then buying the entire quantity Q in the present minimizes the expected cost. Moreover, since p_1 is known while p_2 is uncertain, this also minimizes the expected disutility. Thus, if $p_1 < \mathbb{E}p_2$, then a risk-averse buyer buys Q in the present, as there are no advantages to delaying.

If the current price p_1 is higher than the expected future price $\mathbb{E}p_2$, then buying the entire quantity Q in the future minimizes the expected cost. However, since p_1 is known while p_2 is uncertain, this also yields a higher uncertainty than buying in the present. If p_1 is sufficiently high, though, then the benefit of a lower expected cost outweighs the drawback of a higher uncertainty. We show that for all current prices $p_1 \geq \sigma$ this is the case, where σ is defined as follows (Fig. 2):

Definition 5. *The* **delay threshold price***, denoted σ, is defined as*

$$\sigma = \frac{a + \sqrt{\beta}b}{1 + \sqrt{\beta}}.$$

Thus, if $p_1 > \sigma$, then a risk-averse buyer delays the purchase of the entire quantity Q. Note that if β approaches 1, then σ approaches $\mathbb{E}p_2$. Furthermore, if β approaches ∞, then σ approaches b.

The most interesting case arises if $\mathbb{E}p_2 < p_1 < \sigma$. In this case, a risk averse buyer may spread the purchase over both timeslots. This is a trade-off between expected cost reduction and uncertainty reduction. We give an exact specification on how the purchase is spread.

The following theorem states the optimal action of a risk-averse buyer in all situations described above.

Theorem 2. *The optimal quantity to buy in the present (denoted Q_1^*) is*

$$Q_1^* = \begin{cases} Q & p_1 < \frac{a+b}{2} \\ 0 & p_1 > \sigma \\ \max(0, Q - \frac{|a-p_1 Q|}{\sqrt{\rho}}) & \frac{a+b}{2} < p_1 < \sigma \end{cases}.$$

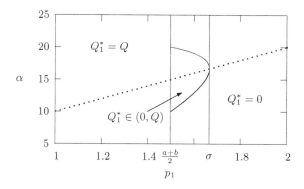

Fig. 2. Optimal quantity to buy in the first timeslot. The dotted line shows $\alpha = p_1 Q$. For points on this line within interval $p_1 \in [\frac{a+b}{2}, \sigma)$, it holds that $Q_1^* = Q$. For $\alpha = p_1 Q$ and $p_1 = \sigma$ all Q_1 are optimal.

The variable ρ depends on the current price p_1 and the distribution over the future price $U[a, b]$ and is defined below. Some special cases are excluded in this equation. If $p_1 = \frac{a+b}{2}$, then all any Q_1 in segment I or II is optimal. If $p_1 = \sigma$ and $p_1 Q \neq \alpha$, then $Q_1^* = 0$. If $p_1 = \sigma$ and $p_1 Q = \alpha$, then any $Q_1 \in [0, Q]$ is optimal.

Definition 6.

$$\rho = \frac{\beta(b - p_1)^2 - (p_1 - a)^2}{\beta - 1}.$$

In the following subsections we prove Theorems 1 and 2.

4.1   Expected Disutility

Here we prove Theorem 1, which expresses the expected disutility in terms of the quantity Q_1 purchased in the present.

Proof. By Definitions 1 and 3, Eqs. (2) and (4) for segments I and II are obtained by computing $\mathbb{E}[u(Z(Q_1))] = \mathbb{E}[Z(Q_1)]$ and $\mathbb{E}[u(Z(Q_1))] = \alpha + \beta(\mathbb{E}[Z(Q_1)] - \alpha)$ respectively. By Definition 3, the expression for segment III is obtained by splitting $\mathbb{E}[u(Z(Q_1))]$ into the following terms:

$$\begin{aligned}
&\mathbb{E}[u(Z(Q_1))] \\
=&\mathbb{E}[u(Z(Q_1))|Z(Q_1) \leq \alpha] \cdot \mathbb{P}(Z(Q_1) \leq \alpha) \\
&+ \mathbb{E}[u(Z(Q_1))|Z(Q_1) > \alpha] \cdot \mathbb{P}(Z(Q_1) > \alpha) \\
=&\mathbb{E}[Z(Q_1)|Z(Q_1) \leq \alpha] \cdot \mathbb{P}(Z(Q_1) \leq \alpha) \\
&+ (\alpha + \beta(\mathbb{E}[Z(Q_1)|Z(Q_1) > \alpha] - \alpha)) \cdot \mathbb{P}(Z(Q_1) > \alpha)
\end{aligned}$$

By Definitions 1 and 4, Eq. (6) for segment III is obtained by computing the probabilities and conditional expectations and by rewriting the expression using calculus.

4.2   Optimal Risk-Averse Consumption

Here we prove Theorem 2. First we state a number of useful properties.

Property 1. $Q_1 \in [0, Q)$ is in segment III (i.e. Eq. (5) is true) if and only if

$$a < \pi(Q_1) < b. \tag{7}$$

Proof. This follows from Definition 4.

Property 2. The derivative of $\pi(Q_1)$ can be expressed in two ways:

$$\frac{\partial \pi}{\partial Q_1} = \frac{\pi(Q_1) - p_1}{Q - Q_1} = \frac{\alpha - p_1 Q}{(Q - Q_1)^2}.$$

Proof. Both expressions follow from Definition 4.

Property 3. The function $\pi(Q_1)$ is monotonic for $Q_1 \in [0, Q)$.

Proof. This follows from the second expression for the derivative of $\pi(Q_1)$ in Property 2. The denominator of this fraction is larger than zero for all $Q_1 \in [0, Q)$. The numerator does not depend on Q_1 and is therefore either positive or negative for all Q_1. Thus, $\pi(Q_1)$ is monotonic.

Property 4. If Q_1 is in segment III, then the derivative of $\mathbb{E}[u(Z(Q_1))]$ is

$$\frac{\partial \mathbb{E}[u(Z(Q_1))]}{\partial Q_1} = \frac{1}{2}\frac{\beta - 1}{b - a}\left[(\pi(Q_1) - p_1)^2 - \rho\right]. \tag{8}$$

Proof. Assume Q_1 is in segment III. The derivative of $\mathbb{E}[u(Z(Q_1))]$ follows from Theorem 1, Definition 6, and the derivative of $\pi(Q_1)$ (Property 2).

Property 5. The expected disutility $\mathbb{E}[u(Z(Q_1))]$ is continuous and differentiable within its domain $[0, Q]$.

Proof. By Eqs. (2), (4), and (6) in Theorem 1 the function $\mathbb{E}[u(Z(Q_1))]$ is continuous and differentiable within each segment I, II, and III. The segments I and III touch at

$$p_1 Q_1 + b(Q - Q_1) = \alpha$$

and the segments II and III touch at

$$p_1 Q_1 + a(Q - Q_1) = \alpha.$$

$\mathbb{E}[u(Z(Q_1))]$ is continuous at the boundaries of the segments, because the expressions of $\mathbb{E}[u(Z(Q_1))]$ for different segments yield the same values in these points. Similarly, $\mathbb{E}[u(Z(Q_1))]$ is differentiable at the boundaries, because the derivatives of $\mathbb{E}[u(Z(Q_1))]$ for different segments yield the same values in these points. For segments I and II, the derivatives of $\mathbb{E}[u(Z(Q_1))]$ can be easily obtained from Theorem 1. For segment III it is given by Property 4.

We use these properties to prove Theorem 2. We distinguish between a low, high, and medium current price: $p_1 \leq \mathbb{E}p_2$, $p_1 \geq \sigma$, $p_1 \in [\mathbb{E}p_2, \sigma]$ respectively. We also briefly discuss the special cases $p_1 = \frac{a+b}{2}$ and $p_1 = \sigma$.

4.3   Low Current Price

Here we prove that, if the current price p_1 is lower than the expected future price, then risk-averse buyers (just like risk-neutral buyers) purchase the entire quantity Q in the present, at price p_1. This is formalized in the following lemma.

Lemma 1. *If* $p_1 < \frac{a+b}{2}$, *then* $Q_1^* = Q$.

Proof. Assume $p_1 < \frac{a+b}{2}$. We will prove that $\mathbb{E}[u(Z(Q_1))]$ decreases monotonically with respect to Q_1, from which it follows that $Q_1^* = Q$. If Q_1 is in segment I or II, then $\mathbb{E}[u(Z(Q_1))]$ is given by Eqs. (2) and (4) respectively. Since $p_1 < \frac{a+b}{2}$, $\mathbb{E}[u(Z(Q_1))]$ decreases monotonically within these segments. We also show that $\mathbb{E}[u(Z(Q_1))]$ decreases monotonically within the segment for which Eq. (5) holds. First note that

$$(b - p_1)^2 > (p_1 - a)^2 \tag{9}$$

holds by rewriting assumption $p_1 < \frac{a+b}{2}$. By this Equation and by Property 1, it holds that

$$(b - p_1)^2 > (\pi(Q_1) - p_1)^2. \tag{10}$$

Furthermore, by Definition 6 and Eq (9) it holds that $\rho > (b - p_1)^2$, and therefore

$$\rho > (\pi(Q_1) - p_1)^2.$$

By this equation and by Property 4, the expected disutility $\mathbb{E}[u(Z(Q_1))]$ has a negative derivative, and therefore decreases monotonically within segment III. Thus, within each segment, $\mathbb{E}[u(Z(Q_1))]$ decreases monotonically. Since $\mathbb{E}[u(Z(Q_1))]$ is continuous (by Property 5), $\mathbb{E}[u(Z(Q_1))]$ also decreases monotonically within its entire domain $Q_1 \in [0, Q]$. Therefore, the highest value in this domain minimizes the expected disutility: $Q_1^* = Q$.

4.4 High Current Price

Here we prove that, if the current price p_1 is higher than σ, then risk-averse consumers delay the purchase of the entire quantity Q. This is formalized in the following lemma.

Lemma 2. *If $p_1 > \sigma$, then $Q_1^* = 0$.*

Proof. Assume $p_1 > \sigma$. We will prove that $\mathbb{E}[u(Z(Q_1))]$ increases monotonically, from which it follows that $Q_1^* = 0$. If Q_1 is in segment I or II, then $\mathbb{E}[u(Z(Q_1))]$ is given by Eqs. (2) and (4) respectively (segments I and II). Since $p_1 > \sigma > \frac{a+b}{2}$, $\mathbb{E}[u(Z(Q_1))]$ increases monotonically with respect to Q_1 within these segments. We also show that $\mathbb{E}[u(Z(Q_1))]$ increases monotonically within the segment III. First note that

$$\beta(b - p_1)^2 < (p_1 - a)^2$$

holds by rewriting assumption $p_1 > \sigma$. This and Definition 6 imply that $\rho < 0$. Therefore, by Property 4, the expected disutility $\mathbb{E}[u(Z(Q_1))]$ has a positive derivative, and therefore increases monotonically within segment III. Thus, within each segment, $\mathbb{E}[u(Z(Q_1))]$ increases monotonically. Since $\mathbb{E}[u(Z(Q_1))]$ is continuous (by Property 5), it also increases monotonically within its entire domain $Q_1[0, Q]$. Therefore, the lowest value in this domain minimizes the expected disutility: $Q_1^* = 0$.

4.5 Medium Current Price

We now show the optimal behavior if the current price is between $\frac{a+b}{2}$ and σ. First, we consider the case in which there is a high certainty on $Z(Q_1) \leq \alpha$.

Lemma 3. *If $\frac{a+b}{2} < p_1 < \sigma$ and $|\alpha - p_1 Q| \geq \sqrt{\rho} Q$, then $Q_1^* = 0$.*

Proof. Assume $\frac{a+b}{2} < p_1 < \sigma$ and $|\alpha - p_1 Q| \geq \sqrt{\rho} Q$. We will prove that $\mathbb{E}[u(Z(Q_1))]$ increases monotonically, from which it follows that $Q_1^* = 0$.

If Q_1 is in segment I or II, then $\mathbb{E}[u(Z(Q_1))]$ is given by Eqs. (2) and (4) respectively. Since $p_1 > \frac{a+b}{2}$, $\mathbb{E}[u(Z(Q_1))]$ increases monotonically within these segments. We also show that $\mathbb{E}[u(Z(Q_1))]$ increases monotonically within the segment III. Note that by Definition 4 it holds that

$$(\pi(Q_1) - p_1)^2 = \frac{(p_1 Q - \alpha)^2}{(Q - Q_1)^2}. \tag{11}$$

Furthermore, by assumption $|\alpha - p_1 Q| \geq \sqrt{\rho} Q$ it holds that

$$\frac{(p_1 Q - \alpha)^2}{(Q - Q_1)^2} \geq \frac{\rho Q^2}{(Q - Q_1)^2}. \tag{12}$$

By Eqs. (11) and (12) it holds that

$$(\pi(Q_1) - p_1)^2 \geq \frac{\rho Q^2}{(Q - Q_1)^2}.$$

Since $\frac{Q^2}{(Q-Q_1)^2} > 1$ it also holds that $(\pi(Q_1) - p_1)^2 > \rho$. Hence, by Property 4 the expected disutility $\mathbb{E}[u(Z(Q_1))]$ has a positive derivative and therefore increases monotonically within segment III. Thus, within each segment, $\mathbb{E}[u(Z(Q_1))]$ increases monotonically. Since $\mathbb{E}[u(Z(Q_1))]$ is continuous (by Property 5), it also increases monotonically within its entire domain $Q_1 \in [0, Q]$. Therefore, the lowest value in this domain minimizes the expected disutility: $Q_1^* = 0$.

So far the optimal behavior was to buy the entire load either in the present or in the future. We now prove the optimal behavior for $\frac{a+b}{2} < p_1 < \sigma$ and $|\alpha - p_1 Q| \leq \sqrt{\rho} Q$, for which the optimal behavior may be to spread the purchase over the present and the future.

Lemma 4. *If $\frac{a+b}{2} < p_1 < \sigma$ and $|\alpha - p_1 Q| < \sqrt{\rho} Q$, then*

$$Q_1^* = Q - \frac{|\alpha - p_1 Q|}{\sqrt{\rho}}.$$

Proof. Assume $\frac{a+b}{2} < p_1 < \sigma$ and $|\alpha - p_1 Q| < \sqrt{\rho} Q$. Note that the first assumption implies $\rho > 0$, so $\sqrt{\rho}$ and therefore the second assumption are well-defined.

We first show the unique solution of $\frac{\partial \mathbb{E}[u(Z(Q_1))]}{\partial Q_1} = 0$ for $Q_1 \in [0, Q)$ in segment III. By Property 4 a necessary condition for such a solution is

$$(\pi(Q_1) - p_1)^2 = \rho. \tag{13}$$

Moreover, this condition is sufficient if we also show that Q_1 is in domain $[0, Q]$ and in segment III. From assumption $\frac{a+b}{2} < p_1 < \sigma$ it follows that Eq. (13) implies $a < \pi(Q_1) < b$, so by Property 1 any Q_1 that satisfies this equation lies in segment III. Furthermore, Eq. (13) has to be satisfied by either $\pi(Q_1) = p_1 - \sqrt{\rho}$ or $\pi(Q_1) = p_1 + \sqrt{\rho}$. Since $\pi(Q_1)$ is monotonic (Property 3) this means there are at most two solutions of $\frac{\partial \mathbb{E}[u(Z(Q_1))]}{\partial Q_1} = 0$ for Q_1. In fact, by Definition 4 and assumption $|a - p_1 Q| < \sqrt{\rho}Q$ it holds that the only solution of $\frac{\partial \mathbb{E}[u(Z(Q_1))]}{\partial Q_1} = 0$ in domain $[0, Q)$ in segment III is

$$Q_1 = Q - \frac{|\alpha - p_1 Q|}{\sqrt{\rho}}$$

which consequently is also the only extremum of $\mathbb{E}[u(Z(Q_1))]$ in segment III. Moreover, since the second derivative of $\mathbb{E}[u(Z(Q_1))]$ with respect to Q_1,

$$\frac{\partial^2 \mathbb{E}[u(Z(Q_1))]}{\partial Q_1^2} = \frac{\beta - 1}{b - a} \frac{(\pi(Q_1) - p_1)^2}{Q - Q_1},$$

is greater than 0, this extremum is the unique minimum within segment III. By the monotonicity of the other segments I and II and since $\mathbb{E}[u(Z(Q_1))]$ is continuous and differentiable for all $Q_1 \in [0, Q)$ (by Property 5), the minimum of $\mathbb{E}[u(Z(Q_1))]$ in segment III is also the unique minimum of $\mathbb{E}[u(Z(Q_1))]$ for $Q_1 \in [0, Q]$.

4.6   Special Cases

We now give a proof for the special cases $p_1 = \frac{a+b}{2}, p_1 = \sigma$.

Lemma 5. *If $p_1 = \frac{a+b}{2}$, then all any Q_1 in segment I or II is optimal. If $p_1 = \sigma$ and $p_1 Q \neq \alpha$, then $Q_1^* = 0$. If $p_1 = \sigma$ and $p_1 Q = \alpha$, then any $Q_1 \in [0, Q]$ is optimal.*

Proof. If $p_1 = \frac{a+b}{2}$, then by Theorem 1 the expected disutility $\mathbb{E}[u(Z(Q_q))]$ for segments I and II is constant. The expected disutility for segment III is higher, because there is uncertainty regarding $Z(Q_1) \leq \alpha$. Therefore, any Q_1 in segment I or II minimizes the expected disutility. If $p_1 = \sigma$, then the same reasoning as in Lemma 2 can be applied, provided that $p_1 Q \neq \alpha$. The only difference is that $\rho = 0$ and the expected disutility has a stationary point for Q_1 such that $\pi(Q_1) = p_1$, but this has no impact on the minimum value, since the expected disutility increases monotonically before and after this point. Thus, $Q_1^* = 0$. However, if $p_1 Q \neq \alpha$, then for all $Q_1 \in [0, Q]$ it holds that $\pi(Q_1) = p_1$, and by

Property 1 it holds that all Q_1 are in segment III. By Theorem 1 it now holds that for all Q_1 the expected disutility equals α.

5   Multiple Segments Piecewise Linear Disutility

So far we have assumed that the piecewise linear disutility function has two segments, separated by a single risk aversion threshold α. One can also consider piecewise linear disutility functions with an arbitrary number of segments. These functions have the useful property that they can be used as approximations of any arbitrary function. Here, we give an expression for the expected multi-segment piecewise linear disutility function, and show it has a form that is very similar to the two-segment piecewise linear disutility function. This may open further research towards a closed-form solution to this optimization problem.

Definition 7. *Let n be the number of segments. Let $\beta_1, \ldots, \beta_{n-1}$ be the parameters that specify the slope of the segments separated by parameters $\alpha_1, \ldots, \alpha_{n-1}$. Convexity is enforced by satisfying $1 < \beta_1 < \cdots < \beta_{n-1}$. Furthermore, let $\alpha_0 = 0$, $\alpha_n = \infty$, and $\beta_0 = 1$. For any $i \in \{0, \ldots, n-1\}$, if $\alpha_i \leq Z \leq \alpha_{i+1}$, then* **the multi-segment piecewise linear disutility function** *is given by*

$$u(Z) = \gamma_i + \beta_i(Z - \alpha_i)$$

where

$$\gamma_i = \sum_{j=1}^{i} \beta_j(\alpha_i - \alpha_{i-1}).$$

The risk-neutral utility function ($n = 1$) and the two-segment piecewise linear disutility function ($n = 2$), which is used elsewhere in this paper (Definition 3), are special cases of the multi-segment piecewise linear disutility function.

The expected disutility for stochastic cost Z has different cases, depending on the probability distribution over the segment $\alpha_i \leq Z \leq \alpha_{i+1}$ in which Z may be. If $n = 1$, then there is only one case, so the expected disutility also has one case: $\mathbb{E}[u(Z)] = \mathbb{E}[Z]$. If $n = 2$, then the expected disutility is given by Theorem 1. This function has three cases: $\mathbb{P}(Z \leq \alpha) = 0, \mathbb{P}(Z \leq \alpha) = 1, \mathbb{P}(Z \leq \alpha) \in (0, 1)$.

For $n > 2$ this can be generalized. Let k be the lowest integer such that $\mathbb{P}(Z \leq \alpha_k) > 0$ and let m be the highest integer such that $\mathbb{P}(Z \geq \alpha_{m-1}) > 0$. Since $1 \leq k \leq m \leq n$, there are $N = \frac{n(n+1)}{2}$ different combinations of $\langle k, m \rangle$, and therefore N different cases of the expected disutility. For arbitrary k, m the corresponding form is given by

$$\mathbb{E}[u(Z)] = \sum_{i=k}^{m} \mathbb{E}[u(Z)|\alpha_{i-1} \leq Z \leq \alpha_i]\mathbb{P}(\alpha_{i-1} \leq Z \leq \alpha_i). \tag{14}$$

In the worst case k and m can be far apart, and moreover, as said, the number of such cases is quadratic. On the one hand, these are all efficiently computable, but for future work we suggest an automatic procedure to construct the cases automatically, based on the analysis in this paper.

6   Conclusion

We have given a closed-form expression for the optimal behavior of a risk-averse buyer with a piecewise linear utility function and a uniformly distributed future price distribution (Theorem 2). If the current price p_1 is lower than the expected future price $\frac{a+b}{2}$, then the optimal behavior is to purchase the entire quantity in the present (Lemma 1). Furthermore, if p_1 is higher than σ, then the optimal behavior is to purchase the entire quantity in the future (Lemma 2). If $p_1 \in [\frac{a+b}{2}, \sigma]$, then the optimal behavior depends on the condition $|\alpha - p_1 Q| \geq \sqrt{\rho} Q$. If this condition holds, then there is sufficient certainty on whether the cost exceed risk aversion threshold α. The buyer is either certain enough that the cost will be lower than α or the buyer thinks the costs will exceed α anyway. Either way, the optimal behavior is to delay the entire purchase, because the expected future price is lower than the current price (Lemma 3). If $|\alpha - p_1 Q| < \sqrt{\rho} Q$, however, there is high uncertainty on whether or not the cost will exceed the risk aversion threshold α. In this case the optimal behavior is to spread the purchase over both timeslots (Lemma 4). Thus, we have derived the first closed-form solution for a two-segment piecewise linear utility function. This gives insight into risk averse buying with two timeslots. Moreover, our solution may open further research and development in finding closed-form solutions for other classes of this problem.

7   Future Work

An interesting line of research is to derive a closed-form solution to the optimization of the expected multi-segment piecewise linear utility function, which we have defined in Sect. 5. Multi-segment $(n > 2)$ piecewise linear utility functions are particularly useful, because they can be used as an approximation of any utility function. For such functions, closed-form expressions could be found using approaches very similar to the ones presented in the current work, where closeness of segment borders may obfuscate the results. Similarly, the results can be extended to other price distributions by modeling and approximating those by piece-wise uniform distributions and following the same line of reasoning.

Another interesting case is the situation when more details are known about the future. Instead of one timeslot with an unknown price, there could be an arbitrary number of timeslots, each with their own price distribution. Since a decision must be made in each timeslot, this problem can be modeled as a Markov Decision Process. Our analysis provides an important first step towards a closed-form analytical solution to this problem.

References

1. Arrow, K.: Aspects of the theory of risk-bearing. Yrjö Jahnsson lectures. Yrjö Jahnssonin Säätiö (1965)
2. Babanov, A., Collins, J., Gini, M.: Harnessing the search for rational bid schedules with stochastic search and domain-specific heuristics. In: Proceedings of the Third International Joint Conference on Autonomous Agents and Multiagent Systems, vol. 1, pp. 269–276. IEEE Computer Society (2004)
3. Best, M., Grauer, R., Hlouskova, J., Zhang, X.: Loss-aversion with kinked linear utility functions. Comput. Econ. **44**(1), 45–65 (2014)
4. Chung, K.-J., Sobel, M.J.: Discounted MDP's: distribution functions and exponential utility maximization. SIAM J. Control Optim. **25**(1), 49–62 (1987)
5. Ermon, S., Conrad, J., Gomes, C.P., Selman, B.: Risk-sensitive policies for sustainable renewable resource allocation. In: IJCAI, pp. 1942–1948 (2011)
6. Fortin, I., Hlouskova, J.: Optimal asset allocation under linear loss aversion. J. Bank. Fin. **35**(11), 2974–2990 (2011)
7. Höning, N., La Poutré, H.: Reduction of market power and stabilisation of outcomes in a novel and simplified two-settlement electricity market. In: Proceedings of the 2012 IEEE/WIC/ACM International Joint Conferences on Web Intelligence and Intelligent Agent Technology, vol. 02, pp. 103–110. IEEE Computer Society (2012)
8. Hou, P., Yeoh, W., Varakantham, P.: Revisiting risk-sensitive MDPs: new algorithms and results. In: Proceedings of the International Conference on Automated Planning and Scheduling (ICAPS), pp. 136–144 (2014)
9. Kahneman, D., Tversky, A.: Prospect theory: an analysis of decision under risk. Econometrica J. Econometric Soc. **47**, 263–291 (1979)
10. Liu, Y., Goodwin, R., Koenig, S.: Risk-averse auction agents. In: Proceedings of the Second International Joint Conference on Autonomous Agents and Multiagent Systems, pp. 353–360. ACM (2003)
11. Liu, Y., Koenig, S.: Probabilistic planning with nonlinear utility functions. In: ICAPS, pp. 410–413 (2006)
12. Minami, R., Silva, V.F.: Shortest stochastic path with risk sensitive evaluation. In: Batyrshin, I., González Mendoza, M. (eds.) MICAI 2012. LNCS (LNAI), vol. 7629, pp. 371–382. Springer, Heidelberg (2013). doi:10.1007/978-3-642-37807-2_32
13. Rabin, M., Thaler, R.H.: Anomalies: risk aversion. J. Econ. Perspect. **15**(1), 219–232 (2001)
14. Robu, V., La Poutré, H.: Designing bidding strategies in sequential auctions for risk averse agents. Multiagent Grid Syst. **6**(5), 437–457 (2010)
15. Vetsikas, I.A., Jennings, N.R.: Bidding strategies for realistic multi-unit sealed-bid auctions. Auton. Agents Multi Agent Syst. **21**(2), 265–291 (2010)
16. Vytelingum, P., Dash, R.K., David, E., Jennings, N.R.: A risk-based bidding strategy for continuous double auctions. In: ECAI, vol. 16, p. 79 (2004)
17. Wakker, P.P.: Explaining the characteristics of the power (CRRA) utility family. Health Econ. **17**(12), 1329–1344 (2008)

Investigation of Learning Strategies for the SPOT Broker in Power TAC

Moinul Morshed Porag Chowdhury[1]([⊠]), Russell Y. Folk[2],
Ferdinando Fioretto[3], Christopher Kiekintveld[1], and William Yeoh[2]

[1] Department of Computer Science,
The University of Texas at El Paso, El Paso, USA
mchowdhury4@miners.utep.edu, cdkiekintveld@utep.edu
[2] Department of Computer Science, New Mexico State University, Las Cruces, USA
{rfolk,wyeoh}@cs.nmsu.edu
[3] Department of Industrial and Operations Engineering,
University of Michigan, Ann Arbor, USA
fioretto@umich.edu

Abstract. The Power TAC simulation emphasizes the strategic problems that broker agents face in managing the economics of a smart grid. The brokers must make trades in multiple markets and, to be successful, brokers must make many good predictions about future supply, demand, and prices in the wholesale and tariff markets. In this paper, we investigate the feasibility of using learning strategies to improve the performance of our broker, SPOT. Specifically, we investigate the use of decision trees and neural networks to predict the clearing price in the wholesale market and the use of reinforcement learning to learn good strategies for pricing our tariffs in the tariff market. Our preliminary results show that our learning strategies are promising ways to improve the performance of the agent for future competitions.

Keywords: Smart grid · Artificial Intelligence · Game theory · Multi agent system · Machine learning

1 Introduction

The traditional energy grid lacks several important features such as effective use of pricing and demand response of energy, customer participation, and proper distribution management for variable-output renewable energy sources [1]. The smart grid has the potential to address many of these issues by providing a more intelligent energy infrastructure [2]. Researchers rely on rich simulations such as the *Power Trading Agent Competition* (Power TAC) [1] to explore the characteristics of future smart grids. In the Power TAC smart grid simulation, brokers participate in several markets including the wholesale market, the tariff market, and the load balancing market to purchase energy and sell it to customers. This game was designed as a scenario for the annual Trading Agent Competition, a research competition with over a decade of history [3].

© Springer International Publishing AG 2017
S. Ceppi et al. (Eds.): AMEC/TADA 2015/2016, LNBIP 271, pp. 96–111, 2017.
DOI: 10.1007/978-3-319-54229-4_7

The wholesale and tariff markets attempt to simulate existing energy markets such as the European or North American wholesale energy markets. The wholesale market is a "day ahead market," where the energy is a perishable good and it allows brokers to buy and sell quantities of energy for future delivery. Market structures like this exist across many different types of perishable goods. So, finding effective, robust, automated bidding strategies for these markets is an important research challenge.

The tariff market is where the major portion of energy purchased from the wholesale market is sold to consumers (e.g., households, offices, etc.). Energy is sold through tariffs offered by the brokers and a goal for the broker is to offer competitive tariffs that attract a large pool of consumers. The overall goal of each broker is to maximize its profit (e.g., by selling energy in the tariff market at a higher price than the purchase price of the energy in the wholesale market).

In this paper, we investigate the feasibility of using learning strategies to improve the performance of our broker, called *Southwest Portfolio Optimizing Trader* (SPOT), in Power TAC. We present our initial work on using decision trees to predict the clearing prices in the wholesale market and the use of an unsupervised reinforcement learning algorithm to learn good strategies for pricing our tariffs in the tariff market. Preliminary results show that these learning strategies hold promise, though we plan to investigate additional improvements to increase the competitiveness of the agent further.

2   Background: Power TAC

Power TAC models a competitive retail power market where the simulation runs for approximately 60 simulated days, and takes about two hours. Broker agents compete with each other by acting in three markets: wholesale market, tariff market and balancing market. It also includes a regulated distribution utility and a real location based population of energy customers during a specific period. Customer models include several entities such as households, electric vehicles, and various commercial and industrial models. Brokers participating in the simulation try to make profit by balancing the energy supply and demand as accurately as possible. By efficiently managing stochastic customer behaviors, weather-dependent renewable energy sources, the broker with highest bank balance wins the competition [4]. SPOT participated in the 2015 Power TAC competition. The Table 1 shows results of the 11 participating agents in 2015 across games with varying numbers of competing brokers.

We only had a couple of months of development before the 2015 tournament, so the main goal was to participate competently without major errors. Overall, our agent achieved this objective, but was not yet competitive with the top agents in the competition. The 2015 agent had preliminary implementation of some of the ideas we describe here, but we have since worked to improve the performance of the agent by updating the learning strategies and decision-making components of the agent.

Table 1. Power TAC 2015 final round results

Name	3 brokers	9 brokers	11 brokers	Total	Total (normalized)
Maxon15 (1st)	186159	3667524	80687243	84540925	3.402
TacTex15 (2nd)	488341	5196258	38755591	44440191	2.221
CUHKTac (3rd)	556792	4000749	35070699	39628240	1.927
AgentUDE	−14748	1162481	52098550	53246283	1.597
Sharpy	−6459	2586534	45130820	47710895	1.564
COLDPower	307197	1334765	14309076	15951038	0.371
cwiBroker	−461511	−1650580	41663592	41663592	0.343
Mertacor	−23099	−139344	32199	−130244	−0.786
NTUTacAgent	−1533793	−10416019	43469971	31520159	−2.202
SPOT	−1570860	−2361785	7521196	3588551	−2.327
CrocodileAgent	−2981460	−13915197	−3318695	−20215352	−6.111

2.1 Wholesale Market

The wholesale market functions as a short-term spot market for buying and selling energy commitments in specific timeslots, where each timeslot represents a simulated hour. At any point in the simulation, agents can participate in auctions to trade energy for the next 24 h, so there are always 24 active auctions. These auctions are periodic double auctions, similar to those used in European or North American wholesale energy markets [5]. Each simulation begins with 14 days pregame data (bootstrap data), which includes data on customers, the wholesale market, and weather data based on the default broker. Brokers can submit bids (orders to buy energy) and asks (orders to sell energy), represented by a quantity and an optional limit price. In addition to the bids of the brokers, several large gencos also sell energy on the wholesale market. The simulation clears the bids by matching buy and sell orders, and determines the clearing price for each auction every day. If the minimum ask price has a higher value than the maximum bid price, then the market does not clear.

The main problem we consider here is learning to predict the clearing prices of these auctions, which can be used by the agent to implement an effective bidding strategy. Previous agents in both Power TAC and earlier TAC competitions have considered similar price prediction problems. AstonTAC is a Power TAC agent that uses a Non-Homogeneous Hidden Markov Model (NHHMM) to forecast energy demand and price [6]. This was the only agent in that competition that was able to buy energy at a low price in the wholesale market and keep energy imbalance low. TacTex13, winner of 2013 Power TAC competition, uses a modified version of Tesauro's bidding algorithm, where they modeled the sequential bidding process as a Markov Decision Process (MDP) for the wholesale market [7]. In the TAC/SCM game, Deep Maize used a Bayesian model of the stochastic demand process to estimate the underlying demand and trend.

It employs a k-Nearest-Neighbors technique to predict the effective demand curves from historical data, self-play games data, and the current game data [8].

2.2   Tariff Market

The Power TAC environment offers the ability for brokers to issue several different types of tariffs three times per simulation day. Each tariff may be as complex or simple as the broker desires though each tariff can only target a single power type such as consumption or production. The most simple type of tariff one may issue is a flat rate tariff that offers a single price per kWh to subscribers. From there, the tariff may be augmented with signup bonuses, or a minimum subscription duration and early termination fee. Tariffs may also be customized to offer tiered usage pricing, time of use pricing, or a daily fee in addition to usage pricing. Tariffs may be issued, revoked, or modified at any time, though the new tariffs will only become available for subscription at the designated 6 h intervals. A tariff is modified by publishing a new tariff with the superseding flag set to the old tariff and then revoking the old tariff. For the purpose of the experiments outlined in this paper, our broker issued a single, simplified flat rate tariff at the beginning of the game and modified it throughout the simulation by superseding the past tariff and revoking the past tariff.

In order to publish the optimal tariff so that we gain both the most subscribers, henceforth referred to as market-share, and the greatest net balance, we utilized an unsupervised reinforced learning technique. This technique is chosen because we want the agent to be able to learn to react in such a way that gains the best possible reward with little interaction from the researchers. To achieve this goal we modeled this problem as a Markov Decision Process (MDP) [9] and utilize the Q-Learning algorithm [10] to discover the optimal policy. Q-Learning involves an iterative process whereby the SPOT agent plays many simulations constantly updating the Q-Value for a given state, action pair. Q-Learning will continue to improve the Q-Values until a convergence is obtained where the Q-Values for each state, action pair change very little per iteration. In order to expedite the convergence of the Q-Learning algorithm, we implemented a distributed system that allowed many simulations to be run simultaneously.

3   Learning in the Wholesale Market

Our baseline broker used a moving average price prediction based on the price history of the agent. To predict a new price for a week ahead specific hour price, the baseline agent uses a weighted sum of the current hour's clearing price, yesterday's predicted clearing price for that specific hour and 6 day ahead same hour predicted price. We have experimented with three different machine learning methods to predict clearing prices in the wholesale market: (*i*) REPTree (a type of decision tree) [11], (*ii*) Linear Regression, and (*iii*) Multilayer Perceptron (a type of neural network). We have also investigated a variety of different features for training the predictors. These include 8 price features that capture information about the recent trading history, such as the clearing price for the previous hour and the prices for the equivalent time slot in the previous day and week. We also include the weather forecast and time of day because the energy production of renewable energy producers (e.g., solar) depends on these factors. The number of participants in the game is included because the amount of competition affects the market clearing price. Finally, we include a moving average of the prices as a convenient way to capture an aggregate price history.

To generate training data, we use simulations with a variety of agent binaries from previous tournaments, as well as a variety of different bootstrap initialization files. We train our models using Weka [12], and evaluate their ability to predict market clearing prices based on the mean absolute prediction error only for auctions that clear (we do not include auctions that do not clear in the error calculations). In the following experiments, we investigate the performance of the models in several areas, including how well they generalize to new agents, different numbers of agents, and how important the different features are to the performance of the predictors.

3.1 Prediction Accuracy Comparisons

We begin with a basic evaluation of the prediction accuracy of the learned models. One of the most significant factors we discovered that influences the accuracy of the models is how we handle auctions that do not clear. In many cases, an auction will have no clearing price due to a spread between the bid and ask prices, which results in the simulation returning null values for these prices. This causes significant problems with the price features we use, as well as the final error calculations. To improve this, we calculate an estimated clearing price for auctions that do not clear by taking the average of lowest ask price and the highest bid price. Figure 1 shows the prediction errors during the course of a single simulation for two different REPTree models trained on 20 games, one with estimated clearing prices and the other without. We also include the errors for a simple moving average price predictor as a baseline for comparison. Each data point shows the average error for all auctions in a window of five timeslots. The data show that both REPTree models outperform the moving average predictor, but the version with estimated clearing prices is dramatically better, and produces much more consistent predictions throughout the entire game. Next, we compare the performance of the three different learning methods with different amounts of training data ranging from 5 to 20 games. We evaluated a variety of different configurations of hidden layers for the Multilayer Perceptron model; only the best one is shown here (MP-20-20, i.e., 2 layer neural network with 20 nodes in each layer). Figure 2 shows the average mean absolute error for the different models based on 5 games of test data. The results show that the decision tree model makes good predictions compared to other models. The decision tree model slowly improves according to the number of games while other models do

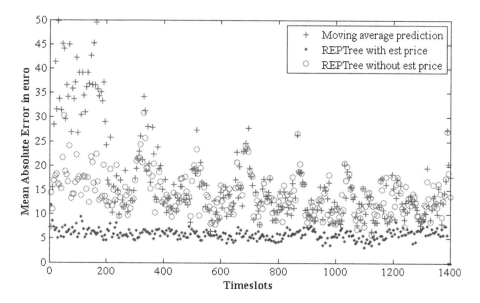

Fig. 1. Effect of clearing price estimation

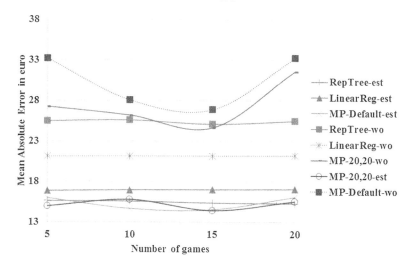

Fig. 2. Comparison of several prediction models by number of games

not show this trend. The default Multilayer Perceptron (1 layer with 18 nodes) with estimated prices shows some improvement in the initial number of games than REPTree but finally looses to REPTree in the 20 game model. In all cases, the models with estimated clearing prices are much better than models without estimated prices.

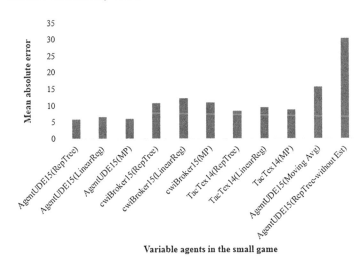

Fig. 3. Comparison of several prediction models

3.2 Evaluation with Different Agents

In the Power TAC competition, broker agents play many games against different opponents with varying strategies. Here, we test how well our predictors generalize to playing new agents that are not in the training data. We test our models on games of the same size, but varying one of the agents in the game between AgentUDE15, cwiBroker15 and TacTex14. All the predictor model are generated from the training dataset where AgentUDE is used. Figure 3 shows the average results for each of the learning methods in the three different agent environments. The REPTree predictor consistently does better than others, though there are differences depending on the pool of opponents. We can also see that the models do best against AgentUDE (which was in the training set), and there is a significant decrease in accuracy when playing either cwiBroker or TacTex. Further work is needed to help the models generalize better to new opponents.

3.3 Evaluation with Different Numbers of Agents

In the competition, broker agents must play in games with varying numbers of opponents. We experiment with different number of brokers in the games, ranging from 3 to 7 brokers. We focus here on the REPTree predictor since it performs better than the others consistently in previous experiments. The 5 agent predictor models trained on data generated from SPOT(Baseline), AgentUDE15, cwiBroker15, SampleBroker, Maxon14 and the 7 agent predictor models use data from SPOT(Baseline), AgentUDE15, cwiBroker15, SampleBroker, Maxon14, Maxon15, COLDPower and CrocodileAgent15. The test data uses the same agents. We also trained a predictor based on a mixed dataset that included the same number of training games, but with a combination of 3, 5, and 7 agent

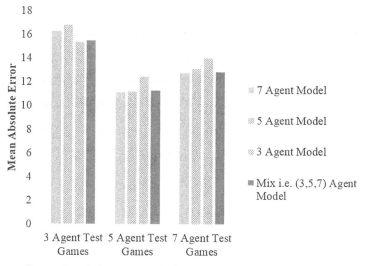

Fig. 4. Comparison for different number of agents

Table 2. Average error for the various agent models

7 agent	5 agent	3 agent	Mixed agent
13.406	13.714	13.958	13.225

games. The data in Fig. 4 shows that, in each case, the model trained on the correct number of agents has the best performance. However, we also note that the mixed model performs very well in all three cases. Table 2 shows the average error of the predictor models over the 3 different test game data, and demonstrates that the average error for the mixed model is better than any of the other three models.

3.4   Using Price Predictions for Bidding

We took the best performing predictor from our experiments (REPTree) and tested whether using these predictions could improve performance for a basic bidding strategy. This strategy attempts to target auctions where the clearing price is predicted to be low, and to buy a higher volume of the needed energy in those specific auctions. Figure 5 shows that using the new predictions and bidding strategy the agent is able to buy a high volume of the needed energy when the average clearing price is lowest against the champion agent Maxon15.

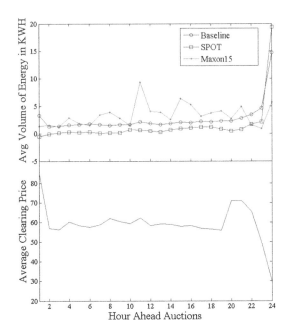

Fig. 5. Comparison for wholesale bidding strategies

3.5   Feature Evaluation

To evaluate which features are the most important for the predictions we used
ReliefFAttributeEvaluation [13] and the Ranker method in Weka to rank our
18 features. We also used the ClassifierSubsetEval method and best-first search
to get the best subset of features from all the features. Table 3 shows the top
7 features using the ranker algorithm and the best subset of features using the
ClassifierSubsetEval method. We ran the subset evaluation on 5, 10, 15, and 20
games and, for all cases, we found a consistent subset of seven features. The
features such as temperature, day of a month, month of a year, number of par-

Table 3. Feature evaluation

Ranked features	Subset evaluation
PreviousHourN_1Price	YesterdayClrPrice
PrevHourClrPrice	PreviousHourN_1Price
PredictedClrPrice	PredictedClrPrice
YesterdayClrPrice	PrevHourClrPrice
AWeekAgoN_1Price	Day
YesterdayN_1Price	HourAhead
PrevOneWeekClrPrice	CloudCoverage

ticipants are ranked low and also out of the best subset. We could potentially discard these types of features while training a predictor model. From the ranked feature column, we see that price features are very important for the REP-Tree predictor model. So, adding additional features of this type may improve performance.

4   Learning in the Tariff Market

We describe how we formulate our problem in the tariff market as a *Markov Decision Process* (MDP) [9] and use Q-learning [10] to learn the optimal policy.

4.1   Formulating the Problem as an MDP

Recall that in the tariff market, the goal is to design tariffs that will result in the largest profit for the broker agent. In this paper, we investigate a restricted version of the problem, where we assume that the broker can only offer flat-rate tariffs, i.e., the price per kWh is uniform across all time steps. However, the broker can vary the price of the flat-rate tariff and the objective is still to maximize the profit of the broker. This problem can be formulated as a *Markov Decision Process* (MDP) [9], defined by the tuple $\langle \mathbf{S}, s_0, \mathbf{A}, \mathbf{T}, \mathbf{R} \rangle$:

- A set of states $\mathbf{S}$. In our problem, we define the set of states to be all possible pairs of $\langle MS, Bal \rangle$, where MS is the percentage of market share controlled by our agent (i.e., the percentage of customers that are subscribing to our agent) and Bal is the overall profit or loss since the start of the simulation (i.e., the amount of money in the "bank"). We discretized MS from 0% to 100% in increments of 5% and Bal from −€2,000,000 to €8,000,000 in increments of €20,000.
- A start state $s_0 \in \mathbf{S}$. In our problem, the start state is always $\langle 0\%, e0 \rangle$ since the agent does not have any subscribers to its tariff and starts with no initial profit or loss.
- A set of actions $\mathbf{A}$. In our problem, the first action of the agent is to publish a new flat-rate tariff at €15 per kWh. Subsequent actions are from the following set of actions:
  - ↑: Increase the price of the tariff by €2.00 per kWh. This is implemented by publishing a new tariff at the higher price and revoking the previous lower-priced tariff.
  - ↔: Keep the price of the tariff. This is implemented by not publishing or revoking any tariffs.
  - ↓: Decrease the price of the tariff by €2.25 per kWh. This is implemented by publishing a new tariff at the lower price and revoking the previous higher-priced tariff.

- A transition function $\mathbf{T} : \mathbf{S} \times \mathbf{A} \times \mathbf{S} \rightarrow [0,1]$ that gives the probability $T(s, a, s')$ of transitioning from state s to s' when action a is executed. In our problem, the transition function is not explicitly defined and transitions are executed by the Power TAC simulator.
- A reward function $\mathbf{R} : \mathbf{S} \times \mathbf{A} \times \mathbf{S} \rightarrow \mathbb{R}^+$ that gives the reward $R(s, a, s')$ of executing action a in state s and arriving in state s'. In our problem, the reward is the gain or loss in profits of the agent, determined by the Power TAC simulator.

A "solution" to an MDP is a policy π, which maps states to actions. Solving an MDP is to find an optimal policy, that is, a policy with the largest expected reward.

4.2 Learning Optimal Tariff Prices

We now describe how to learn the optimal policy of the MDP using Q-learning [10]. We initialize the Q-values of all state-action pairs $Q(s,a)$ to 1,000,000 in order to better encourage exploration [10] and use the following update rule to update the Q-values after executing action a from state s and transitioning to state s':

$$Q(s,a) \leftarrow \alpha \left\{ R(s,a,s') + \gamma \cdot \max_{a' \in \mathbf{A}} Q'(s',a') \right\} \qquad (1)$$

where $\alpha = 0.9$ is the learning rate and $\gamma = 1.0$ is the discount factor.

Parallelizing the Learning Process: In order to increase the robustness of the resulting learned policy, we executed the learning algorithm with 10 different simulation bootstrap files [14]. The different bootstrap files may contain different combinations of types of users, with different energy consumption profiles, energy generation capabilities, etc. In order to speed up the learning process, we parallelize the Q-learning algorithm by running multiple instances of the simulation. We run the simulations in groups of 10 instances, where each instance in the group uses one of the 10 unique bootstrap files. Instead of using and updating their local Q-values, all these instances will use and update the same set of Q-values stored on a central database. Once the simulation of one of the instances ends (the Power TAC simulation can end any time between 1440 to 1800 simulated hours), it will restart with the same bootstrap file from the first time step again.

4.3 Experimental Results

In our experiments, we learn policies against two opposing agents; this scenario corresponds to the 3-agent scenario in the previous Power TAC competition. We characterized possible opposing agents according to their relative competitiveness in the previous years' Power TAC competitions. We learned four different

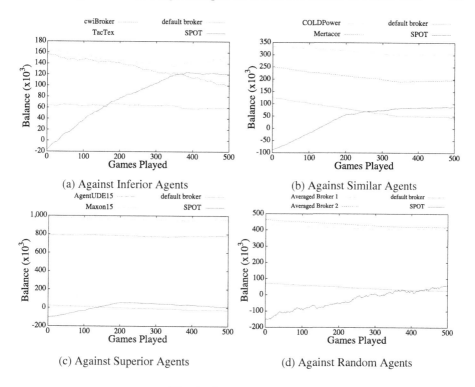

(a) Against Inferior Agents

(b) Against Similar Agents

(c) Against Superior Agents

(d) Against Random Agents

Fig. 6. Convergence rates

sets of Q-values and, equivalently, four different sets of policies against four different types (in terms of their competitive level) of opposing agents:

- SUPERIOR AGENTS: AgentUDE15 and Maxon15.
- SIMILAR AGENTS: Mertacor and COLDPower.
- INFERIOR AGENTS: TacTex14 and CWIBroker14.
- RANDOM AGENTS: Two randomly chosen agents from the set of 6 agents above.

Figure 6 shows the convergence rates for all of the scenarios, where the y-axis shows the final balance at the last time step for each iteration. SPOT is able to learn better policies and improve its final balance with more iterations. To reach convergence, SPOT takes various numbers of iterations according to opponents. SPOT sees the most variance in games where the opponents are randomized. Against a set list of opponents, policy convergence is reached in a limited number of iterations. For example, after approximately 200 iterations convergence is reached against superior brokers.

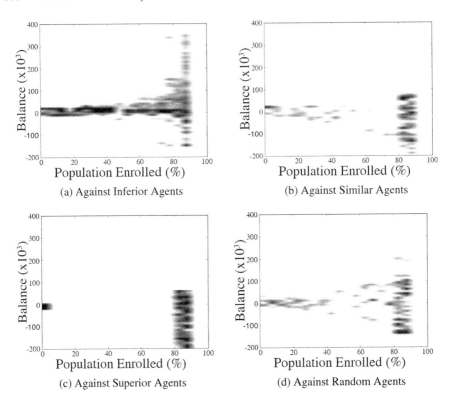

(a) Against Inferior Agents

(b) Against Similar Agents

(c) Against Superior Agents

(d) Against Random Agents

Fig. 7. Explored states

Figure 7 illustrates the explored states in the same scenarios. The color of each state represents the number of times the actions for each state were explored, ranging from black, where all three actions were explored the most, to white, where no actions were explored. The figure shows that more states and actions were explored against inferior agents than against superior agents. Additionally, these results also explain the performance of the agent; against superior agents, our agent was very limited in the states it was able to explore, most times being unable to gain more than 5% of the market share, and when it did get a significant amount it was often at a loss. Thus, it took its best actions and maintained a balance of approximately €50,000.

We evaluated the learned policies against the same set of opposing agents. Figure 8 shows the profit in the tariff market alone of each agent over the various time steps. These results are averaged over 5 different bootstrap files (different from those used in the learning process) and 3 runs per bootstrap file. These results are consistent with the final converged results shown in Fig. 6, where our agent does better against inferior agents than against superior agents.

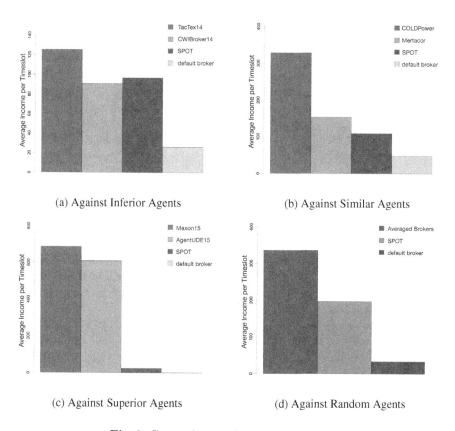

(a) Against Inferior Agents

(b) Against Similar Agents

(c) Against Superior Agents

(d) Against Random Agents

Fig. 8. Comparison against opposing agents

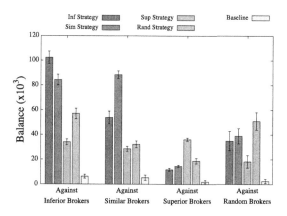

Fig. 9. Profit in the tariff market per timeslot

Figure 9 plots the performance of our agent with each of the four learned policies in addition to an agent with no learned strategy against each pair of opposing agents. Not surprisingly, the results show that the agent with the policy learned through playing against a specific pair of opponents does best when playing against the same pair of opponents (e.g., the agent with the policy learned through playing against superior agents does better than other policies when playing against superior agents). The policy learned through playing against random agents is more robust towards different opponent types, especially compared against the policy learned through playing against superior agents.

5   Conclusions and Future Work

A forward-looking policy is needed between the tariff and wholesale strategy to make consistent profit. The preliminary results in this paper show that the application of learning strategies to broker agents within Power TAC have immediate benefits in both the wholesale and tariff markets separately. However, a more comprehensive study is needed to better harness the strength of these learning approaches. Currently, the evaluations in the wholesale and tariff markets are conducted independently of each other. Therefore, future work includes learning good bidding strategies such as Monte Carlo Tree Search in the wholesale market by taking into account the predicted clearing prices as well as empirically evaluating the coupling effects of the learning strategies between the wholesale and tariff markets.

Acknowledgment. This research is partially supported by NSF grants 1345232 and 1337884. The views and conclusions contained in this document are those of the authors and should not be interpreted as representing the official policies, either expressed or implied, of the sponsoring organizations, agencies, or the U.S. government.

References

1. Ketter, W., Peters, M., Collins, J.: Autonomous agents in future energy markets: the 2012 power trading agent competition. In: Proceedings of the AAAI Conference on Artificial Intelligence, pp. 1298–1304 (2013)
2. Ketter, W., Collins, J., Reddy, P.: Power TAC: a competitive economic simulation of the smart grid. Energy Econ. **39**, 262–270 (2013)
3. Wellman, M.P., Greenwald, A., Stone, P., Wurman, P.R.: The 2001 trading agent competition. Electron. Markets **13**(1), 4–12 (2003)
4. Ketter, W., Collins, J., Reddy, P.P., Weerdt, M.D.: The 2015 power trading agent competition. ERIM Report Series Reference No. ERS-2015-001-LIS (2015)
5. Ketter, W., Collins, J., Reddy, P.: The 2012 power trading agent competition. ERIM Report Series Research in Management (No. ERS-2012-010-LIS) (2012)
6. Kuate, R.T., He, M., Chli, M., Wang, H.H.: An intelligent broker agent for energy trading: an MDP approach. In: Proceedings of the International Joint Conference on Artificial Intelligence (IJCAI), pp. 234–240 (2013)

7. Urieli, D., Stone, P.: TacTex13: a champion adaptive power trading agent. In: Proceedings of the International Conference on Autonomous Agents and Multiagent Systems (AAMAS), pp. 1447–1448 (2014)
8. Kiekintveld, C., Miller, J., Jordan, P.R., Wellman, M.P.: Controlling a supply chain agent using value-based decomposition. In: Proceedings of the ACM Conference on Electronic Commerce (EC), pp. 208–217 (2006)
9. Mausam, Kolobov, A.: Planning with Markov Decision Processes: An AI Perspective. Morgan & Claypool, San Rafael (2012)
10. Abounadi, D.B., Borkar, V.S.: Learning algorithms for Markov decision processes with average cost. SIAM J. Control Optim. **40**(3), 681–698 (2001)
11. Elomaa, T., Kaariainen, M.: An analysis of reduced error pruning. J. Artif. Intell. Res. **15**, 163–187 (2001)
12. Hall, M., Frank, E., Holmes, G., Pfahringer, B., Reutemann, P., Witten, I.H.: The Weka data mining software: an update. SIGKDD Explor. **11**(1) (2009–2015). http://www.cs.waikato.ac.nz/ml/weka/
13. Robnik-Sikonja, M., Kononenko, I.: An adaptation of relief for attribute estimation in regression. In: Proceedings of the International Conference on Machine Learning (ICML), pp. 296–304 (1997)
14. Lauer, M., Riedmiller, M.A.: An algorithm for distributed reinforcement learning in cooperative multi-agent systems. In: Proceedings of the International Conference on Machine Learning (ICML), pp. 535–542 (2000)

On the Use of Off-the-Shelf Machine Learning Techniques to Predict Energy Demands of Power TAC Consumers

Francisco Natividad, Russell Y. Folk, William Yeoh[(✉)], and Huiping Cao

Department of Computer Science, New Mexico State University,
Las Cruces, NM 88003, USA
{fnativid,rfolk,wyeoh,hcao}@cs.nmsu.edu

Abstract. The Power Trading Agent Competition (Power TAC) is a feature-rich simulation that simulates an energy market in a smart grid, where software brokers can buy energy in wholesale markets and sell energy in tariff markets to consumers. Successful brokers can maximize their profits by buying energy at low prices in the wholesale market and selling them at high prices to the consumers. However, this requires that the brokers have accurate predictions of the energy consumption of consumers so that they do not end up having excess energy or insufficient energy in the marketplace. In this paper, we conduct a preliminary investigation that uses standard off-the-shelf machine learning techniques to cluster and predict the consumption of a restricted set of consumers. Our results show that a combination of the popular k-means, k-medoids, and DBSCAN clustering algorithm together with an autoregressive lag model can predict, reasonably accurately, the consumption of consumers.

Keywords: Smart grid · Artificial Intelligence · Multi-agent System · Machine learning

1 Introduction

With the rise in the production of renewable energy in the residential market as well as the proliferation of electric vehicles, there is a concerted effort to transform the conventional power grid into a "smart grid". A feature of this smart grid is an energy market, where software agents can buy and sell energy. In this energy market, transactions can occur with all players in the current energy grid from conventional energy producers with power plants to conventional energy consumers in the residential market.

Rich simulations such as the *Power Trading Agent Competition* (Power TAC) [1] provide an efficient way for researchers to test different possible characteristics of this market before deployment in the real world. In the Power TAC smart grid simulation, a software agent acts as a broker to buy energy in bulk from a wholesale market and sells energy to consumers in a tariff market. The aim of the broker is to maximize its profits through intelligent bidding strategies

© Springer International Publishing AG 2017
S. Ceppi et al. (Eds.): AMEC/TADA 2015/2016, LNBIP 271, pp. 112–126, 2017.
DOI: 10.1007/978-3-319-54229-4_8

in the wholesale market and intelligent tariff designs in the tariff market. This game was developed as a scenario for the annual Trading Agent Competition, a research competition with over a decade of history [2].

For brokers to do well in this competition, one of the key requirements is that they need to be able to predict the energy demands of consumers in the tariff market accurately. An accurate prediction will allow the broker to identify the amount of energy accurately that it needs to purchase in the wholesale market, which can then translate to effective wholesale bidding strategies to purchase energy at the low prices, resulting in larger profits when the energy is sold to the consumers.

In this paper, we report results of our preliminary study, where we use standard off-the-shelf machine learning techniques to identify classes of consumers that have predictable energy requirements. The identification of such classes will allow a broker to design tariffs that specifically target those classes of consumers and exploit their highly predictable energy demands to maximize overall profits. Our results show that a combination of the popular k-means, k-medoids, and DBSCAN clustering algorithm together with an autoregressive lag model can predict, reasonably accurately, the consumption of consumers.

2   Background: Power TAC

Power Trading Agent Competition (Power TAC) [1] is a feature-rich simulation suite available to researchers interested in working on the smart grid problem. Power TAC offers researchers the chance to explore many characteristics of future smart grids by allowing the creation of agents that operate in several different energy markets including the wholesale, the tariff, and the load-balancing markets. The goal of each agent is to acquire energy and sell it at a profit to its customers. This game was designed as a scenario for the annual Trading Agent Competition, a research competition with over a decade of history [2].

The wholesale market attempts to simulate existing energy markets such as the European or North American large energy producer. In Power TAC, the wholesale market is structured as a "day-ahead market," where the energy is a perishable good, which allows brokers to buy and sell quantities of energy for future delivery. Market structures like this exist across many different types of perishable goods, so finding effective, robust, automated bidding strategies for these markets is a significant research challenge.

The tariff market is where the major portion of energy purchased from the wholesale market is sold. Energy is sold to consumers (e.g., households, offices, etc.) through tariffs offered by the brokers. The overall goal of each broker is to maximize its profit (e.g., by selling energy in the tariff market at a higher price than the purchase price of the energy in the wholesale market). Because of this, the broker wishes to offer competitive tariffs that attract a large pool of consumers.

There are a variety of tariff options available for a broker to publish that allows for consumer and prosumer (e.g., consumers that have access to renewable energy such as solar panels) customers. For example, brokers may structure tariffs that are tiered where energy kept below a given threshold is priced low but the price increases when more is required. Another option is to price energy according to the time of the day or day of the week allowing brokers to sell energy at a higher price during peak hours. Power TAC also models customers with electric vehicles and allows brokers to issue specific tariffs that are specialized to their needs or controllable tariffs that can be interrupted if the energy cost is too great.

Simulated consumers can be broken down into two categories: elemental models and factored models. Elemental models define a consumer profile using granular characteristics such as the number of members in the household, the number of working days of the members, and the number of appliances in the household. However, defining elemental models in a simulation might not be efficient in modeling large-population consumers. To alleviate this limitation, factored models are introduced. Factored models can represent profiles of large consumer populations such as hospitals, campuses, apartment complexes, office buildings, etc.

The third major market is the load-balancing market, which functions as an energy equalizer in the Power TAC simulation. The current constraints of the simulation allow for an infinite supply of energy; that is, brokers will never be short on the energy promised to their customers. However, this requires that a broker that is unable to meet energy demands in other markets purchase the remaining energy in the load-balancing market at much higher than average prices. Because of this, it is in a broker's best interest to accurately predict the demand that it is required to fulfill.

3   Power TAC Consumer Demand Prediction

We now describe our approach to better understand if consumers have highly predictable consumption rates that can be exploited in a Power TAC agent. The high-level idea of our approach is as follows:

(1) We generated data for two sets of experiments. In the first smaller controlled experiment, we focused on household elemental models and vary the number of members in the household and the number of working days of the members. In the second larger uncontrolled experiment, we generated data for both factored and elemental models with their default Power TAC configurations.
(2) We used dimensionality reduction techniques to reduce the dimensions of the data points in order to reduce the training time.
(3) We clustered the data using three off-the-shelf clustering algorithms: k-means++ [3], k-medoids [4], and DBSCAN [5].
(4) We predicted the demand of the clusters using two off-the-shelf prediction methods [6]: an autoregressive lag model and a 2-week moving average predictor.

3.1   Data Generation

In Power TAC, a bootstrap file containing bootstrap data is generated as a unique seed for a new game. The bootstrap data is used as the beginning set of consumption patterns per consumer that a broker is allowed to analyze before the start of a game. The bootstrap file contains game parameters and about two weeks or 360 h of historical information (e.g., consumer data, weather data, etc.). Once the game begins, a simulation file containing game data is generated using a bootstrap file that began the game.

In this paper, we analyzed power consumption patterns using two experiments – a smaller controlled experiment with customized Power TAC configurations and a larger uncontrolled experiment with default Power TAC configurations. The first smaller and controlled experiment used 35 different configurations by manipulating two characteristics of a household consumer; the ranges of members in a household and working days were set between 1 and 5 and between 1 and 7, respectively. Note that a household consumer is represented virtually by two loads (a base load and controllable load) with four different tariff shifting properties (non-shifting, smart-shifting, regularly-shifting, and randomly-shifting). This resulted in eight different types of virtual consumers. For each of the 8 types of virtual consumers, there were 35 configurations with 100 distinct bootstrap files generated per configuration. Each game had about 58 days, or 1,399 h, of energy consumption. In total, this experiment generated 28,000 data points of consumption information. The second larger and uncontrolled experiment included all consumers in a default Power TAC game. A typical Power TAC game includes 28 elemental and factored consumers. This experiment produced 100 distinct default bootstrap files and associated game data for a total of 2,800 data points.

Once the data had been generated by the Power TAC games, both the bootstrap and simulation files were prepared for our clustering and prediction algorithms. A modified version of the Power TAC Log Tool[1] was used to perform the extraction of data into a comma separated format (CSV).

The CSV files were transformed into a matrix for bootstrap data $\mathbf{B}$ and game data $\mathbf{G}$. $\mathbf{B}$ contains about two weeks or 360 h of historical consumption data points per consumer:

$$\mathbf{B} = \begin{bmatrix} c_{1,0} & \cdots & c_{1,359} \\ \vdots & \vdots & \vdots \\ c_{N,0} & \cdots & c_{N,359} \end{bmatrix} \quad \text{(bootstrap consumption for } N \text{ consumers)}$$

where $c_{i,j}$ is the energy consumption of consumer i at time step j. Also, the bootstrap data for consumer i is indexed by $\mathbf{B}_i$.

---

[1] https://github.com/powertac/powertac-tools.

For each bootstrap file, there is an associated simulation file with game data $\mathbf{G}$, where the game data for consumer i is indexed by $\mathbf{G}_i$.

$$\mathbf{G} = \begin{bmatrix} c_{1,360} & \cdots & c_{1,1758} \\ \vdots & \vdots & \vdots \\ c_{N,360} & \cdots & c_{N,1758} \end{bmatrix} \qquad \text{(simulation consumption for } N \text{ consumers)}$$

All bootstrap and game data are paired and represented by matrix $\mathbf{D}$.

$$\mathbf{D} = \begin{bmatrix} \mathbf{B}_1 & \mathbf{G}_1 \\ \vdots & \vdots \\ \mathbf{B}_N & \mathbf{G}_N \end{bmatrix} \qquad \text{(paired consumption data)}$$

The rows in matrix $\mathbf{D}$ are then shuffled and split in half into a training dataset and a test dataset. Training bootstrap data is represented by $\mathbf{B}_{train}$ and training game data is represented by $\mathbf{G}_{train}$. Similarly, test bootstrap data is represented by $\mathbf{B}_{test}$ and test game data is represented by $\mathbf{G}_{test}$.

3.2   Dimensionality Reduction

Principal Component Analysis (PCA) is a technique that is widely used for applications such as dimensionality reduction, lossy data compression, feature extraction, and data visualization [7]. PCA can be defined as the orthogonal projection of a dataset onto a lower dimensional linear space, known as the principal subspace, such that the variance of the projected data is maximized [8]. Principal components were calculated using *Singular Value Decomposition* (SVD) on the covariance matrix of a training bootstrap dataset. SVD creates three matrices: left singular vectors represented as a matrix $\mathbf{U}$, where each column is a unit vector representing a principal component; a singular values matrix $\mathbf{V}$ that has the variance represented by each principal component; and a right singular matrix, which was ignored. Using the singular values $\mathbf{V}$, one can select P principal components from M dimensions to retain a certain percentage of the total variance R using the following equation:

$$R = \frac{\sum_{i=1}^{P} \mathbf{V}_i}{\sum_{i=1}^{M} \mathbf{V}_i} \tag{1}$$

Before applying PCA, the training bootstrap dataset $\mathbf{B}_{\text{train}}$ should be standardized. In other words, the training bootstrap dataset should be rescaled to have zero mean and unit variance using the z-score normalization in Eq. (2). Calculating the z-score requires the mean $\mathbb{E}[\mathbf{B}_{\text{train}}]$ and standard deviation $\sigma_{\mathbf{B}_{\text{train}}}$ [9].

$$\text{z-score} = \frac{\mathbf{B}_{\text{train}} - \mathbb{E}[\mathbf{B}_{\text{train}}]}{\sigma_{\mathbf{B}_{\text{train}}}} \tag{2}$$

Once $\mathbf{B}_{train}$ is standardized, SVD was applied to generate the principal components. The principal components were selected by solving Eq. (1) with $R \geq 0.9$, representing ninety-percent retained variance. Then, $\mathbf{B}_{train}$ was projected onto a lower dimensional subspace defined by the selected principal components.

3.3   Clustering

We now describe how we clustered the training bootstrap dataset $\mathbf{B}_{train}$. We used the following off-the-shelf clustering algorithms: k-means++, k-medoids, and DBSCAN. k-means++ is based on a well known partitioning based algorithm called k-means [3]. k-means++ adds a heuristic when initializing the cluster centroids used in k-means, then uses the original k-means algorithm. A known problem with the k-means algorithm is its weakness with the presence of noise, which can cause it to fail to converge [9]. Algorithm 1 presents the pseudocode of k-means++. In the k-means pseudocode, $D(x)$ denotes the shortest distance from a data point to the closest center we have already chosen [3].

Algorithm 1. k-means++ algorithm

1: **procedure** k-MEANS++(X, k)
2:      arbitrarily choose a data point from X as centroid $\mathcal{C}_1$.
3:      for each $i \in \{2, \dots, k\}$, choose a data point from X with probability $\frac{D(x)^2}{\sum_{x \in X} D(x)^2}$ as centroid $\mathcal{C}_i$.
4:      **repeat**
5:          For each $i \in \{1, \dots, k\}$, set the clusters $\mathcal{C}_i$ to be the set of points in X that are closer to c_i than those points that are to c_j for all $j \neq i$.
6:          For each $i \in \{1, \dots, k\}$, set c_i to be the center of mass of all points in $\mathcal{C}_i : c_i = \frac{1}{|\mathcal{C}_i|} \sum_{x \in \mathcal{C}_i} x$.
7:      **until** $\mathcal{C}$ no longer changes
8: **end procedure**

We also explored the partitioning-based algorithm *Partitioning Around Medoids* (PAM), a popular approximation algorithm of k-medoids designed by Kaufman *et al.* [4]. PAM uses two phases: a build phase, where initial k medoids are selected arbitrarily, and a swap phase, where the algorithm attempts to find a substitution for a current medoid with a non-medoid that reduces the within-cluster distance. PAM is shown in Algorithm 2 and in this paper is referred to as k-medoids.

Algorithm 2. k-medoids PAM algorithm

1: **procedure** k-MEDOIDS(X, k)
2:      arbitrarily choose k data points from X as the initial medoids.
3:      **repeat**
4:          for each non-medoid data point, (re)assign it to the cluster with the nearest medoid.
5:          select a non-medoid data point, swap with a current medoid that reduces the total within-cluster distance.
6:      **until** no change
7: **end procedure**

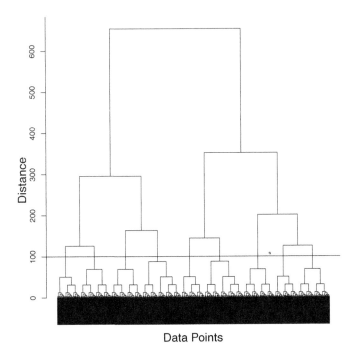

Fig. 1. Dendrogram of our dataset

To define the number of clusters k for k-means and k-medoids, we used two methods. The first is through hierarchical clustering, which creates a hierarchy that can be presented as a dendrogram. Figure 1 shows an example of a dendrogram. The dendrogram represents related data, and each successive relation creates the hierarchy. Therefore, it provides a visual tradeoff between the number of clusters and the size of each cluster. The larger the *distance* value for which a cut is made, the fewer the number of clusters and the larger the size of the clusters. For example, if we chose to cut at *distance* = 100, we will have $k = 9$ clusters, which are about equal size.

The second method to choose k is the elbow method, which is based on increasing the number of clusters to help reduce the sum of within-cluster distances of each data point to its cluster representative. We first select a small k and then slowly increment it until $\sqrt{\frac{N}{2}}$ [9], where N is the number of data points in the dataset. Figure 2 shows an example of the total within-cluster distance as a function of the number of clusters k for the k-means algorithm. The goal is to choose k at the "elbow," which is when increasing k does not significantly reduce the within-cluster distances. A reasonable "elbow" for our figure is at $k = 12$, which is indicated by an arrow.

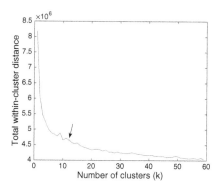

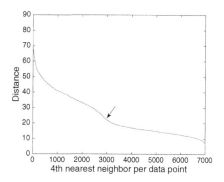

Fig. 2. Tradeoff between within-cluster distance and number of clusters k

Fig. 3. Tradeoff between distance ϵ and number of data points whose 4th nearest neighbor is within ϵ

Algorithm 3. DBSCAN algorithm

1: **procedure** DBSCAN(X, ϵ, δ)
2:     mark all data points in X as unvisited
3:     **repeat**
4:         randomly select an unvisited object x;
5:         mark x as visited;
6:         **if** the ϵ-neighborhood of x has at least δ points **then**
7:             create a new cluster C and add x to C;
8:             set Π as the set of points in the ϵ-neighborhood of x;
9:             **for** each point x' in Π **do**
10:                 **if** x' is unvisited **then**
11:                     mark x' as visited
12:                     **if** ϵ-neighborhood of x' has at least δ points **then**
13:                         add those points to Π
14:                     **end if**
15:                 **end if**
16:                 **if** x' is not yet a member of any cluster **then**
17:                     add x' to C
18:                 **end if**
19:             **end for**
20:             output C
21:         **else**
22:             mark x as noise
23:         **end if**
24:     **until** no object is unvisited
25: **end procedure**

Finally, *Density-Based Spatial Clustering of Applications with Noise* (DBSCAN) is a density-based clustering algorithm that uses a similarity heuristic to find groups that contain a defined minimum number of data points δ within a defined ϵ-distance. The algorithm selects a data point at random and greedily adds data points that reside within ϵ of the start data point. Once the minimum number of data points is obtained, it will attempt to expand the cluster by continuously clustering more data points within ϵ from any data point in the cluster. Algorithm 3 shows the pseudocode of DBSCAN.

DBSCAN is different from k-means and k-medoids in that it requires a minimum number of data points δ to define a cluster and a maximum distance ϵ to associate dense neighbors. These parameters can be estimated using methods devised by Ester et al. [5]. For example, in Fig. 3, $\delta = 4$ and $\epsilon = 22.49$.

3.4 Prediction

We now describe how we learn the parameters of prediction methods using the game training datasets $\mathbf{G}_{\text{train}}$. We used two off-the-shelf methods to predict the energy consumption of consumers. The first is a *moving average* with a two week or 336 h window defined by:

$$x_t = \mathbb{E}[x_{t-336} + \cdots + x_{t-1}] \tag{3}$$

which takes two weeks of the known consumption in the past and averaging for an estimated next consumption value, x_t, at consumption hour t.

The second is a variant of the *classical autoregressive model* (AR) [6] defined as:

$$x_t = w_1 \cdot x_{t-h} + w_0 \tag{4}$$

where x_t is the predicted future energy consumption; w_1 and w_0 are weights and the model uses the value from a fixed "lag" in the past x_{t-h}; where h is the lag value. This variant equation is used because it performed well with the periodic consumption behavior of the household consumers. To determine the best lag value, we attempted to find consumption patterns that may exist in the time series data. Using the equation:

$$\hat{\gamma}(h) = \frac{1}{m} \sum_{i=1}^{m-h} (x_{i+h} - \bar{x})(x_i - \bar{x}) \tag{5}$$

we found the sample autocovariance of the time series data [6], where h is the lag and m is the number of time steps in the time series. Then, using the equation below:

$$\hat{\rho}(h) = \frac{\hat{\gamma}(h)}{\hat{\gamma}(0)} \tag{6}$$

we can compute the sample autocorrelation with the sample autocovariance of the original time series shifted by h hours $\hat{\gamma}(h)$ over the sample autocovariance of the original time series $\hat{\gamma}(0)$. Figure 4 plots an example sample autocorrelation and one can visualize that there is a peak correlation at 24-hour intervals.

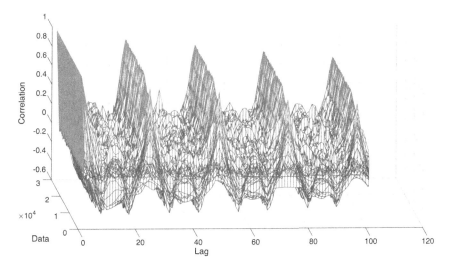

Fig. 4. Sample autocorrelation as a function of the lag

Therefore, the variant autoregression lag model in Eq. (4) uses the lag value of 24 simulated hours in the past.

4   Experimental Results

Recall that we have controlled and uncontrolled experiments. We ran our experiments with the three clustering algorithms described in Sect. 3.3 and used the two prediction algorithms described in Sect. 3.4 to understand the advantages of clustering. To evaluate our algorithms on the test datasets, we associate the test bootstrap data for each consumer to the most similar cluster and used the prediction model of that cluster to predict the consumption in the test game data associated to that test bootstrap data.

We used $k = \{6, 10\}$ for the controlled experiments of base and controllable loads defined by the hierarchical clustering and elbow methods for the k-means and k-medoids clustering algorithms, and we set $\delta = 4$ and $\epsilon = \{11.77, 16.34\}$ for base and controllable loads, respectively, for the DBSCAN algorithm. Similarly, we used $k = 2$ for the uncontrolled experiments of mixed both load types, and we set $\delta = 4$ and $\epsilon = 0.75$ for the mixed load types. We also used the lower and upper limits of k being 1 cluster and N clusters, a cluster per training bootstrap data point. This provided us an idea of a possible lower and upper bound for predictive error using partitioning based algorithms k-means and k-medoids.

Note, in our experiments we found k-means++ and k-medoids to have very similar results during prediction. Hence, we only discuss k-means++ because it had a slightly better result than k-medoids. We used the *Mean Squared Error* (MSE) to analyze the prediction error of both prediction methods. The MSE was computed using:

$$\text{MSE} = \frac{1}{n \cdot m} \sum_{i=1}^{n} \sum_{j=1}^{m} (\hat{c}_{i,j} - c_{i,j})^2 \tag{7}$$

where $\hat{c}_{i,j}$ is predicted energy consumption of consumer i during hour j, $c_{i,j}$ is the actual energy consumption of consumer i during hour j, n is the number of consumers in the test dataset, and m is the number of time steps in the time series.

In the smaller controlled experiments, Tables 1 and 2 tabulate the prediction MSE for k-means and DBSCAN, respectively. For both clustering algorithms, the autoregressive lag model outperformed the moving average for base loads. The reason is that it has a more predictable consumption pattern. On the other hand, the autoregressive lag model and the moving average model performed similarly for controllable loads. The reason is that the consumption of controllable loads is more erratic. A more granular view of per-cluster MSE is presented in Figs. 5, 6, 7 and 8.

Table 1. Controlled experiment prediction MSE with k-means++

k	Load type	Moving average	Autoregressive lag model
1	Base	1.4148e−05 kWh	5.8561e−06 kWh
6	Base	1.4148e−05 kWh	5.8545e−06 kWh
10	Base	1.4148e−05 kWh	5.8425e−06 kWh
7000	Base	1.4148e−05 kWh	5.9506e−06 kWh
1	Controllable	1.8476e−05 kWh	1.8691e−05 kWh
6	Controllable	1.8476e−05 kWh	1.8229e−05 kWh
10	Controllable	1.8476e−05 kWh	1.8201e−05 kWh
7000	Controllable	1.8476e−05 kWh	1.7819e−05 kWh

Table 2. Controlled experiment prediction MSE with DBSCAN

ϵ	Load type	Moving average	Autoregressive lag model
11.77	Base	1.4148e−05 kWh	5.8536e−06 kWh
16.34	Controllable	1.8476e−05 kWh	1.8685e−05 kWh

Table 3. Uncontrolled experiment prediction MSE with k-means++

k	Load type	Moving average	Autoregressive lag model
1	Both	1.9750 kWh	0.5161 kWh
2	Both	1.9750 kWh	0.4999 kWh
1400	Both	1.9750 kWh	0.4928 kWh

Table 4. Uncontrolled experiment prediction MSE with DBSCAN

ϵ	Load type	Moving average	Autoregressive lag model
0.75	Both	1.9750 kWh	0.4925 kWh

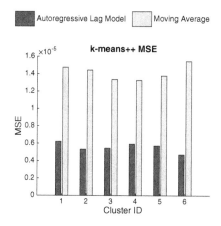

Fig. 5. Prediction MSE: Base load in controlled experiment with k-means++ $(k = 6)$

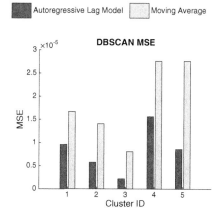

Fig. 6. Prediction MSE: Base load in controlled experiment with DBSCAN

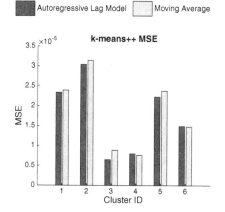

Fig. 7. Prediction MSE: Controllable load in controlled experiment with k-means++ $(k = 6)$

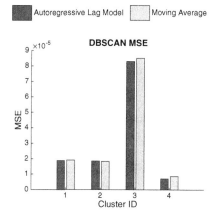

Fig. 8. Prediction MSE: Controllable load in controlled experiment with DBSCAN

In the larger uncontrolled experiments, Tables 3 and 4 tabulate the prediction MSE for k-means and DBSCAN, respectively. In both clustering algorithms, the autoregressive model also outperformed the moving average. The per-cluster view is presented in Figs. 9 and 10, where the y-axis is in log scale.

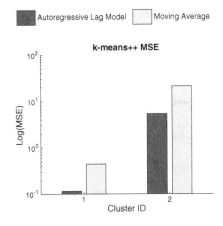

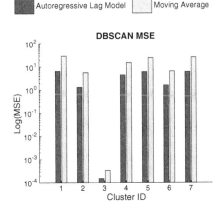

Fig. 9. Prediction MSE: Uncontrolled experiment with k-means++ $(k = 2)$

Fig. 10. Prediction MSE: Uncontrolled experiment with DBSCAN

5   Related Work

While there is a large number of Power TAC brokers that have competed in the past Power TAC competitions including AgentUDE15[2], Maxon15[3], Mertacor[4], COLDPower [10], TacTex14 [11], and CWIBroker14 [12], many of the approaches used by the brokers are not published publicly. As such, it is difficult to accurately identify the types of learning approaches taken by the agents. We describe below a sample of brokers that *do* publish their approaches and describe how we differ from them in our learning methods.

Parra Jr. and Kiekitveld [13] investigated the use of a large number of algorithms including linear regressions, decision trees, and k-nearest neighbors, all implemented on WEKA, to predict customer energy usage patterns in Power TAC. Their analysis used weather and energy consumption to perform analysis on different types of consumers in a Power TAC simulation. The main difference between their work and ours is that we used dimensionality reduction techniques as well as clustering prior to using prediction algorithms. Unfortunately, their results show that their techniques were not successful in finding a good model without a high error.

Urieli and Stone [11] also use learning algorithms in their TacTex14 broker, where they cluster consumers not by their energy usage but by their type. For example, office complex consumers are all clustered together independent of the number of occupants in the office complex, which is not known to the broker. They then use a locally weighted linear regression model to predict the energy consumption of those clustered consumers.

---

[2] http://www.powertac.org/wiki/index.php/AgentUDE15.

[3] http://www.powertac.org/wiki/index.php/Maxon15.

[4] http://www.powertac.org/wiki/index.php/Mertacor2015.

Finally, the approach taken by Wang *et al.* [14] is the most similar to ours, where they too cluster customers according to their energy usage using the k-means algorithm. However, their prediction methods are different, where they propose two methods. The first predicts the future consumption based on a weighted sum of the current consumption and the historical consumption and the second uses logistic regression based on historical usage data and weather data. As they also discussed the strategies of their broker for the other parts of the competition (i.e., the wholesale, imbalance, and tariff markets), they show empirical results on how their broker performed overall. As such, it is not known how effective their prediction algorithms are. In contrast, we show that our autoregressive lag model, which is significantly simpler and computationally efficient, has a small error and illustrate the underlying reason for this behavior, which is the high correlation in energy consumption in 24-hour intervals.

6 Conclusions and Future Work

In this preliminary study, we show that off-the-shelf clustering and prediction algorithms can be effectively used to classify consumers based on the predictability of their energy consumptions. We show that the k-means, k-medoids, and DBSCAN clustering algorithms coupled with an autoregressive lag model can predict energy consumption of consumers with reasonable accuracy. These results show that there is a strong temporal structure to the energy consumptions. Finally, we also plan to exploit the strong temporal correlations and integrate the clustering and prediction algorithms into an actual Power TAC broker agent for the competition.

Acknowledgments. This research is partially supported by NSF grants 1345232 and 1337884. The views and conclusions contained in this document are those of the authors and should not be interpreted as representing the official policies, either expressed or implied, of the sponsoring organizations, agencies, or the U.S. government.

References

1. Ketter, W., Peters, M., Collins, J.: Autonomous agents in future energy markets: the 2012 power trading agent competition. In: Proceedings of the AAAI Conference on Artificial Intelligence, pp. 1298–1304 (2013)
2. Wellman, M.P., Greenwald, A., Stone, P., Wurman, P.R.: The 2001 trading agent competition. Electron. Mark. **13**(1), 4–12 (2003)
3. Arthur, D., Vassilvitskii, S.: k-means++: the advantages of careful seeding. In: Proceedings of the ACM-SIAM Symposium on Discrete Algorithms, pp. 1027–1035 (2007)
4. Kaufman, L., Rousseeuw, P.: Clustering by Means of Medoids. North-Holland, Amsterdam (1987)
5. Ester, M., Kriegel, H.P., Sander, J., Xu, X.: A density-based algorithm for discovering clusters in large spatial databases with noise. In: Proceedings of the Conference on Knowledge Discovery and Data Mining, pp. 226–231 (1996)

6. Shumway, R., Stoffer, D.: Time Series Analysis and Its Applications: With R Examples. Springer Texts in Statistics. Springer, New York (2010)
7. Jolliffe, I.: Principal Component Analysis. Springer Series in Statistics. Springer, New York (2002)
8. Bishop, C.: Pattern Recognition and Machine Learning. Information Science and Statistics. Springer, New York (2013)
9. Han, J., Pei, J., Kamber, M.: Data Mining: Concepts and Techniques. The Morgan Kaufmann Series in Data Management Systems. Elsevier Science, Amsterdam (2011)
10. Serrano, J., de Cote, E.M., Rodríguez, A.Y.: Fixing energy tariff prices through reinforcement learning. In: Proceedings of the International Workshop on Agent based Complex Automated Negotiations (2015)
11. Urieli, D., Stone, P.: Tactex'13: a champion adaptive power trading agent. In: Proceedings of the International Conference on Autonomous Agents and Multi-agent Systems, pp. 1447–1448 (2014)
12. Liefers, B., Hoogland, J., La Poutré, H.: A successful broker agent for power TAC. In: Ceppi, S., David, E., Podobnik, V., Robu, V., Shehory, O., Stein, S., Vetsikas, I.A. (eds.) AMEC/TADA 2013–2014. LNBIP, vol. 187, pp. 99–113. Springer, Cham (2014). doi:10.1007/978-3-319-13218-1_8
13. Parra Jr., J., Kiekintveld, C.: Initial exploration of machine learning to predict customer demand in an energy market simulation. In: Proceedings of Workshop on Trading Agent Design and Analysis (2013)
14. Wang, X., Zhang, M., Ren, F., Ito, T.: GongBroker: a broker model for power trading in smart grid markets. In: International Conference on Web Intelligence and Intelligent Agent Technology, pp. 21–24 (2015)

A Genetic Algorithmic Approach
to Automated Auction Mechanism Design

Jinzhong Niu[1(✉)] and Simon Parsons[2]

[1] Guttman Community College, City University of New York, New York, USA
`jniu@gradcenter.cuny.edu`
[2] Department of Informatics, King's College London, London, UK
`simon.parsons@kcl.ac.uk`

Abstract. In this paper, we present a genetic algorithmic approach to automated auction mechanism design in the context of CAT games. This is a follow-up to one piece of our prior work in the domain, the reinforcement learning-based grey-box approach [14]. Our experiments show that given the same search space the grey-box approach is able to produce better auction mechanisms than the genetic algorithmic approach. The comparison can also shed light on the design and evaluation of similar search solutions to other domain problems.

Keywords: Genetic algorithms · Auction mechanism design · Double auctions · JCAT

1 Introduction

Auction mechanisms play an essential role in electronic commerce and in market-based control and resource allocation in computer systems. A major challenge in these domains is to design auction mechanisms that exhibit desired properties. Automated mechanism design aims to solve the problem of mechanism design in an automated fashion, typically by searching some space of possible mechanisms [3,5,20].

One piece of our prior work in this area is [14], in which we presented a what we called *grey-box* approach to automated design of double auctions in the context of TAC Market Design Competition (or the CAT Game) [15]. In the grey-box method, we use a tree model to represent the search space and associate an n-armed bandit problem solver [23, Chap. 2] to each node where multiple partial solutions to the same part of the problem exist. The n-armed bandit problem solvers select building blocks so that complete auction mechanisms can be constructed and evaluated in CAT games. The performance of each sampled auction mechanism in CAT games is then used as feedback for those building blocks in the mechanism. Our experiments showed that the grey-box search was able to produce better auction mechanisms than those manually crafted by participants in the first CAT Game.

As the tree model is independent of search methods, one follow-up question that arises naturally is: *How would the grey-box method perform compared to*

© Springer International Publishing AG 2017
S. Ceppi et al. (Eds.): AMEC/TADA 2015/2016, LNBIP 271, pp. 127–142, 2017.
DOI: 10.1007/978-3-319-54229-4_9

other search methods? Indeed, other search methods have been used in auto-mated auction mechanism design, though focusing on some particular aspects of an auction mechanism. For instance, Cliff [3] used a simple *genetic algorithm* (GA) to explore a continuum of probabilities of the next shout in an auction coming from a seller (or a buyer) and Phelps *et al.* [20] used *genetic program-ming* (GP) in acquiring pricing rules for double auctions. In this paper, aiming to answer the question raised above, we investigate how effective simple GAs are in automated auction mechanism design based on the same tree model (search space) as used in the grey-box search.

We first briefly review the grey-box method as well as the search space of dou-ble auctions in the domain of CAT games in Sect. 2. Due to the space constraint, detailed descriptions of these and other background information are not included here but can be found in [14].[1] Then Sect. 3 introduces the GA search method and Sect. 4 describes the GA experiments we carried out and interprets the experi-mental results. Section 5 further draws contrasts and makes connections between the grey-box method and various evolutionary computational solution concepts and techniques, and finally concludes.

2   A Brief Review of the Grey-Box Method

The grey-box method aimed to search for auction mechanisms in the domain of the CAT Game, an annual event held from 2007 through 2011 to foster research in electronic market mechanism design [15]. In a CAT game, participants each operate an electronic double-auction marketplace and the marketplaces compete against each other for market share and profit. Traders are software agents pro-vided by the game organizers. Each trader is armed with a marketplace selection strategy as well as a bidding strategy so that the trader can choose a marketplace to bid and trade in. A CAT game lasts a certain number of trading days. Each trader has a chance before the start of each day to select a marketplace to trade during that day and the marketplace can impose various charges on traders, admission, transaction fee, etc. At the end of the day, each marketplace receives a daily score between 0.0 and 1.0, a combination of three components with equal weights: share of trader population attracted, share of profit, and percentage of successful trade offers. The marketplace, or indeed the auction mechanism designed for the marketplace, that receives the highest cumulative score wins the game. The execution of CAT games is supported by JCAT [16], the open source software package that we also used to run the grey-box experiments [14] and the GA experiments in this paper.

In the grey-box method, the search space is modeled as a tree, which is depicted in Fig. 1, an abbreviated version of Fig. 1 in [14]. The tree model illus-trates how building blocks are selected and assembled level by level. There are (and) nodes, or nodes, and (leaf) nodes in the tree. An (and) node combines a set of building blocks, each represented by one of its child nodes, to form a compound building block. The root node, for example, is an (and) node assembling *policies*,

---

[1] [14] is available at http://www.sci.brooklyn.cuny.edu/~jniu/research/publications/.

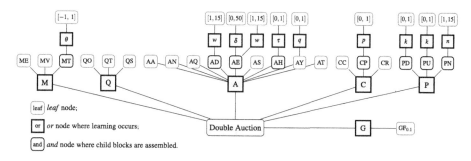

Fig. 1. The search space of double auctions modeled as a tree.

one on each major aspect of an auction mechanism (M for matching policy, Q for quoting policy, A for shout accepting policy, C for clearing condition, P for pricing policy, and G for charging policy),[2] to construct an auction mechanism. An **or** node represents the decision making of selecting a building block from the candidates represented by the child nodes of the **or** node. This selection occurs not only for those major aspects of an auction mechanism, i.e. M, Q, A, C, and P, but also for minor components, for example, a learning component for an adaptive policy (in a similar way to that in which Phelps *et al.* learned a trading strategy [19]), and for determining optimal values of parameters in a policy, like θ in MT and k in PD. A (leaf) node represents an atomic block that can either be for selection at its **or** parent node or be further assembled into a bigger block by its (and) parent node. A special type of (leaf) node in Fig. 1 is that with a label in the format of $[x, y]$. Such a $([x, y])$ node is a convenient representation of a set of (leaf) nodes that have a common parent—the parent of this special (leaf) node—and take values evenly distributed between x and y for the parameter labeled at the parent node. Note that both the grey-box search and the GA search to be introduced below consider only mechanisms using a fixed charging policy, denoted as $GF_{0.1}$. This simplification aims to avoid the slow exploration in the particular corner of the search space for charging policy, which involves significantly more parameters and variations than those for other policies.

The grey-box method combines techniques from reinforcement learning, e.g., solutions to n-armed bandit problem [23], and evolutionary computation, e.g., the use of a Hall of Fame [21]. The general idea of this algorithm is to use n-armed bandit learners to choose building blocks when needed so as to construct auction mechanisms based on the tree model in Fig. 1, to run CAT games to evaluate the constructed mechanisms, and to keep good mechanisms in a Hall of Fame.

In the tree model, **or** nodes contribute to the variety of auction mechanisms in the search space and are where exploitation and exploration occur. We model each **or** node as an n-armed bandit learner that chooses among

---

[2] A taxonomy of policies in this domain of auction mechanisms is described in detail in [17].

candidate blocks, and we use the simple softmax method [23, Sect. 2.3] to solve this learning problem.[3] Solving all the n-armed bandit learners in the tree will uniquely determine a configuration of an auction mechanism, which is exactly how an auction mechanism is sampled in the search space. The sampled mechanisms can then be put into a CAT game for evaluation. The game score of a sampled mechanism not only suggests how good the mechanism itself is, but is also an indicator of the performance of the building blocks that are used in the mechanism. If a building block is due to the selection of an n-armed bandit learner among the child nodes of the corresponding $\boxed{\text{or}}$ node, the game score can be readily used as the feedback for the building block. All such feedback to a building block cumulatively serves as the expected return, or what we call the *quality score*, of the building block. Thus, after a game completes, the quality scores of building blocks that are children of an $\boxed{\text{or}}$ node are updated, and so are the way how an auction mechanism is sampled in the space in later steps.

In each CAT game that is run to evaluate sampled mechanisms, we include four fixed, well known, mechanisms plus selected mechanisms that performed well at previous steps and are from the Hall of Fame. The fixed set of four mechanisms in every CAT game includes two clearing house (CH) mechanisms—CH_l and CH_h—and two continuous double auction (CDA) mechanisms—CDA_l and CDA_h—with one of each adopting the $GF_{0.1}$ policy, charging a *low* 10% fee on trader profit and the other charging a *high* 100% fee on trader profit. The CH and CDA mechanisms have been used in the real world for many years and were found competitive in the context of CAT games as well. The selection of Hall of Famers to compete in the CAT game is based on the same softmax method as used in choosing building blocks at each $\boxed{\text{or}}$ node. More details on how the Hall of Fame is maintained and Hall of Famers are selected can be found in [14].

3   The Genetic Algorithmic Approach

To compare the effectiveness of the grey-box approach with other search methods, we carried out a new set of experiments, searching the same solution space as used in the grey-box experiments based on the classic GA [6,11].

Encoding Individual Mechanisms. In these GA experiments, each individual auction mechanism is not represented by a binary string as in a typical GA, but by a tree structure, since each individual auction mechanism can be viewed as the result of making selections at the $\boxed{\text{or}}$ nodes in the tree model in Fig. 1 (it is exactly the case in the grey-box experiments), and thus be conveniently represented by the tree structure after the unselected branches of the $\boxed{\text{or}}$ nodes are cut off from the tree model. For example, the tree on the left side in Fig. 2 represents the auction mechanism $\mathsf{ME} + \mathsf{QS} + \mathsf{AD}_{w=3} + \mathsf{CP}_{p=0.4} + \mathsf{PU}_{k=0.7} + \mathsf{GF}_{0.1}$.

---

[3] The same solution was adopted in designing marketplace selection strategies for trading agents in CAT games. However the two scenarios may need different parameter values. The market selection scenario should favor choices that give a good profit—a cumulative measure—while here we require effective exploration to find a good mechanism in the foreseeable future—a one-time concern.

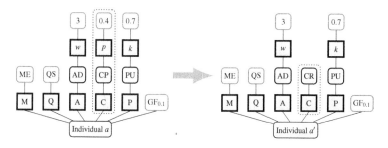

Fig. 2. An illustration of mutation in the GA, before mutation on the left side and after mutation on the right side. The replaced and replacing subtrees are both enclosed by dotted lines.

Mutation and Crossover. The tree-based encoding of an individual requires specialized mutation and crossover operators, due to the hierarchical construction and the different types of node in the tree. The diversity of auction mechanism individuals in the space originates from the [or] nodes, so mutation and crossover occur only at [or] nodes. To apply mutation to an individual, it is decided probabilistically, based on the *mutation rate*, at each [or] node in its tree-based encoding whether the node selects a different child node from the tree model. If yes, the original child (and its children if any) is replaced by the new child, which is uniformly selected from all the possible choices other than the original one. If the new child requires its own descendants, the whole subtree is added. Descendants that are [or] nodes make their selections randomly, in contrast to the way in the grey-box experiments where selections are made based on the quality scores of different choices. Figure 2 demonstrates an example of mutation on the auction mechanism given above, with the encoding before mutation on the left side and the encoding after mutation on the right side. The node C is the only place where mutation occurs and as a result the branch $CP_{p=0.4}$ is replaced by CR, both enclosed by dotted lines.

Crossover occurs between two auction mechanism individuals in the GA experiments, and only at [or] nodes similar to what happens with mutation. To perform crossover, indeed single-point crossover, between two individuals, the [or] nodes that appear in both trees and have different children respectively in the two trees are collected; then one of these collected nodes is selected randomly as the place to possibly perform the crossover; and finally it is decided probabilistically, based on the *crossover rate*, whether or not to perform the crossover, and if yes, the two appearances of the selected node in the two trees switch their children. Figure 3 demonstrates the crossover between two individuals—identified as a and b in the figure respectively. In Fig. 3, the [or] nodes at which crossover can be performed are marked with •, including M, Q, P, and p. A and C are excluded because their children in the two trees respectively are also identical, while θ and p in individual a and n in individual b are excluded because they appear in only one of the two trees. Random selection among the eligible nodes picks P. After a probabilistic test based on the crossover rate is taken and turns out to

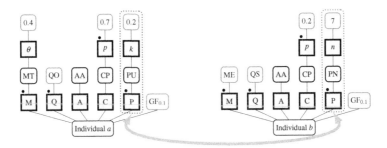

Fig. 3. An illustration of crossover in the GA between two individuals. The [or] nodes at which crossover can be performed are marked with • in the original encodings. P is selected to be the place where crossover is actually performed. The two subtrees with P as the root in the two trees are swapped and enclosed by dotted lines.

Algorithm 1. The GA-AMD algorithm.

```
Input: B, FM
Output: HOF

1  begin
2  │   HOF ← ∅
3  │   for g ← 1 to NUM_OF_GENERATIONS do
4  │   │   if g = 1 then
5  │   │   │   P ← Init-Population(B)
6  │   │   else
7  │   │   │   P ← Select-Population(P)
8  │   │   │   P ← Crossover-Population(B, P, r_co)
9  │   │   │   P ← Mutate-Population(B, P, r_m)
10 │   │   P ← Randomize(P)
11 │   │   for i ← 1 to |P|/NUM_OF_SAMPLES do
12 │   │   │   G ← Create-Game()
13 │   │   │   SM ← ∅
14 │   │   │   for m ← 1 to NUM_OF_SAMPLES do
15 │   │   │   │   SM ← SM ∪ {P[(i − 1) ∗ NUM_OF_SAMPLES + m]}
16 │   │   │   EM ← Select(HOF, NUM_OF_HOF_SAMPLES)
17 │   │   │   Run-Game(G, FM ∪ EM ∪ SM)
18 │   │   │   foreach M ∈ EM ∪ SM do
19 │   │   │   │   Update-Market-Score(M, Score(G, M))
20 │   │   │   │   if M ∉ HOF then
21 │   │   │   │   │   HOF ← HOF ∪ {M}
22 │   │   │   │   if CAPACITY_OF_HOF < |HOF| then
23 │   │   │   │   │   HOF ← HOF − {Worst-Market(HOF)}
```

---

be positive, the subtrees $PU_{k=0.2}$ in a and $PN_{n=7}$ in b, both enclosed by dotted lines in the figure, are swapped, producing two new individuals.

The GA Algorithm. The skeleton of the GA algorithm that is used in our GA experiments is given in Algorithm 1. These GA experiments adopt the same search space of auction mechanisms, the same set of fixed auction mechanisms to evaluate the fitnesses of the mechanisms sampled from the space, and the same idea of using a Hall of Fame to produce output as in the grey-box experiments.

Function. Init-Population.

Input: $\mathbb{B}$
Output: $\mathbb{P}$

1 **begin**
2 | $\mathbb{P} \leftarrow \varnothing$
3 | **for** $i \leftarrow 1$ **to** SIZE_OF_POPULATION **do**
4 | | $M \leftarrow$ Create-Market()
5 | | **for** $t \leftarrow 1$ **to** NUM_OF_POLICYTYPES **do**
6 | | | $B \leftarrow$ Select($\mathbb{B}_t$, 1)
7 | | | Add-Block(M, B)
8 | | $\mathbb{P} \leftarrow \mathbb{P} \cup \{M\}$

The initial generation of auction mechanism individuals in each GA experiment is created by randomly sampling the search space in exactly the same way as at the beginning of the grey-box search until a certain number (SIZE_OF_POPULATION) of individuals are obtained (see Function Init-Population). Each of the subsequent generations is created through steps of selection, crossover, and mutation from the previous generation. The selection step, shown in Function Select-Population, is a combination of *elitism* and *roulette wheel selection*. Elitism selection keeps a certain number of fitter individuals in the next generation based on the *elitism rate*, which determines the size of the portion of the population to be considered as elite individuals. Roulette wheel selection fills the rest of the population by probabilistically selecting among all the individuals in the previous generation. The probability of an individual being selected each time is proportional to its fitness, which is its average daily score in the game that it participated in during the evaluation of the previous generation. This type of selection has a known problem that individuals with low fitnesses have little chance to get selected when the fitnesses of individuals differ dramatically. Due to the scoring scheme of the CAT game, the typical daily score of an auction mechanism ranges from 0.1 to 0.5, so the usual drawback of roulette wheel selection does not have big impact in this GA algorithm. The individuals that are picked in roulette wheel selection then go through the crossover and mutation steps. In the crossover step, shown in Function Crossover-Population, individuals are paired up and each pair is probabilistically recombined (Crossover-Individuals() in Line 7) as we described above and illustrated in Fig. 3. In the mutation step, shown in Function Mutate-Population, individuals are each probabilistically mutated (Mutate-Individual() in Line 7) as we described above and illustrated in Fig. 2.

To evaluate a generation of auction mechanism individuals, all the mechanisms are randomly divided into groups. For each group, a CAT game is created, and, similar to those games in the grey-box experiments, this CAT game also includes a set of fixed market mechanisms and a certain number of mechanisms sampled from the Hall of Fame. After the game, the Hall of Fame is updated

---

Function. Select-Population.

> **Input:** $\mathbb{P}$
> **Output:** $\mathbb{P}'$

1 begin
2 | $\mathbb{P}' \leftarrow \varnothing$
3 | Descending-Sort ($\mathbb{P}$)
4 | $n_e \leftarrow$ SIZE_OF_POPULATION $* r_e$
5 | for $i \leftarrow 1$ to n_e do
6 | | $\mathbb{P}' \leftarrow \mathbb{P}' \cup \{\mathbb{P}[i]\}$
7 | $s \leftarrow 0$
8 | for $i \leftarrow 1$ to SIZE_OF_POPULATION do
9 | | $s \leftarrow s +$ Score ($\mathbb{P}[i]$)
10 | for $i \leftarrow n_e$ to SIZE_OF_POPULATION do
11 | | $k \leftarrow$ SIZE_OF_POPULATION
12 | | $r \leftarrow$ Uniform ($0,s$)
13 | | for $j \leftarrow 1$ to SIZE_OF_POPULATION do
14 | | | $r \leftarrow r -$ Score ($\mathbb{P}[i]$)
15 | | | if $r <= 0$ then
16 | | | | $k \leftarrow j$
17 | | | | break
18 | | $\mathbb{P}' \leftarrow \mathbb{P}' \cup \{\mathbb{P}[k]\}$

Function. Crossover-Population.

> **Input:** $\mathbb{B}$, $\mathbb{P}$
> **Output:** $\mathbb{P}'$

1 begin
2 | $\mathbb{P}' \leftarrow \varnothing$
3 | $n_e \leftarrow$ SIZE_OF_POPULATION $* r_e$
4 | for $i \leftarrow 1$ to n_e do
5 | | $\mathbb{P}' \leftarrow \mathbb{P}' \cup \{\mathbb{P}[i]\}$
6 | for $i \leftarrow 1$ to (SIZE_OF_POPULATION $- n_e$)/2 do
7 | | $\mathbb{P}' \leftarrow \mathbb{P}' \cup \{$Crossover-Individuals ($\mathbb{B}$, $\mathbb{P}[n_e + i * 2 - 1]$, $\mathbb{P}[n_e + i * 2], r_{co}$)$\}$

---

to incorporate the scores of the participating Hall of Famers and include new individuals from the generation that performed well. The way in which the Hall of Fame is manipulated is exactly the same as in the grey-box experiments. As mentioned above, the average daily scores of the individuals are used as their fitnesses in the selection step.

Function. Mutate-Population.

Input: $\mathbb{B}$, $\mathbb{P}$
Output: $\mathbb{P}'$

```
1  begin
2  |   P' ← ∅
3  |   n_e ← SIZE_OF_POPULATION * r_e
4  |   for i ← 1 to n_e do
5  |   |   P' ← P' ∪ {P[i]}
6  |   for i ← n_e to SIZE_OF_POPULATION do
7  |   |   P' ← P' ∪ {Mutate-Individual(B, P[i], r_m)}
```

---

4   Experimental Setup and Results

In the GA experiments, each game is configured to evaluate two individuals from the population as in the grey-box experiments. To compare the performances of the two approaches, the population consists of 20 individual auction mechanisms at each generation and evolves over 20 generations so that each GA experiment makes use of approximately the same number of CAT games in total (200) as in a grey-box experiment.[4] Some experiments based on the GA may have a population of thousands of individuals or even more. Our experiment cannot support a population of this size due to the high computational cost of running CAT games. The 20 generations and the population of 20 individuals are the result of balancing the two parameters under the constraint of the total number of CAT games to run. The elitism rate, r_e, the crossover rate, r_{co}, and the mutation rate, r_m, are set to be 0.1, 0.7, and 0.05, which are typical in the GA experiments reported in the literature [7,10]. Table 1 summarizes the values of parameters and inputs of Algorithm 1 in our GA experiments.

To provide a better comparison, we ran two sets of GA experiments, one without crossover and the other with it. Figures 4 and 5 show the daily scores of the four fixed auction mechanisms and the top Hall of Famers over time in two sets of GA experiments together with those from the grey-box experiments. All the results are averaged over 40 runs. Note that the x axes in the subfigures are *step* (as in the grey-box experiments), or equivalently the number of games that have been run, rather than *generation* that is common in plotting results from

---

[4] As the Hall of Fame is empty at the beginning of each GA experiment, the first CAT game includes four individuals from the population, so the total number of games to evaluate the 20 generations is actually 199. But the difference of one game can be negligible. In theory, it is possible to design the experiments to run exactly the same number of CAT games as long as NUM_OF_GENERATIONS × SIZE_OF_POPULATION = 402 and SIZE_OF_POPULATION%2 = 0, however the integer solutions—201 and 2, or 67 and 6—to this equation are not practical for the GA as SIZE_OF_POPULATION is too small.

Table 1. The values of parameters and inputs of the GA experiments.

Parameter	Value	Parameter	Value
NUM_OF_GENERATIONS	20	r_e	0.1
SIZE_OF_POPULATION	20	r_{co}	0.7
NUM_OF_SAMPLES	2	r_m	0.05
NUM_OF_HOF_SAMPLES	2	τ^{a}	0.3
CAPACITY_OF_HOF	10	α^{a}	1
NUM_OF_POLICYTYPES	5	FM	$\{CH_l,\ CH_h,\ CDA_l,\ CDA_h\}$

[a] τ and α are parameters in the softmax solver used by the Select(HOF, NUM_OF_HOF_SAMPLES) function, which is exactly the same in the grey-box search in [14].

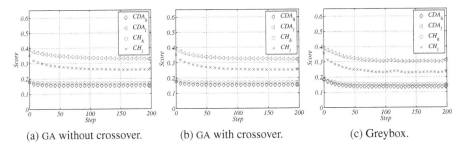

(a) GA without crossover.   (b) GA with crossover.   (c) Greybox.

Fig. 4. Scores of the four fixed auction mechanisms in the two sets of GA experiments, one without crossover and the other with crossover, and those in the first set of grey-box experiments, each averaged over 40 runs. (c) is originally Fig. 2(a) in [14].

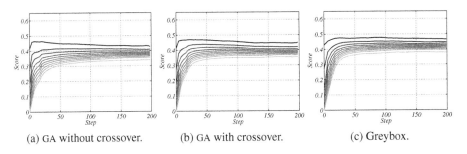

(a) GA without crossover.   (b) GA with crossover.   (c) Greybox.

Fig. 5. Scores of the Hall of Famers in the two sets of GA experiments, one without crossover and the other with crossover, and those in the first set of grey-box experiments, each averaged over 40 runs. (c) is originally Fig. 2(b) in [14].

GA experiments. This presentation makes it easier to compare the results of the GA experiments with those from the grey-box experiments.

Plots in Fig. 4a and b, from the two sets of GA experiments respectively, exhibit the similar pattern as those in Fig. 4c, which are from the grey-box experiments. The scores of the four fixed auction mechanisms are at approximately the same

Table 2. The average daily scores of the best fixed auction mechanism and the best Hall of Famers in the CAT games at the end of the GA experiments, and those at the end of the first set of grey-box experiments. In parentheses are the standard deviations. The scores in the second row are significantly different from each other at the 95% confidence level and so are those in the third row.

Auction mechanism	GA without crossover	GA with crossover	Greybox[a]
Best fixed mechanism (CDA_l)	0.3260 (0.0224)	0.3203 (0.0230)	0.3101 (0.0659)
Best Hall of Famers	0.4275 (0.0233)	0.4496 (0.0340)	0.4652 (0.0210)
Worst Hall of Famers	0.3389 (0.0255)	0.3554 (0.0192)	0.3790 (0.0219)

[a]The values in this column are originally from [14].

positions across the three cases and then all descend until they settle down around certain values. These auction mechanisms ended up with the same relative ranking positions in these different cases. The difference is that in the end each of the four auction mechanisms settles down with different scores in different cases, the highest in the GA without crossover and the lowest in the grey-box search. This suggests that the auction mechanisms explored in the grey-box experiments are overall the most competitive while those explored in the GA experiments without crossover are the least competitive. This further indicates that the grey-box search is more effective than both versions of the GA search and as expected crossover plays an important role in the GA. Figure 5 indicates exactly the same. Figure 5a and b, from the two sets of GA experiments respectively, show that the scores of the Hall of Famers increase dramatically at the beginning of the experiments and flatten out at the end around certain positions that are lower than those in Fig. 5c.

Table 2 lists respectively the average scores of the best fixed auction mechanism, and the best and worst Hall of Famers at the end of the two versions of GA experiments and the grey-box experiments. At the 95% confidence level, any two values in the second row or any two values in the third row are significantly different from each other. That is to say that the Hall of Famers produced by the grey-box experiments are significantly better than those produced by the GA experiments. The scores of the best fixed auction mechanism in the three cases agree to this finding, but they are not significantly different. This less significance is possibly due to the fact that the CAT game is not a zero-sum game, since the transaction success rate of a mechanism in a CAT game is relatively independent from the performance of its opponents, which counts for one third of its total score. Thus the gain of a stronger auction mechanism does not necessarily mean the same amount of loss of the losing mechanism given that all the rest of the configuration remains the same.[5]

To further investigate the effectiveness of the grey-box search in comparison with the GA search, we ran additional experiments to let the Hall of Famers produced by the grey-box experiments and the two sets of GA experiments compete against each other directly. Each of the three sets of experiments produced dozens

---

[5] One example is that the scores of CDA_h and CH_h flatten out much earlier during the experiments than the scores of CDA_l and CH_l in all the three cases in Fig. 4.

Table 3. The average daily scores of the Hall of Famers produced by the GA experiments and the first set of grey-box experiments in direct competition in CAT games. In parentheses are the standard deviations. The scores are significantly different from each other at the 95% confidence level.

GA without crossover	GA with crossover	Greybox
0.3481 (0.0201)	0.3643 (0.0188)	0.4155 (0.0291)

of the Hall of Famers (69 from the grey-box experiments, 45 from the GA experiments without crossover, and 71 from the GA experiments with crossover).[6] We ran 100 CAT games with eight auction mechanisms in each game, which includes two of the fixed auction mechanisms, CDA_l and CH_l, and two randomly selected auction mechanisms from each of the three set of Hall of Famers. Other than this, the CAT games are configured exactly the same as we did in the grey-box experiments and the GA experiments. Table 3 lists the average daily scores of the three set of auction mechanisms. At the 95% confidence level, the scores of the Hall of Famers from the grey-box experiments are significantly higher than those from either set of the GA experiments. We showed in [14] that the grey-box search was able to find mechanisms that are stronger than well known double auction mechanisms when competing directly in CAT games and are better than mechanisms that were reported in the literature in term of various economic properties and confirmed that the grey-box search can consistently produce similar results when, for example, the capacity of the Hall of Fame varies. This work provides one more piece of evidence for the superiority of the grey-box approach by comparing the results of the grey-box experiments and those of experiments based on different versions of the classic GA.[7]

5   Discussions, Future Work, and Summary

In this section, we draw contrasts and make connections between the grey-box approach and evolutionary computational approaches including GAs, GPs, and their variants. First, we can compare our grey-box approach to prior work on automated auction mechanism and trading strategy acquisition based on simple GAs, including Cliff *et al.* [4] and Phelps *et al.* [19] as well as ours reported here. A simple GA, or SGA, evolves genomes, or binary strings, using selection, crossover, and mutation operators, while the grey-box approach evolves a vector of quality scores, each for a pre-defined building block, and explores the solution space by biasing those building blocks that lead to better solutions. A SGA

---

[6] A Hall of Famer may come from more than one run of the same experiment.

[7] We actually ran additional sets of GA experiments with crossover, each with a different crossover rate, 0.1, 0.4, or 1.0, in contrast to 0.7 that was used in the GA experiments described in the text. It turned out that the GA experiments using 0.7 produced the best results and hence only the results of this set of experiments were included in the text in the comparison against those of the grey-box experiments.

maintains a set of sampling points in the solution space and tries to arrive at points of higher fitness that are accessible by applying the operators, while the grey-box approach tends to view the solution space along multiple dimensions simultaneously, maintain a hyperplane that divides the solution space into slices, adjust the sizes of the slices, and identify and explore more in those of high fitness.

A popular theory that intends to explain the effectiveness of SGAs in many optimization domains is the *building block hypothesis*, or BBH [11,13]. The BBH argues that certain building blocks of low *order* and low *defining length*, called *schemata*,[8] in the genome play a substantial role in constructing genomes of high fitness. The operators of SGAs enable the process to concentrate sampling in subspaces that are identified by these schemata and further in the common areas of these subspaces that have increasing fitness through mixing different schemata. Based on this argument, Thierens and Goldberg [24] indicated that computational expense grows exponentially with the difficulty of the problem, in terms of the number of schemata and the orders of schemata. Efforts have been made to address this issue with SGAs and improvements to SGAs were proposed by either explicitly exploring to identify schemata or implicitly using special operators to avoid breaking possible schemata in the sampled solutions [2,12]. The grey-box approach has similarities to these advanced GAs[9] since the grey-box approach explicitly considers the building blocks for auction mechanisms and biases its search towards the corners in the search space that correspond to high quality blocks.

The idea of the grey-box approach is in particular similar to that of the *compact* GA , or CGA, which was introduced by Harik *et al.* [9]. A CGA represents the population as a probability vector, rather than as a set of binary strings, where the ith component of the probability vector gives the probability that the ith bit of an individual's genome is 1. Compared with SGAs, CGAs have compact representations and work well in practice. The view of evolving a vector of real-valued quality scores in our grey-box approach (and the use of a real-valued array of probabilities in the CGA) should be distinguished from *real-coded genetic algorithms* [8]. In the former case, the vector of real numbers maintains a global view of the conceived fitness landscape of the problem domain or can be considered as a summary of the whole population of individuals if such a population exists, while in the latter case, a vector of real-coded values uniquely determines an individual in the solution domain and one only sees a global view of the fitness landscape when considering all the individuals and their fitness values.

The tree-based model of auction mechanisms in our work bears similarities on the surface to the tree structures in GP, though the tree structure in the

---

[8] A schemata is typically represented in the form, for example, ****01*1***, where * can match 0 or 1. The defining length of a schemata is the maximal distance between bits with deterministic values, and the order of a schemata is the number of bits with deterministic values.

[9] These are sometimes called *competent genetic algorithms*.

former case represents the whole search space and quality scores of building blocks reflect the fitness landscape of the space while tree structures in the latter each represent one individual in the search space and contains no information themselves about how fit they are.

Another topic in evolutionary computation that is related to grey-box search is the problem of early convergence to suboptimal solutions. In the grey-box experiments, parameters of the softmax exploration method in the n-armed bandit problem solvers were carefully set up so that sampling in the search space starts with near randomness and gradually biases modestly towards areas that are fitter than others. Techniques employed in evolutionary computation to address the problem of premature convergence, including *fitness sharing, crowding*, and mutation with high rate, are based on similar considerations [11,22]. For example, fitness sharing lowers the fitness of an individual by a certain amount, which basically reflects the number of similar individuals in the population, so that similar individuals with high fitness will not be able to prevail in the next generation. In so doing, the whole population could remain diverse, approaching multiple optima in the space in parallel if applicable. In fact, as a piece of future work, these techniques can be incorporated into our GA experiments to see if the experiments can produce similar or even better results than the grey-box experiments.

Finally, our grey-box approach should be distinguished from Ronald A. Fisher's work in *population genetics* [1]. Fisher, in his research on Mendelian inheritance, assumed that—as paraphrased by Sewall Wright[10]—

> ...each gene is assigned a constant value, measuring its contribution to the character of the individual (here fitness) in such a way that the sum of the contributions of all genes will equal as closely as possible the actual measures of the character in the individuals of the population.

Wright disagreed with the view of the linear additive contribution of genes and insisted that, based on his experimental work, genes favorable in one combination are extremely likely to be unfavorable in another. Our grey-box approach is not based on Fisher's argument, although the vector of quality scores undoubtedly converges and better auction policies would obtain higher scores if the argument holds in the case of auction mechanisms. When the argument does not hold, which we believe is the case based on our experience with the experiments using CAT games, our grey-box approach may help to obtain insights on which auction policies can make better or bad combinations, and on how to design new, better policies that work better with others.

To summarize, the main contribution of this work is that we apply two different search methods in the same solution space and make a fair comparison between the two approaches, the first piece as we are aware of in the context of experimental auction mechanism design. As the search methods are domain independent, considerations in designing our algorithms and experiments and

---

[10] A co-founder of the field with Fisher and a critic of Fisher's approach.

the discussions above can shed light on the design and evaluation of similar search solutions to other domain problems.[11]

Acknowledgments. Support for this work was provided by PSC-CUNY Award 68800-00 46, jointly funded by the Professional Staff Congress and the City University of New York. The authors acknowledge resources from the computational facility at the CUNY High Performance Computing Center, which is operated by the College of Staten Island and funded, in part, by grants from the City of New York, State of New York, CUNY Research Foundation, and National Science Foundation Grants CNS-0958379, CNS-0855217 and ACI 1126113.

References

1. Burjorjee, K.M.: The fundamental problem with the building block hypothesis. CoRR, abs/0810.3356 (2008)
2. Chen, Y.-P., Goldberg, D.E.: Convergence time for the linkage learning genetic algorithm. Evol. Comput. **13**(3), 279–302 (2005)
3. Cliff, D.: Evolution of market mechanism through a continuous space of auction-types. Technical report HPL-2001-326, Hewlett-Packard Research Laboratories, Bristol, December 2001
4. Cliff, D.: Explorations in evolutionary design of online auction market mechanisms. Technical report HPL-2003-80, Hewlett-Packard Research Laboratories, Bristol, July 2003
5. Conitzer, V., Sandholm, T.: Automated mechanism design for a self-interested designer. In: Proceedings of the Fourth ACM Conference on Electronic commerce (EC 2003), pp. 232–233. ACM, New York (2003)
6. Forrest, S.: Genetic algorithms: principles of adaptation applied to computation. Science **261**, 872–878 (1993)
7. Goldberg, D.E.: Genetic Algorithms in Search, Optimization and Machine Learning. Addison-Wesley Longman Publishing Co. Inc., Boston (1989)
8. Goldberg, D.E.: Real-coded genetic algorithms, virtual alphabets, and blocking. Complex Syst. **5**, 139–167 (1990)
9. Harik, G.R., Lobo, F.G., Goldberg, D.E.: The compact genetic algorithm. IEEE Trans. Evol. Comput. **3**, 523–528 (1999)
10. Haupt, R.L., Haupt, S.E.: Practical Genetic Algorithms, 2nd edn. Wiley, New York (2004)
11. Holland, J.H.: Adaptation in natural and artificial systems. The University of Michigan Press, Ann Arbor (1975). Reprinted by MIT Press, Cambridge (1992)
12. Li, Z., Goodman, E.D.: Exploring building blocks through crossover. In: Kang, L., Cai, Z., Yan, X., Liu, Y. (eds.) ISICA 2008. LNCS, vol. 5370, pp. 707–714. Springer, Heidelberg (2008). doi:10.1007/978-3-540-92137-0_77
13. Mitchell, M., Forrest, S., Holland, J.H.: The royal road for genetic algorithms: fitness landscapes and GA performance. In: Varela, F.V., Bourgine, P. (eds.) Toward a Practice of Autonomous Systems: First European Conference on Artificial Life, pp. 245–254. MIT Press, Cambridge (1991)

---

[11] Similar comparisons between reinforcement learning-based approaches and evolutionary computational approaches do exist in other domains. Further discussions of these comparisons are however beyond the scope of this paper and are not possible due to the space constraint.

14. Niu, J., Cai, K., Parsons, S.: A grey-box approach to automated mechanism design. In: David, E., Larson, K., Rogers, A., Shehory, O., Stein, S. (eds.) AMEC/TADA-2010. LNBIP, vol. 118, pp. 47–61. Springer, Heidelberg (2012). doi:10.1007/978-3-642-34200-4_4

15. Niu, J., Cai, K., Parsons, S., Gerding, E., McBurney, P.: Characterizing effective auction mechanisms: insights from the 2007 TAC Mechanism Design Competition. In: Padgham et al. [18], pp. 1079–1086

16. Niu, J., Cai, K., Parsons, S., Gerding, E., McBurney, P., Moyaux, T., Phelps, S., Shield, D.: JCAT: a platform for the TAC market design competition. In: Padgham et al. [18], pp. 1649–1650. Demo Paper

17. Niu, J., Cai, K., Parsons, S., McBurney, P., Gerding, E.: What the 2007 TAC market design game tells us about effective auction mechanisms. J. Auton. Agents Multiagent Syst. **21**(2), 172–203 (2010)

18. Padgham, L., Parkes, D.C., Müller, J.P., Parsons, S. (eds.): 7th International Joint Conference on Autonomous Agents and Multiagent Systems (AAMAS 2008), IFAAMAS, Estoril, 12–16 May 2008

19. Phelps, S., Marcinkiewicz, M., Parsons, S., McBurney, P.: A novel method for automatic strategy acquisition in n-player non-zero-sum games. In: Proceedings of the Fifth International Joint Conference on Autonomous Agents and Multi-agent Systems (AAMAS 2006), pp. 705–712. ACM Press, New York (2006)

20. Phelps, S., Parsons, S., Sklar, E., McBurney, P.: Using genetic programming to optimise pricing rules for a double auction market. In: Proceedings of the Workshop on Agents for Electronic Commerce, Pittsburgh (2003)

21. Rosin, C.D.: Coevolutionary search among adversaries. Ph.D. thesis, University of California, San Diego (1997)

22. Sareni, B., Krähenbühl, L.: Fitness sharing and niching methods revisited. IEEE Trans. Evol. Comput. **2**(3), 97–106 (1998)

23. Sutton, R.S., Barto, A.G.: Reinforcement Learning: An Introduction. MIT Press, Cambridge (1998)

24. Thierens, D., Goldberg, D.E.: Mixing in genetic algorithms. In: Proceedings of the Fifth International Conference on Genetic Algorithms, San Francisco, pp. 38–47. Morgan Kaufmann Publishers Inc. (1993)

Autonomous Power Trading Approaches
of a Winner Broker

Serkan Özdemir[(✉)] and Rainer Unland

DAWIS, University of Duisburg-Essen, Schützenbahn 70, 45127 Essen, Germany
{serkan.oezdemir,rainer.unland}@icb.uni-due.de

Abstract. The future smart grid will bring new actors such as local producers, storage capacities and interruptible consumers to the existing electricity grid along with the challenge of sustainability. Intermediary power actors, i.e., brokers, will take the burden of financial management, during the integration of these customers. This paper describes the mathematical modelling, formalization and the design of decision making systems of a winner broker agent, AgentUDE14, which competed in Power Trading Agent Competition 2014 Final (Power TAC). In this work, we divide the main trading problem into sub problems and then formalize and solve them individually to reduce the mathematical complexity. In the wholesale market, we propose a dynamic programming approach whereas our retailer algorithm uses an aggressive tariff publication policy, which exploits tariff fees, such as early withdrawal penalty and bonus payment. We show the results that AgentUDE14 is a successful agent in many metrics, analyzing the tournament data from Power TAC 2014 Finals.

Keywords: Autonomous trading · Learning agents · Smart grid · Multi-agent

1 Introduction

Smart grids have turned into an exciting area for researchers and business. New power actors with exciting concepts and ideas constantly join the market and reshape its structure and course of actions. Besides, some governments have already declared their energy transition policies, e.g. Germany with its Energiewende concept. Within Energiewende, Germany will permanently shut down all its 17 nuclear power plants by the end of 2022 [9]. Meanwhile, fossil fuel based electricity production is likely to be replaced by massive renewable energy production capabilities [5, 16].

Power TAC is an open source, smart grid simulation platform, which extends agent-based computational economics and brings competitive electricity markets and broker-centric smart grid design into a unique multi-agent simulation platform. In Power TAC, agents act as retail brokers in a local power distribution region, purchasing power from a wholesale market as well as from local sources, such as homes and businesses with solar panels, and selling power to local customers and into the wholesale market. Retail brokers must solve a supply-chain problem in which the product is infinitely perishable, and supply and demand must be exactly balanced always [1, 2].

We take the broker's trading problem as individual trading problems for each of the electricity market that AgentUDE involves. In the wholesale market, we design a responsive

© Springer International Publishing AG 2017
S. Ceppi et al. (Eds.): AMEC/TADA 2015/2016, LNBIP 271, pp. 143–156, 2017.
DOI: 10.1007/978-3-319-54229-4_10

hybrid model for price forecasting, using dynamic programming techniques and Markov Decision Process. We use a belief function to adjust predicted values, derived from exponentially smoothed values of market clearing prices (MCP). In the retail market, AgentUDE focuses on the manipulation of tariff parameters to earn more from customers' penalties. This was a quite new strategy for the Power TAC 2014 Final games and resulted in decent amount of profit. Detailed investigations into the effects of the AgentUDE14 business strategies showed that AgentUDE14 achieved a serious portion of its profit through Early Withdrawal Penalties (EWP) and Bonus Payments (BP).

Thanks to its overall business strategy and, especially, its aggressive tariff strategy, AgentUDE14 won the Power TAC 2014 finals despite being the newest kid on the competition. This paper discusses and analyzes the trading performance of AgentUDE, using the data from an international competition.

2   Related Work

Smart grid multi-agent systems were applied in many complex applications, using open-source agent platforms, such as JADE [17], Agent.GUI [18], ZEUS [19] and JACK [14]. The leading application area is micro grids [16], especially in resource scheduling and cost optimizations.

In the field of competitive markets, Power TAC is one of the leading frameworks, which enables competitive benchmarking in many dimensions (see Sect. 3). One of the most cited paper was published by the TacTex team, the winner of the Power TAC 2013 competition. TacTex formalizes broker's trading problem as Markov Decision Process to abstract the mathematical modelling of the problem. On the other side, it optimizes its customer tariffs through an algorithm, called "Lookahead-policy for Autonomous Time- constrained Trading of Electricity" [3].

Another publication is from the AstonTAC team. It focuses on the trading in the wholesale market using Markov Decision Processes for the formalization and Non-Homogeneous Hidden Markov Models to deal with future trends [4].

The last broker related paper was published by the cwiBroker team. They took the second place in Power TAC 2014 and 2015 competitions, utilizing a trading technique that uses the equilibrium in continuous markets [8].

One of the most comprehensive research papers is published by [13]. The paper reviews reinforcement learning approaches from the decision-support perspective in smart electricity markets. Besides this work, many existing papers have confirmed that MDP is one of the proven ways of handling time-sequential problems [3, 4, 10].

In our wholesale market module, we use a hybrid electricity price forecasting approach, using several reinforcement learning methods [6, 7] and MDP, which is a modified version of MDP design, introduced by [3]. We use an exponential smoothing operator along with a belief function which is proposed by [10].

3   The Power Trading Agent Competition

Smart grid simulation platforms have become more and more popular as liberalized electricity markets and decentralized power generation challenge the volatile balance of electricity demand and supply. Simulations aim to address these challenges to create a vision of sustainable smart grid ecosystems. Power TAC is a data driven platform that brings electricity brokers and smart market concepts together. Figure 1 depicts the high-level structure of Power TAC.

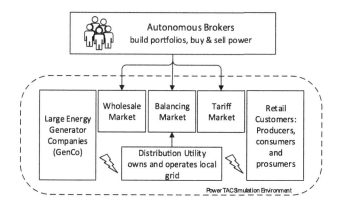

Fig. 1. Major elements of the Power TAC scenario.

In this Power TAC scenario, broker agents remotely trade in simulated electricity markets to increase their profits. Brokers are challenged to match their supply and demand by means of trading in retail and wholesale electricity markets. The broker that achieves the highest overall profit over all runs of the finals is the winner of the competition. The 2014 version of Power TAC is best described in [1, 2].

The platform integrates various smart grid actors such as customer models, retail markets, wholesale markets, a distribution utility (DU), and autonomous electricity brokers within a single distribution area, currently a city. The main actors within Power TAC are now described in more detail:

– *Electricity Brokers* are business entities that trade as intermediaries to attain good results for their own accounts. They try to attract customers by publishing electricity tariffs in the retail market, i.e. tariff market. The so-called DU closely monitors all brokers in order to evaluate their demand and supply behavior. Imbalanced energy is subject to penalties, which may result in a profit loss. Therefore, brokers must trade in the Wholesale Market in order to cover their net demand.
– *Customers* are small and medium sized consumers and producers such as households or small companies but also electric vehicles. They interact with the environment through electricity tariffs. An aggregator may act on behalf of a group of customers, e.g. parking lots. They can buy or sell electricity, subscribing to appropriate tariffs which are defined in power type, time and money domains.

- *Generator Companies* (GenCo) represent the large power generators or consumers. These actors trade in the Wholesale Market and manage their commitments for the next few hours up to several weeks.
- *The Distribution Utility* (DU) operates the grid and manages the imbalances in real-time. It is assumed that the distribution utility owns the physical infrastructure. It charges brokers for their net distributed energy per kWh, known as distribution fee. It also manages imbalances and charges brokers for their imbalanced energy, called balancing fee.

A Power TAC tournament consists of a set of games, grouped in different game sizes, e.g. with three, five and seven players. The game size indicates the number of competing broker agents. In addition to competing teams, a built-in default broker is always included in games, i.e. it means two brokers and the default broker compete in a three-player game. The default broker is the only retailer for all customers at the beginning of each game, during the so-called bootstrap period. During this period, activity logs are stored to give first relevant, necessary information to the competing brokers. Once all brokers are permitted to join in, they are meant to compete for customers.

After all games have ended, profits are summed up and normalized on the basis of each individual game size. The broker with the highest aggregated profit is the winner.

A Power TAC game takes up to a random time slot count, starting from one, cf. Fig. 2 for the activities in a time slot. In the paper, we refer to the current time slot t and time distance δ to future auction hour (see Table 1 to read more about the notation):

1. Brokers receive signals at every timeslot, like current cash balance, cleared prices of timeslots $cp_t, cp_{t+1}, \ldots, cp_{t+23}$, and published tariffs by all brokers.
2. Brokers ought to submit orders to the Wholesale Market in order to procure an energy amount E^f, which must be predicted prior to delivery hours.
3. At the end of a timeslot, a broker's cash account is updated based on the profit

$$\sum_i T_i E_i^t - \sum_j cp_t^j E_t^j.$$ T_i is the tariff price of the energy unit (kWh) and E_i^t denotes the distributed energy amount at timeslot t, under tariff i. $\sum_j^{24} cp_t^j E_t^j$ denotes the cost of procuring the energy amount E_t^j at timeslot t. Imbalance penalty $\left(\sum_i E_i^t - \sum_j^{24} E_t^j \right) P$ is debited from the broker's cash account, using the balancing fee of P (per unit).

4. In addition to the tariff value, tariff activities like customer subscriptions or withdrawals are subject to payment due to bonuses or early withdrawal penalty parameters of the according tariffs.
5. Brokers pay a distribution fee for each energy unit if power is to be distributed/transferred or if local power is traded in the Wholesale Market. The fee is exempted in case of market brokerage. Another exemption applies if local production (energy from customers) is consumed in the same area (by customers).
6. At the end of the timeslot, all brokers get all necessary information, like information about net distribution, imbalance volumes, as well as tariff transactions.

7. Customers initially subscribed to the tariff of the default broker. After all other brokers joined in they evaluate at each timeslot the existing tariffs based on their energy profile. For more details, [11] presents a comprehensive explanation of the consumption model.

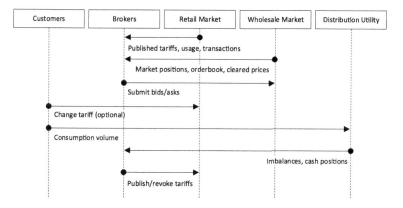

Fig. 2. Timeslot sequence diagram from a brokers' point of view.

Table 1. Summary of all relevant notations.

Symbol	Definition
t	Current time slot t, i.e., order hour
δ	Time slot proximity. Time slot distance of t to the power delivery hour
$cp_{t,\delta}$	MCP of the wholesale market ordered at t with δ
$\tilde{cp}_{t,\delta}$	Price-driven forecasted price at t with δ
EWP	Early withdrawal penalty, which is paid from customers to brokers
BP	Bonus payment is paid to customers, in case of a successful tariff subscription
C	Number of customers with respected attribute, e.g. subscriber, total customers
D_t	Distribution volume at timeslot t
$N_{t,f}$	Needed power, calculated at timeslot t. for the procurement at future timeslot f

Apart from the modules mentioned above, the simulation platform acts as a top-level coordinator for customers, brokers and the DU. It especially also provides necessary real-world data, such as weather forecasts, and manages the tariff market.

4   AgentUDE14 at a Glance

In the Power TAC 2014 Finals, 72 games were played. Out of these, 16 games were with 8 players, 35 games were with 5 players and 21 games were with 3 players. AgentUDE and cwiBroker dominated the games by realizing the best profits. AgentUDE took the first place in game sizes 5 and 8 and third place in game size 3.

The broker abilities of AgentUDE can be divided into three groups: Wholesale, retail and balancing market activities. Each module has its own predictive model and data structure to create and transmit messages to the Power TAC core.

The wholesale trading module of AgentUDE uses a hybrid dynamic programming approach, which tracks historical market data. This enables the broker to predict market trends regardless of weather conditions. Statistics revealed that wholesale market costs of brokers do not vary much from each other [20]. Therefore, retail activities are better understood by interpreting the diversity of the individual tariff publication policies of the brokers. On the other side, AgentUDE deploys an aggressive tariff strategy. Especially in the beginning of a game, it is trying to offer the cheapest tariff. The idea is to speculate on contract length, EWP and BP. There are two main goals in the retail strategy: To provoke other brokers to publish cheaper tariffs and in order to persuade customers to change their tariffs. This triggers tariff penalties which are accounted as profit for the losing broker. The results of this strategy are presented in the next subsections.

Table 1 defines the key parameters that are used in the paper. Here, time slot proximity refers to the time between order hour and delivery hour. For example, bidding at 18:00 for the power delivery at 20:00 means that the proximity is two.

4.1   Wholesale Market Activities

Wholesale trading is a vital issue for all brokers to minimize their imbalanced energy. Additionally, brokers are challenged to buy the cheapest possible energy to be more flexible in the retail market. For profitability reasons, customers tend to switch to the cheapest tariff available according to their knowledge.

Figure 3 shows the cleared bidding and asking prices of AgentUDE. Apparently, these cost prices make sense if the balance of the market is not important. The cost can be decreased by a stingy bidding policy. However, it eventually results in a poor market balance performance. Therefore, the broker developers are encouraged to deploy tactical and strategical decision-support models so that the net imbalance can be avoided. Then, the overall wholesale costs decrease.

Figure 4 illustrates the prediction performance of AgentUDE under different game sizes. In 8 player games, the success rate is higher than with smaller game sizes since the market is more stable due to the large number of participants.

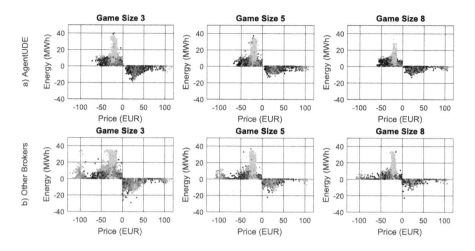

Fig. 3. Cleared bids and asks of AgentUDE and other brokers in Power TAC 2014 Finals. Negative prices show the payments from brokers for a certain amount of bought energy. In the same way, a positive price refers to a received payment for a certain amount of sold energy. Grey tones indicate the time proximity. The light grey color indicates a time slot in the far future of the game. The latter can mean up to 24 h. Likewise, the black color indicates the near future; i.e., a sooner delivery.

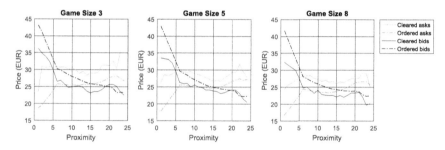

Fig. 4. The average cleared wholesale prices and the trading performance of AgentUDE in Power TAC 2014 Finals.

Table 2 lists the number of tariffs and the wholesale bidding and selling costs of brokers. "$N_{tariffs}$" is the total number of published tariffs. Frequency expresses the publication cycle in terms of time slots. "P_{bids}" and "P_{asks}" stand for the average bidding and asking prices. The energy consumption share of AgentUDE of the total energy consumption is 22.9%. Furthermore, after cwiBroker AgentUDE is the second-best broker when it comes to lowest market costs.

AgentUDE's bidding process takes place in two steps: Electricity price forecasting and strategic bidding. In the first step, future prices are predicted, using a number of machine learning techniques. In the final step, these forecasted prices are transformed into strategic prices, taking balancing cost into account.

Table 2. The number of tariffs and wholesale trading averages of the brokers in Power TAC 2014 Finals.

Broker	$N_{tariffs}$	Frequency	P_{bids} ($€/MWh$)	P_{asks} ($€/MWh$)
AgentUDE	3791	27	22.70	28.90
cwiBroker	1071	97	22.49	27.60
CrocodileAgent	1106	94	43.11	13.08
Maxon	1426	73	23.15	53.30
Mertacor	2732	38	26.36	–
coldbroker	607	171	27.87	27.49
default	144	725	29.10	26.49
TacTex	1670	62	22.94	19.81

Electricity Price Forecasting. In this section, we outline the design of our MCP-based forecasting model and compare our wholesale bidding performance with other broker agents, using the data from Power TAC 2014 Finals.

Price forecasting is one of the most established area in the time-series analysis [12]. However, due to reasons given in the abstract and introduction of the paper, energy markets are getting closer to a non-stationary position. Daily price spikes, rapidly changing trends require a hybrid forecasting solution.

Analyzing the Power TAC games, we see that the price signals are usually stationary and seasonal. Therefore, we can pick a simple seasonal autoregressive integrated moving average (SARIMA) model. In the auto- and partial-autocorrelations, we see a strong seasonality at lag 24 as well as a non-seasonal spike at lag 1. For simplicity, we ignore the moving averages and take $SARIMA(1, 0, 0)x(0, 1, 0)_{24}$ model to describe the forecasting problem. Therefore, the formula can be rewritten as:

$$\hat{Y}_{t+1} = \left(Y_t - Y_{t-24}\right) + Y_{t-23} \tag{1}$$

where $\hat{Y}_{t+1}$ is the prediction of the next time slot at current time slot t whereas Y values denote historical prices. The problem in the formula is the age of some regression terms such as Y_{t-23} and Y_{t-24}. Motivating from the strong correlation in partial autocorrelation of seasonal difference, we replace those aged regression terms with a robust model, using dynamic programming technique so that our forecasting model can avoid price spikes caused by outlier historical prices.

In this section, we outline the design of our forecasting model. On the background, we use a dynamic programming technique to implement the similar-hour concept [10]. The similar-hour concept is based on searching past data for hours with characteristics similar to the predicted hour. For example, the trader agent has the same historical patterns at 02:00 on different days of the week. In other words, the agent uses the same data, while submitting bids to 03:00, 04:00, ..., 02:00 (next day). Therefore, we use MDPs to handle our time-sequential decisions, as formally described by [6]. Each hour of day (24) is represented by a Markov Process. It means that at each time slot, there are 24 concurrent bidding processes. Each process has 25 states. One of those states is terminal state {completed}. The rest of the states denote the timeslot proximity between order hour and delivery hour. Let P_{14} be the process of delivery hour 14:00. Then P_2 is in the state 6 and 1 at the order hours 08:00 and 13:00, respectively. Our MDP is defined as follows:

- States: $S \in \{1, \ldots, 24, completed\}$
- Terminal state: $\{completed\}$

- Reward: $R(s', a) = \begin{cases} 1: & s' = \{completed\} \\ 0: & otherwise \end{cases}$
- Actions: $a_s \in \mathbb{Z}$
- Transitions: State s transitions to $'completed'$, if a bid clears. Otherwise, it transitions to $s - 1$.

Here, action values are limit prices, provided by a value function $V^*(s)$. The value function basically maximizes the expected sum of rewards, and theoretically replaces the term $(Y_{t-23} - Y_{t-24})$, given in Formula 1. The model of the environment is represented by a belief function $f(s, a)$, which is a modified version of a work by [3] and influenced by Q-learning concept [7]. However, Tesauro keeps the probability of a given price by harvesting historical data. In our case, we only keep the weights of changes of two sequential MCP's as the problem defined in Formula 1. Therefore, the belief function $f(s, a)$ points to weights of $a \in \xi_a$, given a state s, where higher values mean higher probability of reward occurrence where ξ_a is the set of actions, $\{a \in \mathbb{Z}| -500 \le a \le 500\}$. Since our reward function is a kind of counting process, we are interested in the reward occurrence in the belief function. The action with highest probability ought to result in transition to $\{completed\}$.

As time proceeds to $t + 1$, the belief functions $f(s, a)$ is updated for $\forall a \in \xi_a$, as MCPs broadcasted to brokers. In brief, MCP's are supervising and reforming the belief function based on the market results. Therefore, the agent does not need to act to learn and update its model. Following formula updates the belief function, using a learning rate α and a reward function. Note that only MCP's are positively rewarded whereas other actions are rewarded with a zero value. This way, in turn, provides a normalization process on the action-state vector:

$$f_{t+1}(s_t, a_t) = f_t(s_t, a_t) * \alpha + R(s_{t+1}, a_t) * (1 - \alpha) \tag{2}$$

$$s_{t+1} = \begin{cases} 'completed':MCP = a_t \\ s_t - 1:otherwise \end{cases} \tag{3}$$

where (2) and (3) are subject to $0 \le \alpha \le 1$.

To solve this MDP, we use value iteration method to find the expected sum of rewards. The value function $V^*(s)$ takes a probability density function (pdf), $F_s(a)$ where μ and σ parameters of the normal distribution are obtained from the values of $f(s, a)$, given a state s for $\forall a \in \mathbb{Z}$. Following value function, $V^*(s)$ solves our MDP and creates a bid value, using an exponential smoothing operator. Here, the exponential smoothing operator refers to the non-seasonal auto regression term in Formula 1.

$$V^*(s) = \begin{cases} cp'_s:s = 24 \\ cp'_{s+1} + \arg\max_a F_s(s):otherwise \end{cases} \quad (4)$$

where exponential smoothing operator is defined as $cp'_s = cp_s(\beta) + cp'_s(1 - \beta)$ and subject to $0 \le \beta \le 1$. Since there is no seasonal difference available at state $s = 24$. Therefore, we only use an exponential smoothing value. If $s < 24$, then smoothed value is summed with seasonal difference, which implemented within a belief function.

Strategic Bidding. Forecasted prices usually known as truthful information. However, these predictions are not directly submitted to markets by brokers. In order to make the model comparable, forecasted prices must be transformed into strategic prices. Forecasted prices constitute 24 price distributions where μ_{hour} and σ_{hour} are mean and standard deviation of an hour. We finalize the transformation in two steps:

- Strategic prices $[1, 2, \ldots, 24] = [balancingPrice, \ldots, (\mu_{t+24} - \sigma_{t+24})]$
- Strategic prices $[1, 2, \ldots, 24] * = [1 + p_{t+1,\delta=1}, \ldots, 1 + p_{t+24,\delta=24}]$

where probability of $p_{t,\delta}$ is defined as:

$$p_{t,\delta} = \frac{\sum^{clearingProximity=proximity} trading\ volume_t}{\sum trading\ volume_t} \quad (5)$$

In the first step of the transformation, we assign prices to enabled auctions, starting from the first standard deviation before the mean up to the balancing price. The balancing price is a dynamic variable which is recalculated at every time slot, based on the balancing market reports. Higher proximities are likely to get lower prices. In the second step, we take trading volume into the account. To do that, we scan historical trading volumes, tracking the same bidding proximities. Higher volume probability means higher strategic price for the given proximity.

4.2   Retail Market Activities

AgentUDE applied a unique strategy on the retail side in the competition, which substantially differentiated it from the other brokers: It first published aggressive tariffs, usually the lowest tariff values, complemented by customer binding measures such as EWP and BP. Due to the competition, this strategy provoked other brokers to publish lower tariffs. This lower prices smoothly convinced customers of AgentUDE to switch their tariffs. This triggered the payment of EWPs, which resulted in additional profit. This strategy provided a 20% contribution to the overall profit of AgentUDE.

All the games start with several uncertainties such as market status (production and consumption capacities) and the number of competitors. Broker agents are not aware of their competitors' trading strategies. Thus, initial tariffs are set based on experimental values per game size.

As a part of the retailer strategy, AgentUDE always sets an EWP value if the tariff value to be published is the currently lowest in the market. Otherwise, EWP is not set since it would harm the attractiveness of the tariff. The tariff value (i.e. unit price of electricity in EUR/kWh) is determined, analyzing the brokers' procurement costs and competitors' activities. Our cost predictor takes the most recent cleared wholesale market prices and the distribution fee into account, tracking the last *n* days where n is an experimental value. Another variable, called "minimum of competitor's", scans the tariff repository to find the most competitive tariff. AgentUDE assigns market costs and adds a profit margin (experimental value) to the tariff value, if the tariff value is greater than other tariff values in the tariff repository. Otherwise, "minimum of competitor's" is assigned to the tariff value, multiplying the value with a competition factor (experimental value). More details can be found in our previous publication [15].

Table 3 compares the tariff fee performances of all brokers. Surprisingly, only AgentUDE and TacTex benefitted from tariff fees. Here, the profit increases with the increase of the number of players.

Table 3. Overall average profits of brokers from tariff fees in Power TAC 2014 Finals.

Broker	Game size 3 (EUR/ game)	Game size 5 (EUR/ game)	Game size 8 (EUR/ game)
AgentUDE	410.893 (6 games)	277.335 (20 games)	698.067 (14 games)
CrocodileAgent	13.583 (5 games)	12.835 (17 games)	8.537 (14 games)
Mertacor	4.615 (4 games)	3.168 (17 games)	987 (8 games)
TacTex	811.864 (2 games)	599.021 (6 games)	508.912 (14 games)

To gain even more profit from this strategy, some requirements must be met: Active customer and a tough competitor. First, customers have to see some profitable tariffs on the desk before leaving their current retailer. If not, customers tend to ignore the existing tariffs and stay in their tariff. In this case, the strategy offered by AgentUDE does not work well. Second, a broker has to offer competitive tariffs so that customers can see them and change their tariffs if it is really profitable for them. As a proof of this claim, competitive and non-competitive brokers were monitored in 3 player games below.

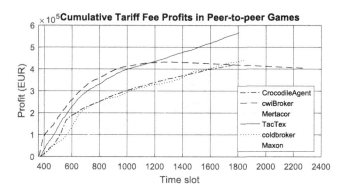

Fig. 5. Cumulative tariff fee earnings of AgentUDE that are collected through 3 player games.

Figure 5 reflects the tariff fee earnings of AgentUDE in the 3 player games between AgentUDE and the other competing broker (other than the default broker). Apparently, TacTex, CrocodileAgent and cwiBroker allowed AgentUDE to gain more profit while Mertacor, Maxon permitted less. In the same fashion, this symbiotic relationship is proportional to the official results given in previous sections. Another result is that TacTex, cwiBroker and AgentUDE offer the most profitable tariffs to the customers and convince them to change their tariffs.

4.3   Balancing Market Activities

Brokers must meet their demand and supply. If not, they might lose a serious portion of their profits for paying a huge imbalance fee. The most challenging issue at this point is to predict future consumptions. AgentUDE uses the consumption data of customers to make predictions. However, this method does not always provide reasonable results since it does not consider changing conditions such as the weather. The balancing market tool signals brokers to pay attention to their imbalance status. However, brokers are challenged to predict their future demand. AgentUDE predicts its customer demand, through:

$$N_{t,f} = N_{t-1,f} * \omega + \left(D_t * \frac{D_{T-24}}{D_{t-24}} \right) * (1 - \omega) \qquad (6)$$

where N is the needed energy and D is distribution volume at the current time slot t for the future time slot f. The weight is $0 < \omega < 1$. Consequently, needed energy is adjusted with imbalance signal and the final amount of needed energy is submitted to the whole-sale market.

Figure 6 illustrates the magnitude of cumulative imbalance volumes and net payments to DU from brokers. In this figure, negative and positive volumes are regarded as absolute values, thus, summed up regardless of their signs. On the left figure, it can be seen that AgentUDE, TacTex and cwiBroker ended up almost with the same imbalance. However, the net payment amounts of TacTex and cwiBroker are greater than the amount that AgentUDE paid (right figure). This indicator shows that, unit benefit (net imbalance/net payment) of AgentUDE is higher than others.

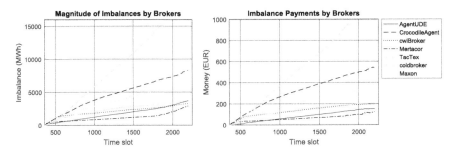

Fig. 6. The cumulative volume of negative and positive imbalances.

5   Future Work and Conclusion

AgentUDE seems to be a successful broker in terms of profitability. However, there are still pending issues to be improved prior to next Power TAC competitions. One of the more important issues is to improve efficiency in the wholesale trading business. Even though AgentUDE has a decent performance in comparison with other brokers, it still requires more accuracy to increase its competitiveness over other brokers. One chance for improvement is to better integrate weather forecasts in the price predictions for the wholesale market.

Another improvement is the utilization of unused power actors. In the Power TAC environment there are a number of new generation power actors such as storage units or controllable customers. However, most of the brokers as AgentUDE do not benefit from them. On the other side, the DU encourages brokers to publish producer tariffs by means of waiving distribution fee if the produced energy is consumed in the same local area. Despite this attractive offer, only AgentUDE and CrocodileAgent benefitted from this opportunity. However, it is officially announced at the Power TAC developer website that the number of producers and electric vehicles will be increased dramatically. It means that another improvement is needed to balance local production and consumption. No doubt, utilizing these components improves the overall efficiency and profitability of the broker.

This paper presented the trading strategies of AgentUDE. Based on the statistics which were discussed in this paper three significant outcomes for the retail, wholesale and balancing market activities can be identified:

Firstly, the wholesale market performances of the given brokers do not differ much. It can clearly be seen that all the brokers deliver a decent market performance based on their demand profiles. Thus, the first outcome is wholesale activities do not contribute much to the overall profit outcome of brokers.

Secondly, the retail strategies of the brokers reveal a great deal of variety. What allows AgentUDE to be one step ahead of its competitors is its aggressive tariff strategy. The results show that AgentUDE earns a serious portion of its profit by tariff fee speculations. This strategy leaves Agent-UDE in a more comfortable and flexible position against other brokers.

It is noteworthy to remark that all the data and results presented in the paper are valid for the specific releases of the brokers and Power TAC during the 2014 competition. The simulation environments as well as the brokers get stronger and stronger with time and growing experience. Additionally, new teams bring nice fresh wind to the competition. The Power TAC core modules have also been updated. At this point, success remains a relative term, especially in such a dynamic and progressive simulation environment. AgentUDE team will continue to update its broker as part of the smart grid studies at the University of Duisburg-Essen.

References

1. Ketter, W., Collins, J., Weerdt, M.: The 2016 Power Trading Agent Competition. ERIM Report Series (2016)

2. Ketter, W., Collins, J., Reddy, P.: Power TAC: a competitive economic simulation of the smart grid. Energy Econ. **39**, 262–270 (2013)
3. Urieli, D., Stone, P.: TacTex'13: a champion adaptive power trading agent. In: Proceedings of the Twenty-Eighth AAAI Conference on Artificial Intelligence, pp. 465–471 (2014)
4. Kuate, R.T., He, M., Chli, M., Wang, H.H.: An intelligent broker agent for energy trading: an MDP approach. In: Proceedings of the Twenty-Third International Joint Conference on Artificial Intelligence, pp. 234–240 (2014)
5. Federal Environmental Agency (FEA). Energieziel 2050: 100% Strom aus erneuerbaren Quellen. http://www.umweltbundesamt.de/publikationen/energieziel-2050. Accessed 11 April 2014
6. Sutton, R.S., Barto, A.G.: Reinforcement Learning: An Introduction, vol. 1(1). MIT Press, Cambridge (1998)
7. Watkins, C.J.C.H., Dayan, P.: Q-learning. Mach. Learn. **8**(3–4), 279–292 (1992)
8. Liefers, B., Han, P.L., Hoogland, J.: A successful broker agent for power TAC. Agent-Mediated Electron. Commer. **187**(2014), 99–113 (2014)
9. Morris, C., Pehnt, M.: Energy Transition: The German Energiewende. Heinrich Böll Stiftung (2014)
10. Tesauro, G., Bredin, J.L.: Strategic sequential bidding in auctions using dynamic programming. In: Proceedings of the First International Joint Conference on Autonomous Agents and Multiagent Systems: Part 2, pp. 591–598. ACM, July 2002
11. Reddy, P.P., Veloso, M.M.: Factored models for multiscale decision-making in smart grid customers. In: AAAI, July 2012
12. Weron, R.: Electricity price forecasting: a review of the state-of-the-art with a look into the future. Int. J. Forecast. **30**(4), 1030–1081 (2014)
13. Peters, M., Ketter, W., Saar-Tsechansky, M., Collins, J.: A reinforcement learning approach to autonomous decision-making in smart electricity markets. Mach. Learn. **92**(1), 5–39 (2013)
14. Howden, N., et al.: JACK intelligent agents-summary of an agent infrastructure. In: 5th International Conference on Autonomous Agents (2001)
15. Ozdemir, S., Unland, R.: A winner agent in a smart grid simulation platform. In: 2015 IEEE/WIC/ACM International Conference on Web Intelligence and Intelligent Agent Technology (WI-IAT), vol. 2. IEEE (2015)
16. Smart Grid. http://energy.gov/oe/services/technology-development/smart-grid. Accessed 12 Oct 2016
17. Bellifemine, F., Poggi, A., Rimassa, G.: JADE–A FIPA-compliant agent framework. In: Proceedings of PAAM, vol. 99, pp. 97–108 (1999)
18. Derksen, C., Branki, C., Unland, R.: Agent.GUI: a multi-agent based simulation framework. In: 2011 Federated Conference on Computer Science and Information Systems (FedCSIS). IEEE (2011)
19. Nwana, H.S., et al.: ZEUS: a toolkit and approach for building distributed multi-agent systems. In: Proceedings of the Third Annual Conference on Autonomous Agents. ACM (1999)
20. Babic, J., Podobnik, V.: An analysis of power trading agent competition 2014. Agent-Mediated Electron. Commer. **187**(2014), 1–15 (2014)

Author Index

Printed in the United States
By Bookmasters